Louis XVI

D1026757

Louis XVI

John Hardman

Yale University Press

New Haven & London · 1993

To my father

To the memory of my mother

Set in Baskerville by Best-set Typesetter Ltd., Hong Kong
Printed and bound in Great Britain by The Bath Press, Avon

Library of Congress Cataloging-in-Publication Data

Hardman, John.
　　Louis XVI / John Hardman.
　　　p.　cm.
　　Includes bibliographical references (p. 254) and index.
　　ISBN 0–300–05719–9 (hbk.)
　　ISBN 0–300–06077–7 (pbk.)
　　1. Louis XVI. King of France, 1754–1793.　2. France—Kings and rulers—Biography.　3. France—History—Louis XVI, 1774–1793.
　4. France—History—Revolution.　1789–1793.　I. Title.
DC137.H37　1993
944′.035′092—dc20　　　　　　　　　　　　　　　　　92–13117
　[B]　　　　　　　　　　　　　　　　　　　　　　　　　　CIP

A catalogue record for this book is available from the British Library.

Contents

List of Illustrations

The following illustrations are between pages 152 and 153.

Preface

Louis XVI was the only one of the Bourbon kings before the Revolution not to have been given a sobriquet, such as the Just, the Great or the Well-beloved. His withdrawn character made him seem colourless. How can one write about a king who shortly before his execution told Malesherbes, 'I would rather let people interpret my silence than my words'? Often Louis would answer a direct question with silence, evasion or a disconcerting change of subject. He should have been dubbed Louis the Silent.

Rather than trying to 'interpret his silence', most historians have fallen back on stereotypes: most general histories treat him in a hostile or dismissive way, as a man ignorant or unconcerned about the great events of his times; most biographies, on the other hand, tend towards hagiography. Yet with patience his silence can be interpreted in its context and indeed supplemented by his surviving letters and the letters and diaries of those who were in daily contact with him, particularly ministers and those in the ministerial milieu. An attempt can be made to dispel the clouds of ignorance which two hundred years after his death still envelop major areas of the King's life. Was he, for instance, able and well-informed or stupid and ignorant? How did the political system function? Was Louis dominated by Marie-Antoinette or did he exclude her from policy-making? Did he accept the Revolution or did he want to restore the Ancien Régime?

Some judgements, of course, might apply at the beginning of the reign but not at the end. The pivotal point was 1787, the date of Louis's great personal reform initiative presented to the Assembly of Notables. This is reflected in the organization of this work: Part I, ending in 1786, deals with the King's role in a theoretically absolute monarchy and presents him as eccentric but assured, particularly in the fields of foreign policy and finance; Part II shows Louis confronting the early assemblies, Notables, Estates-General and the National Assembly, and the disintegration alike of the regime and of his personal composure;

Preface

Part III focuses on Louis's attitude towards the Revolution as embodied in the Constitution of 1791. In general, as Louis's political role is reduced, his character, refined by suffering, becomes more sympathetic. This is reflected in the treatment of the three sections of this book: whereas Part I is largely a political history, much of which has never been written, in Part III episodes such as the flight to Varennes and Louis's imprisonment and execution, which generate dramatic rather than intellectual excitement, are given in some detail.

I should like to thank Dr Munro Price for communicating to me his doctoral thesis on Vergennes and Breteuil and putting at my disposal his transcription of Louis's letters to Vergennes. This book is the better for our discussions, particularly the sections on the Guines and Diamond Necklace Affairs. I should also like to thank Rebecca Cameron for carrying out an essential task for me in Paris.

Introduction

When the future Louis XVI was born in 1754 a period of political stability had just ended and one of economic expansion, when the population of France increased to twenty-five million, was coming to an end. Twenty years later the Comte de Maurepas, chief minister to the young Louis XVI, would seek to re-create what came to be seen as a golden age of the monarchy, when he had been a respected young minister under the premiership of Cardinal Fleury. In the continuum of French history, periods of stability alternated with ones of crisis. The past did not serve as a fixed point of reference for political debate: few Frenchmen could honestly say, with those who offered Cromwell the crown of England, 'we know what a king can do'. Contradictions were never far from the surface. There was reverence for the person of the king, many attributing to him thaumaturgical properties; he was the 'Eldest son of the Church', 'The most Christian king', the descendant of Saint Louis, yet the king's person was often subjected to violence: the first of the Bourbons, Henri IV, had been assassinated in 1610, and Damiens nearly succeeded in assassinating Louis XV in 1757. Louis XVI expected, and hoped, that he would be assassinated rather than formally tried in 1792.

The monarchy was old, the Bourbons being a branch of the Capetian dynasty which had ruled France since 987, but during the civil war known as the Fronde (1648–53) that very antiquity had been turned against it as Parisians darkly hinted that the monarchy was too old for long continuance. The 'absolute' monarchy which Louis XIV had finally established—after Richelieu's attempts in that direction had provoked the Fronde—was relatively new and perceived as such. Barnave, for example, seeing how easily the Crown re-asserted its authority in 1771, observed 'mais le pouvoir était encore neuf'.

Absolute monarchy had never meant total power. The king was considered to be limited by his Christian conscience and by the Fundamental Laws or unwritten constitution, largely undefined but

1

including the Salic Law which forbade succession to the throne by or through women. More practically, 'absolutism' was limited because the range of government was narrow, being largely confined to the conduct and financing of foreign policy and its continuation by means of war. This led to some expansion of government administration, especially rapid under Louis XV, and 'justice as the mode of royal government gradually gave way to administration'.[1] Nevertheless, absolutism in practice meant unlimited authority within a limited sphere; not much was done by the State, but that little was done by the royal government, not by the king or not by the king alone. The 'absolute' power of the French monarchy did not consist in the personal power of the monarch; the Bourbon kings — Louis XIV had been an exception — did not tend to exhibit a strong personal policy. Absolutism consisted rather in the theoretical legislative self-sufficiency of the decisions taken by 'the king in his Council'. The preamble to royal edicts usually concluded with the formula: 'On these grounds, on the advice of our Council, and of our own sure knowledge, absolute power and royal authority we ordain . . .' 'On the advice of our Council' was not just an empty phrase designed to give re-assurance that 'the king's religion had not been surprised'. The words meant what they said: it was characteristic of the Bourbon kings to rule by counsel. As Dauphin, the future Louis XVI put it thus: '. . . the third characteristic which distinguishes legislative volition from the private whim of the prince is that of being an advised [*délibéré*] volition. Councils are of the essence of the monarchy.'[2]

The kings received advice through the *Conseil d'État*, and whenever they sought informal advice and information, such as by opening private correspondence, it was generally to the detriment of good government. The Council was in theory one body which for practical purposes met at different times with different personnel and functions, judicial, administrative and political: even the thirty-two Intendants who ruled the provinces bore the official title *Commissaire départi du Conseil*. The two emanations of the Council which most directly concerned the king were the *Conseil d'en haut*, which discussed foreign policy (generally on Sundays and Wednesdays), and the *Conseil des Dépêches*, which met on Tuesdays and Saturdays to discuss internal matters. Under Louis XVI the *Conseil d'en haut* was usually called simply the *Conseil d'État*; technically, only its members were called *ministres*.

In theory the decisions of the Council were akin to a judicial judgment which should be reached by pleading both sides, like adversaries in a court of law. This procedure should even be adopted in foreign policy. Thus in 1785 the Foreign Secretary, Vergennes, could write to Louis XVI: 'The duty of Your Majesty's ministers is to lay before him the pros and cons . . . of the possible courses of action and to await, in respectful silence, for the orders which he is pleased in his wisdom to give them.'[3] It was not for Vergennes to tell his master that he should abide by the majority opinion, but this was clearly understood. Louis XV once complimented a young *maître des requêtes* on his *rapport* to the Council, saying that he personally agreed with its conclusions but that they would have to follow the majority view. Often, especially in the period after about 1750, the Council was divided, so that under Louis XV and XVI the institutionalized Bourbon tendency to take a great deal of advice frequently led to an appearance of indecisiveness.

Under Louis XV, the Council was the main decision-making body. Some of the most important decisions of Louis XVI were also taken by the Council, particularly in the early stages of the Revolution. Most of the time, however, the Council acted as a rubber stamp for decisions which had already been taken in ad hoc comités of the King and the relevant ministers or sometimes simply by the King in his weekly *travail* or working-session with the individual ministers. The *travail* was the basic unit of government. It gave each minister substantial autonomy, particularly financial. If in the course of the *travail* a *ministre-ordonnateur* (paymaster) obtained the King's signature, he could spend what he pleased: the need for the restraint of a central budget was a problem rarely addressed and never solved by the kings.

There were six departmental ministers: the Chancellor, the four Secretaries of State — for Foreign Affairs, War, Marine (navy and colonies) and the *Maison du Roi* — and the *Contrôleur-général des finances*. The tasks of the first four are self-explanatory; the *Contrôleur*, apart from Finance, had administrative tasks which made him a sort of Minister of the Interior. So too did the Minister for the Maison through his responsibility not only for the Court but for Paris and for the *pays d'état*. Indeed, during the reorganization of the ministries in the time of the Revolution, it was the Ministry of the Maison which became that of the Interior. In the preceding period there were damaging jurisdictional conflicts between the Contrôle and the Maison, facilitated by the autonomy of the *travail*.

Ministerial recruitment underwent a significant change during the 1750s which was ultimately to undermine the loyalty of the King's principal agents. Louis XIV may not have appointed 'bourgeois' ministers but he restricted his choice to the administrative robe, the 'robe' of this noblesse de robe referring to the lawyer's gown. A typical minister had begun his career preparing cases for the Council as a *maître des requêtes* prior to his appointment as an Intendant. Dynasties of such *noblesse d'État* emerged, the most famous being that of the Phélypeaux which under Louis XV provided a minister for the Marine

(Maurepas) and one for the Maison (Saint-Florentin). Such families acquired a common ethos and purpose — briefly to develop the power of the King by making France more centralized and more uniform. Louis XIV had deterred the grands seigneurs from wanting ministerial office by the simple expedient of divorcing title from power. Hence the seigneurial-sounding *Surintendant des finances* became the *Contrôleur* (an accounting term connoting bourgeois attention to detail). Such was the power of words in a hierarchical society that no grand seigneur ever became *Contrôleur-général*.

Secrétaire, too, had something of the connotations of its modern namesake. Apart from considerations of *dérogeance* (loss of caste), the grands seigneurs simply lacked the training to run a complex department: when after nearly a century they took on certain ministries, at first they employed *adjoints* to do the donkey work and offended their robe colleagues by 'treating them almost as bourgeois'. The decisive step came in 1758 when Louis XV asked the maréchal-duc de Belle-Isle to become secretary of state for war. He had just dismissed both his experienced war and naval ministers in the middle of a war and needed an expert regardless of the political consequences (even from a military point of view the move was hardly a success as France was defeated heavily by both land and sea). Belle-Îsle, however, far from seizing the chance of power (his grandfather, Fouquet, had been the last Surintendant), only accepted after a deputation of his fellow-peers had assured him that it would involve no *dérogeance*. He was the last of his kind to entertain such doubts and soon the court aristocracy were demanding at least the service ministries as of right.[4]

The King and his Council governed in association with the royal courts known as the parlements. The Parlement of Paris, *the* Parlement, whose jurisdiction covered half of France, and the twelve provincial parlements were courts of appeal. They also had considerable administrative powers ranging from control of the grain trade to control of public meetings, from censorship of the press to the regulation of guilds. Much of this was carried out in conjunction with or rivalry to the lieutenant de police, the subordinate of the Minister for the Maison. The parlements are best remembered, however, for their political, even constitutional role: in the absence of representative institutions, notably the Estates-General, the parlements gave a 'simulated consent' to royal legislation.

The Estates-General of Clergy, Nobility and Third Estate had never performed the task of representation well: in 1356 they had lost the 'power of the purse' when the nobility, in return for personal exemption, had allowed the King the right to collect the main direct tax, the *taille*, without consultation and in perpetuity. This had meant that the powers — and indeed the usefulness to the kings — of the Estates had dwindled: they tended to be summoned only during royal minorities or in times of troubles and invariably ended in failure or internal wrangling as when they had last met in 1614.

The connection between the political power of the Parlement and the absence of the Estates was well understood by the more perceptive, and generally the parlementaires and ministers kept silent on a matter which enhanced the powers of both. For the period between the meeting of the Estates in 1614 and their meeting in 1789 can be defined as that of the absolute monarchy and of the classical period of the Ancien Régime. Its main constituents were the Crown and the parlements, which were able to thrive in the absence of representative institutions and were the two main casualties of the French Revolution.

All this implies a partnership between Crown and Parlement to ensure the success of 'simulated consent'. The King's most solemn enactment, the Edict, occurred when the Lettres Patentes drafted in the Council were 'registered' in the parlements. There was a difference of emphasis between the conciliar and the parlementaire view of what registration entailed. The conciliar view was that registration was necessary to show that the King was speaking *ex cathedra* but was no more than a promulgation. For parlementaires, registration involved 'verifying' whether the proposed legislation conformed with natural justice and the Fundamental Laws. If they thought that it did not, the parlements 'remonstrated' with the King who, after a series of exchanges, either modified his legislation or enforced it by appearing in person at a *lit de justice*.

The theory behind the *lit* was based on the Roman Law maxim that 'in the presence of the delegator, the powers of the delegate cease'. The parlements did not represent 'the nation' but the king. When the king-magistrates had found it impossible to dispense the growing volume of justice in person, sitting in popular imagination under an oak tree, they had delegated powers to their parlement as a matter of practical convenience. They could, however, always resume their judicial functions, and at a *lit* the magistrates were supposed to mumble their dissenting opinions inaudibly. In normal times the parlements accepted the finality of the *lit de justice*, whilst the king was reluctant to employ them because controversial legislation, particularly taxation, was less likely to be obeyed if it was known to have been enforced. This view of basic harmony was held by many at the time and is shared by some historians.[5]

An opposite view considers normal times to have been few and far between. The Parlement, after all, had armed Parisians against the king during the Fronde and had driven him out of Paris. As a result, Louis

XIV deprived the Parlements of the right of remonstrating until they had registered the legislation. The Duc d'Orléans, who became regent when Louis XV succeeded at the age of five in 1714, had restored this right in return for the Parlement's annulling of Louis XIV's will. Thereafter, the Parlement had grown bolder with every succeeding year until by the middle of the century they were denying the finality of the *lit de justice*, issuing *arrêts de défence* forbidding obedience to legislation so passed, and, bolstering their political power with their judicial, going on judicial strike, a serious matter in such a litigious society. There was a contradiction in the parlementaire's position which was never resolved. As Bailey Stone has put it: '. . . the judges championed the centrality of the monarchy in French history, law and administration; yet, simultaneously they championed property and individual rights and privileges in such a way as to challenge the practical continuation of that monarchy.'[6] In other words the practice became more important than the theory.

The matters of practical dispute between the Crown and the Parlement mainly concerned religion and finance. In its search for uniformity, including religious conformity, the Crown sought to stamp out the sect of Jansenism, a Catholic heresy which shared with Calvinism a belief in predestination and efficacious grace. It had many adherents in the Parlement, which responded by attacking the Jesuits, regarded as the spearhead of the assault on the Jansenists. The Parlement succeeded so well that in 1764 a reluctant Louis XV was forced to expel the Jesuits from France. Victory denied the parlementaires a source of conflict but left them with an ideology of resistance which they had adapted from Jansenism.[7] It was based on the stance of 'persecuted orthodoxy'. They were defending the King from an ultra-montane papacy. They were resisting the mortal King's momentary legislative volition in the name of 'his immortal will as expressed in the fundamental Laws'. They attacked 'ministerial despotism' to preserve the King, the notion of 'ministerial despotism' being the oppositional version of 'the King's religion surprised'. This way of thinking was to have a long life. It is present in the central fallacy of Rousseau's *Du Contrat social*, that it is not what one actually believes that matters but what one would believe if properly informed — the justification for totalitarian rule. It was to haunt Louis XVI during the Revolution when the émigrés claimed to represent what would have been his policies if he were free.

Financial matters became controversial around the middle of the century because of the increasing cost of warfare. Montesquieu, a president in the Parlement of Bordeaux, wrote in the section of *De l'esprit des lois* (1748) dealing with taxation: 'A new distemper has spread itself over Europe, infecting our princes and inducing them to maintain an exorbitant number of troops.' This was a little unfair; at the end of Louis XIV's reign there had been more Frenchmen under arms than there were to be at any time before 1914. Under Louis XV, however, the Navy expanded and under Louis XVI further naval expansion was to cripple the finances of the monarchy. Moreover, Louis XIV had restricted his taxation of the nobility to emergency measures, the *capitation* and the *dixième*, which were regarded as the equivalent of the feudal levy and were withdrawn as soon as the wars ended. Controversially, Louis XV instituted his *vingtième*, payable by all landowners, in 1749, i.e. the year after the conclusion of the War of the Austrian Succession. He evidently regarded it as a permanent tax. The parlementaires, however, all of whom were noble and most of whom were landowners, persisted right until the end of the Ancien Régime, in the belief that 'taxation was but a temporary inconvenience'.[8] Since the *vingtième* was regarded as temporary, the parlementaires took a dim view of the Crown's attempts to root out noble tax-evasion by *vérifications* or by a *cadastre*, a survey of the nation's landed wealth. In the 1787 Assembly of Notables, Angran d'Allerai could still claim '. . . that there was no permanent tax without privileged exemptions, but that he conceded that it was fair that with a temporary tax exemptions should not be claimed'.[9] Nothing was more calculated to cause a judicial strike than the threatened introduction of a *cadastre*.

The monarchy did not seek to tax the nobility through choice. It was accepted that the peasantry, four-fifths of the population, could not pay any more and should rather be relieved; physiocratic dogma and administrative difficulties spared the growing commercial wealth of the towns (which consequently grew even richer); which only left the nobility and clergy (who, however, managed to get out of paying the *vingtième* and continued with their voluntary and therefore inadequate 'Free Gift'). The nobility's ultimate response was to demand the convocation of the Estates-General. This was both a logical demand, an echo of the American colonists' 'no taxation without representation', and a historical one: their consent in the Estates of 1356 to let the King tax the peasants at will had been conditional on his agreeing not to tax them. It can in general be said that obtaining the consent of the taxpayer does bring in greater revenues, if the ruler is prepared to pay the political price. Ancien Régime finance was always hand-to-mouth, characterized by 'fiscalism'. The kings of England tended to have less power than those of France but, despite having the resources of a much poorer country at their disposal, they also tended to win the succession of wars between them, most recently the Seven Years War (1756–63), when France had to cede Canada, among other territories, and agree to the presence of an English commissioner to ensure that Dunkirk remained unfortified.

By 1770 comparisons between France and England favoured the realm of George III in almost every respect. The economic expansion of France which had lasted since 1730 had come to an end. The *Contrôleur-général* told Louis XV in 1769 that government finances threatened a catastrophe. The parlements, using the weapons described, allowed Louis XV less effective power than George III possessed; unconstitutionally they had made him a constitutional monarch. They had forced him to expel the Jesuits; forced his Contrôleur, Bertin, to abandon his *cadastre*; in 1765 they had even annulled the proceeding of the General Assembly of the Church of France, on the grounds that they sought to encroach on the civil power, employing the familiar argument that they were 'plus royaliste que le roi'. In the midst of his degradation, the King did show a flash of spirit in the *séance de flagellation* of 1766. In his speech to the Parlement based on the work of a young *maître des requêtes*, Charles Alexandre de Calonne, Louis XV majestically affirmed that 'legislative power belongs to me unfettered and undivided'.[10] The *séance* revived the King's spirits for a few days, but it was only words. Moreover, in the Duc de Choiseul, the King's leading minister, the parlements had an ally who was prepared to favour the extent of their claims if only because he needed them to finance a war of revenge against England.

Indeed, one perceptive if eccentric observer, the Marquis de Bouillé, considered that Choiseul, through increasing pensions to parlementaires, was responsible for bringing the Parlement into the centre of political life (he also considered that the process had debauched the parlementaires).[11] Miromesnil, the *premier président* of the Parlement of Rouen, put it slightly differently: Louis XV's fear of the parlements was 'puerile', 'or rather a split in the Ministry made them seem formidable'.[12] Cardinal Fleury, who died in 1743, had maintained a united ministry, but under Louis XV's personal rule splits had developed; whether or not they were encouraged by the King to maintain his independence remains unclear. Malesherbes dates this to the quarrel between Machault and the Comte d'Argenson and 'all the following ministers who have involved the courts in their ministerial disputes'.[13] The rival ministers maintained their own faction in the Parlement. Thus the role of the Parlement is ambiguous: was it the chosen battlefield for ministers to fight out their rivalries or a foyer of resistance to government?

This ambiguity was present when the King crushed the Parlement during the events known as the Maupeou coup d'état or the Revolution of 1771. Was it the case that the Chancellor Maupeou, appointed in 1768, 'attacked the Parlement in order to attack Choiseul' and supplant him as the leading minister[14] or was Maupeou expressing the King's exasperation with the Parlement's encroachments, culminating in its conduct over the trial of the Duc d'Aiguillon? D'Aiguillon was governor of Brittany, ministerial aspirant and the ally of the King's new *maîtresse en titre* Jeanne Bécu, Comtesse du Barry. D'Aiguillon was the subject of an investigation by the Parlement into whether he had bribed witnesses to prove that La Chalotais, *procureur-général* of the Parlement of Rennes, had written poison-pen letters concerning the King. To clear his honour d'Aiguillon asked that he be tried by the Parlement, a request to which the King acceded — wrongly, for the Parlement was able to turn the affair into a trial of the government. When the King cancelled the trial and declared d'Aiguillon innocent, the Parlement defiantly voted an *arrêt d'indignité* against d'Aiguillon forbidding him to exercise the rights of his peerage.

Maupeou was not displeased to see a potential rival left with a stain on his honour, nor to have the opportunity to return the Parlement's provocation with interest, which was taken by the disciplinary edict of 3 December 1770 reaffirming the legislative self-sufficiency of the King and forbidding the Parlement to use the weapons of mass resignation or judicial strikes. The Parlement responded precisely by a mass resignation, but both sides manœuvred. In the interval Maupeou told the King that Choiseul was secretly supporting the Parlement and that he was planning to involve France in war with England over the Spanish Bourbons' claims to the Falkland Islands, further tightening the grip of the Parlement through the King's need for war-funds. This was too much for the King, a pacifist *avant la lettre* who was conscious that royal finances were so bad that the Contrôleur Terray had been forced to carry through a partial bankruptcy that year. On Christmas eve, Choiseul was dismissed and exiled to his estates at Chanteloup. All Maupeou's efforts could not prevent d'Aiguillon from succeeding him as Foreign Secretary six months later.

If Maupeou had been merely attacking Choiseul through the Parlement, he would now have made peace with that body, but he did not. On the night of 19/20 January musketeers roused each parlementaire and asked him to state in writing whether he would resume dispensing justice on the morrow. Those who consented soon retracted and the parlementaires were exiled, not as heretofore to some agreeable town such as Pontoise but, often singly, to isolated and desolate places. Unable to gain any defectors from the Parlement, Maupeou replaced it by the rival conciliar body, the *Grand Conseil*, and reduced its vast jurisdiction by the creation of six *Conseils supérieurs*. The refractory Parlement of Rouen was abolished, as were those of Douai and Metz, and replaced by *Conseils supérieurs*; the remaining parlements were remodelled. In April 1771 Maupeou suggested replacing all the parlements with *Conseils supérieurs*, but Louis XV refused on the grounds that it would foster an impression of despotism.

There is indeed a belief among recent Anglo-Saxon historians,[15] following a widespread contemporary opinion, that despotism is precisely what Maupeou established. Maupeou had shown that the King's power was not subject to restraint either in theory or in practice. The fact that the coup was bloodless, carried out in the provinces by a 'Conseiller d'état sans escorte', served only to emphasize the point.[16] The King was above the law, of which he was the sole interpreter. The vindictiveness of Maupeou's exiles further demonstrated its arbitrary nature. Doyle also argues that the Parlement never recovered from the blow. These historians make the further point that the coup permanently altered people's perception of the monarchy and led to the demand for constitutional safeguards. The view was earlier expressed by de Tocqueville: 'The disappearance of the French Parlement, an institution almost coeval with the monarchy, made the Nation vaguely aware of standing on the threshold of an age of violence and instability, when anything might happen.'[17]

Many contemporaries undoubtedly shared this view. De Tocqueville's great-grandfather, Malesherbes, in a private letter, talked not just of 'ministerial despotism' but of the personal despotism of the King: 'In fact, the King has no particular liking for this man [Maupeou] but he is greatly attached to his despotism.'[18] He believed that Maupeou had raised an issue that might one day change the constitution and even the dynasty. The *premier président*, faced with the disciplinary edict, should have secretly told the King that the Parlement was only a court of law and that in future the King must 'address himself directly to his subjects in the most suitable way suggested by his wisdom'.[19] Diderot thought that Maupeou had rent the 'spider's web' which hid the face of despotism; and the tax-farmer Augeard that 'it is necessary that the King must be master of the Parlement but that no one should realize it'.[20]

Not everyone shared such a view or shares it now. Modern French historians tend to qualify the 'despotism' of the Maupeou coup with 'enlightened', emphasizing its positive, enabling aspects and linking it to a movement affecting other European monarchies at the time.[21] The support of Voltaire, who wrote an *Éloge de Maupeou*, is adduced as well as the abolition of venality of office and the tips or *épices* which litigants had to give to the judges, and above all, the plans that were being drawn up to abolish seigneurial courts and redeem feudal dues.

Maupeou and his secretary Lebrun were working on a codification of French laws which after the Revolution, when Lebrun was Third Consul, became the basis for the Code Napoléon.

The coup is best seen, however, as a return to the traditional royal policy of seeking centralization and uniformity in alliance with the Third Estate and at the expense of the aristocracy, whether represented by feudal barons or in the eighteenth century by the parlementaires. Maupeou was innately conservative, and at his installation he wore three different robes, one of which had not been seen within living memory. Educated by the Jesuits, he remained an ardent supporter, attempting to have the order recalled, though failing to carry this in the Council. He believed the exiled Parlement to be infected with the spirit of the philosophes, and was particularly worried by distortions of the French language in parlementaire remonstrances, such as novel uses of the words *liberté, citoyen*, and *patriote*, which 'he portrayed [to Lenoir], as harbingers of an approaching revolution'.[22]

These debates were not conducted internally between the Council and the Parlement, and this was one of the grievances of the King against the Parlement. Yet however much he blamed them for publishing remonstrances which should have been penned exclusively to 'enlighten his religion', he in his turn increasingly used the preambles to his edicts for purposes of propaganda. In an absolute monarchy, the King is at least in theory the only public person, the only court of appeal.[23] If a minister of Louis XIV had been told he was 'popular' he would have been bewildered or angry. By 1760, however, the influence of 'public opinion' or the 'political class', or what Talleyrand called *la société*, on the Government was probably as strong as it was in England. Yet because France did not have representative institutions, the precise impact of *la société* is hard to convey, nor was it fully assimilated into the political thinking of the time. According to Talleyrand: 'France gave the impression of being composed of a certain number of *sociétés* with which the Government was obliged to reckon. . . . The power of what is called in France *la société* was prodigious in the years preceding the Revolution and even throughout the last century. . . . In a country where the Constitution is lost in the mists of the time the influence of *la société* is bound to be immense.'[24]

La société exerted its influence principally at Paris, where royal loans had to be floated and debts serviced, and at the Court of Versailles. The Court still retained its original character of being the King's Household: some of the largest departments catered for his personal needs — the *garde-robe*, for instance, looked after his clothes, the *bouche* his food, and so on. All its officers, however grand, were there to perform a menial if stylized domestic duty, such as handing the King his shirt at his *lever*, the ceremony at which he got up and dressed, or his night-cap at the *coucher*. The Abbé de Veri delighted in calling Court officials glorified valets. Indeed, Louis XVI often gave more affection and confidence to his genuine servants than to his decorative ones. The fiction that the Court officers were performing a service led to inefficiency and prevented the creation of purely honorific chamberlains to buy support, as happened at other courts.[25]

The often peripatetic court had been 'rendered sedentary' and expanded when Louis XIV had established it at Versailles in the 1670s as a way of cutting off the great nobles from their territorial bases of power in the provinces. He denied them power but could not prevent them from acquiring influence. It was influence only because the Court did not have the official position in goverment which even Louis XIV never denied to the parlements. In any case the grandees no longer wanted power, at least in the bureaucratic form in which it was now exercised. Nevertheless, they maintained their links with the local élites and lobbied ministers in favour of their provinces: success nourished their connection. The various family and factional interests at Court were organized in such a way as to reach the King's ear and so informally to influence decisions, as well as to obtain contracts and sinecures.

At the summit were the households of the adult members of the Royal Family, the 'children of France', i.e. the children or grandchildren of a king, there being no fewer than twelve such households in 1789, all extensive. Then there were the more distant relatives, the Princes of the Blood, who were kept distinct from the run of the nobility by the operation of the Salic Law, which gave them an interest in the administration of a crown they or their descendants might inherit. The junior Bourbons, the Condés and the Contis, were far too distantly related to make this a realistic ambition, but the immensely rich House of Orléans, descended from Louis XIV's brother, never gave up hope. Established at Paris in the Palais Royal, they already had immense wealth and this assumed threatening proportions in 1769 when the Duc de Chartres, son of the Duc d'Orléans, married the daughter of the Duc de Penthièvre, the inheritor of the vast fortune created by Louis XIV for his legitimated bastards. Beneath the Princes of the Blood came the *princes étrangers*, notably the members of the House of Lorraine and the Rohan, the descendants of the autonomous Dukes of Brittany. The *princes étrangers* ranked above the *gens titrés*, as dukes were called. Then came the ordinary noble families headed by the Noailles, who dominated the allocation of court office under Louis XV and the Montmorency. The lesser families grouped themselves with one or more of the above.

Those with the most influence on the kings, however, were not perhaps the original inmates of Versailles but those who came from outside: Louis XV's mistresses, Louis XVI's Queen; and, under Louis XVI, the Polignacs, who were imported into the château for a political purpose (see below, pp. 54–6). For the birth, wealth and *charge* of a courtier were of little political consequence unless they led to access to the King. When Louis de Rohan was made *grand-aumônier* in 1777, Marie-Antoinette told her mother: 'In any case [the office] of grand-aumônier does not give him any contact with me and he won't have much conversation with the King, whom he will only see at his *lever* and at church.'[26] Access to the King's private apartments was tightly controlled. The King's more official contacts were regulated by the *premier gentilhomme de la chambre* and his private or secret ones by the *premier valet de chambre*. There were four *premiers valets*, each serving for three months in the year. Their status was ambiguous — they were generally taken from the upper bourgeoisie or lesser nobility — but not their importance, which was reflected in the high cost of their *charges*, 200,000 livres.[27]

In any case, the kings spent most of their time with members of the Council and most of the rest hunting, a largely silent or at least wordless pursuit: hunting and business ('mes affaires'), Louis XV told his grandson the Duke of Parma, were his twin passions, omitting in a family letter the passions for which he is more famous.[28] The ministers were the key men and the King gave them any social standing they needed. Symbolically, the court *règlement* of 1732 restricted the *noblesse présentée*, i.e. those who could attend formal receptions or private royal entertainments, *either* to those who could prove nobility back to 1400 *or* to the relatives of ministers.

The influence of courtiers, however, could become power when, in addition to soliciting the pensions which were necessary to maintain their lifestyle at Versailles, they also, from the 1750s, became ministers: the political importance of the Rohan, for instance, increased greatly when Louis XV made the Duc de Rohan-Soubise a *ministre*, though without a portfolio. As the court aristocracy became, in Calonne's words, 'seized with ministerial mania',[29] the Court became increasingly 'politicized', and on the great issues of the day (the respective roles of the Austrian Alliance and of the Parlements) were polarized between what was sometimes called the party of *lumières* and the *dévots*.

The former instituted the 'diplomatic revolution' of 1756 when France made an alliance with her traditional enemy, the Austrian Habsburgs. They also favoured a policy of entente towards the parlements and were often anti-clerical and sympathetic to the philosophes. The King's mistress Madame de Pompadour headed this grouping and, after her death in 1762, the Duc de Choiseul. Choiseul came of an extremely old and fairly prominent family from Lorraine. This duchy had passed to France in 1766 but its dispossessed duke had married Maria Theresa, the daughter and heiress of the last male Habsburg, Charles VI, who had died in 1740. Though Choiseul did not conclude the Austrian alliance, he was most fitted to maintain it. Louis XV himself had reservations about the alliance which found expression in his secret diplomacy, *le secret du roi*. This was designed to balance the new alliance by continuing the traditional French diplomacy of alliance with Poland, Sweden, Turkey and the lesser German states — a policy which would form the cornerstone of Louis XVI's diplomacy.

There had, however, always been a traditionalist, *dévot* alternative available to Louis XV, personified by his only son, the Dauphin Louis Ferdinand, with ministers in the wing such as members of the Richelieu-d'Aiguillon family ready to implement it: the Richelieu family in particular deplored the Austrian alliance as the negation of the policies of their collateral ancestor, the Cardinal. The Dauphin hated the Austrian alliance and hated Choiseul for undermining royal authority, for being a free-thinker and above all for expelling the Jesuits. After that event, he contemplated ceasing to attend the Council, 'lest he condone the iniquity', but compromised by attending in silence and glowering across the table at Choiseul.[30] When the Dauphin died in 1765, his heir, the future Louis XVI, was only eleven, but his unmarried aunts Adélaïde and Victoire, the patrons of Maupeou, took over their brother's role as protector of the *dévot* party at Court. This was the tradition into which the future Louis XVI was born.

PART I

Years of Hope

1
Early Life

Parentage and ancestry

From childhood up, History was the favourite reading of Louis-Auguste, successively Duc de Berry, Dauphin and King of France as Louis XVI. The work he returned to most was David Hume's *History of England*: on the occasion of Hume's visit to France in 1763, the nine-year-old Berry made him a pretty speech and got his younger brothers the Comte de Provence and the Comte d'Artois to do the same. Artois, who was only six, forgot his lines. Berry had inherited his penchant for history from his mother, Maria-Josepha, daughter of Augustus III, Elector of Saxony and King of Poland, but Hume's *History* was also a favourite with his father, Louis the Dauphin, born in 1729, the only son of the King, Louis XV. The Dauphin particularly liked the section in Hume's work relating to the death of his direct ancestor Charles I, which pampered his extreme morbidity. The life of the martyr-king was in turn to feed his son's *amor fati*.

Marie-Josèphe was the second wife of the Dauphin (his first, a Spanish Infanta of whom he was passionately fond, had died in childbirth) and she only won his affection at considerable personal cost, moderating her natural vivacity to conform to his melancholy ways (he was bored by hunting, gaming and the theatre, though he enjoyed playing the violin) and pompous religiosity (he published prayers under pseudonyms). In 1750 she gave birth to a daughter, in 1751 to the Duc de Bourgogne, in 1753 to the Duc d'Acquitaine, who died the following year, and on 23 August 1754 to the Duc de Berry. Berry was followed by the Comte de Provence (later Louis XVIII) and the Comte d'Artois (later Charles X), by another sister, Clôtilde, and finally in 1764 by his sister Elizabeth, the constant companion of his last years.

In naming his first two sons, the Dauphin had discharged his debt to his relatives; he was to pay off the interest by naming his fourth, Provence, Louis-Stanislas-Xavier after his maternal grandfather

Stanislas, the deposed King of Poland. In naming his third son, who was not expected to be king, he was free to indulge a personal preference. The Dauphin chose Louis-Auguste, the Christian names of the canonized Louis IX (1214–70). Saint Louis was not just a personal favourite with the Dauphin, it was through descent from him that the Bourbons, in the person of Henri IV, claimed the throne on the assassination of Henri III in 1589, no direct ancestor having reigned in the intervening centuries. The choice of his Christian names, as with Sterne's hero, was to condition the character of their recipient: the king-saint was held up to his namesake as a model from the cradle to the scaffold when, according to tradition, his confessor exhorted him with the words: 'Fils de Saint Louis, ascendez au ciel.' When he was twelve, Marie-Josèphe told her son: 'What a king Louis IX was! He was the arbiter of the world.[1] What a saint! He is the patron of your august family and the protector of the monarchy. May you follow in his footsteps![2]

The children of the Dauphin and their Saxon mother were sometimes scathingly referred to as 'Dresden knicknacks', but it was only the Duc de Berry who inherited the fair complexion, the bulging powder-blue eyes (*œil-du-roi* was to be a colour in the palette of the Sèvres porcelain factory during his reign) and the strong, cumbersome frame of the Saxon Welphs. Burgundy, Provence and Artois had the dark gimlet eyes of their father, who had inherited them from his Polish mother, Maria Lesczinska. Berry's distinctive hooded eyelids and heavy eyebrows were also quite unlike those of his brothers and his character too was to appear heavy in comparison with the hauteur of Bourgogne, the wit of Provence and the dashing charm of Artois — the only one of them to have inherited Louis XV's good looks.

The Duc de Bourgogne was his parents' favourite and lived in an atmosphere of adulation. In 1755 *Le Mercure de France* informed its readers that the four-year-old displayed 'a decided taste for arms' and in 1758 that he showed 'firmness for one of such tender years'. He seems to have bullied Berry a little and he cheated him at cards, which Berry particularly resented as he had no liking for cards in any case: when he was sixteen his confessor attempted to overcome this dislike, advocating playing cards as social cement for the Royal Family, but he never played more than the occasional game of whist.

In eighteenth-century France royal children, as indeed those of the Court families, saw very little of their parents and that usually on ceremonial occasions. Up to the age of seven they were supervised by the *Gouvernante des Enfants de France*. The current Gouvernante was the Comtesse de Marsan of the House of Rohan. There was little affection between Berry and Mme de Marsan, who lavished her attention on Bourgogne as the heir, and her affection on Provence, as the most immediately engaging.

On 8 September, when he was just over six, Berry was 'put into the hands of the men', which meant exchanging the Governess for a Governor, the atrabilious Duc de la Vauguyon, the friend and former *menin*, or official playfellow of the Dauphin as a boy. Under his direction, a preceptor and various subpreceptors and tutors would carry out the education of the Prince. At this time Berry was given the diamond shoe-buckles his brother had outgrown and went straight from the strange, long, babyish robes which young princes wore to the dress of an adult. Berry's formal education had begun a year early because the health of his brother Bourgogne had deteriorated and it was thought a companion would do him good. For seven months Berry ministered to the brother he adored, but on Easter morning 1761 he died, of tuberculosis, leaving Berry the ultimate heir to the throne.

The loss of the Duc de Bourgogne, considered a precocious child, was a devastating blow to the Dauphin, who had placed all his hopes on him (he considered that Louis XV was running the country so badly that there was no hope of a recovery in his own lifetime).[3] Without transferring these hopes to Berry, the Dauphin nevertheless closely supervised the education of his children, made them work hard and personally examined them on their progress every Wednesday and Saturday.

The education of Louis XVI has been the subject of a meticulously and imaginatively documented study by Mme Girault de Coursac.[4] In contrast to the traditional view of Louis-Auguste as a dull and lazy boy, she concludes that he was a precocious child, excelling particularly at 'science' subjects such as mathematics, physics and geography. Her claims are based on an attempt to reconstruct his lessons from the publications of his tutors. In 1768, when Louis-Auguste was fourteen, Le Blonde dedicated his *Éléments d'Algèbre* to his royal pupil, writing in the preface: '. . . the pleasure you found in the solution of the majority of the problems it contains and the ease with which you grasped the key to their solution are new proofs of your intelligence and the excellence of your judgement . . .' The *Éléments d'Algèbre* contains linear simultaneous equations, quadratic equations, the concept of real and imaginary numbers, and progressions and series. The Abbé Nollet, in the preface to *L'Art des Expériences* of 1770, the basis of his university course of experimental physics, claims a similar degree of comprehension for the royal dedicatee. Unfortunately, Mme de Coursac does not discount the degree of flattery necessarily involved in such dedications, though to be credible flattery must bear some relationship to truth and it would be impressive if the boy had merely been set without solving many such problems. The only controlling evidence that can be adduced is the sound understanding of the intricacies of public finance he was to display as king, exemplified by his memorandum of 1787.[5]

Louis-Auguste's mastery of geography, demonstrated by his superb map of the environs of Versailles now in the Bibliothèque Nationale, has never been in doubt.[6] His tutor was the distinguished cartographer Philippe Buache, the protégé of the Comte de Maurepas, former Minister for the Marine, who enjoyed the protection of the Dauphin. Another of Maurepas's protégés was the Latin tutor, the Abbé de Radonvilliers, who inspired his pupil with an abiding love of the language. His favourite Latin author was Tacitus, admired for his laconic style: his own letters, written for economy on quartered paper, were to achieve Tacitean brevity if not wit.

Louis-Auguste's interest in the factual rather than the theoretical or speculative — when king, he used 'schématique' as a favourite term of abuse — is reflected in his library, which consisted mainly of technical or scientific treatises, works of history and classical authors. There were only two works of romantic fiction, of which one was *Robinson Crusoe*.

His training in the theory of kingship is summarized in *Les Réflexions sur mes entretiens avec M. le Duc de La Vauguyon*, on which he started work when he was thirteen. Following a suggestion of the Dauphin's, La Vauguyon asked the historian Moreau and the Jesuit Berthier to draw up some maxims concerning kingship. Moreau, who was later made the historiographer royal, was to become the leading exponent of traditional royal absolutism. La Vauguyon then discussed the maxims fully with his royal pupil, who between 1767 and 1769 condensed them into thirty-three reflections. It is a competent job; Louis-Auguste has thoroughly absorbed the maxims, adding words or sentences of his own, and it will be possible to trace their influence throughout his reign, but without sparkle or verbal felicity. As befits an enterprise planned by the Dauphin, the reflections are imbued with the spirit of traditional French kingship which he espoused: orthodox Catholicism and a narrow interpretation of the role of the Parlement. They do not, however, exhibit a blinkered adherence to the old tenets: though one 'must hold in horror those who refuse [God] their homage' — here the young prince is thinking of the philosophes — equally 'one must notice changes in the language and modes of speech in order thoroughly to understand the spirit of the age'. In the same spirit, of knowing the enemy, for he never had the slightest doubt that they were the enemy, one of his first purchases on receiving a regular allowance was their organ, the *Encyclopédie*.

The *Réflexions* provide a clue as to why Louis's abilities have been consistently undervalued both by his contemporaries and his historians.

He was naturally timid, but this quality was reinforced by his tutors' stress on the need for *retenue* — a key word throughout his life[7] — meaning sometimes 'reserve' and sometimes 'restraint'. Louis's timidity was shared to a lesser extent by Louis XV and even by Louis XIV and may be said to be a Bourbon characteristic. Thus Louis XIV was informed, in connection with the education of his son the Grand Dauphin: 'Though timidity, common with children who posses judgement, prevents them from speaking, this silence stems from *retenue*, not stupidity.' Berthier even develops the theory that such timidity is a necessary royal characteristic, though his pupil does not incorporate this section in his *Réflexions*.

These tendencies were reinforced by the injunction in 1770 of Louis-Auguste's confessor, the Abbé Soldini, 'Never let people read your mind' ('Ne vous laissez jamais pénétrer'), which finds an echo in two despatches of the Austrian Ambassador, Mercy-Argenteau that year: 'His sombre and reserved character have so far rendered him impenetrable' (14 July); and, on 17 December: 'one cannot predict the impressions that are made on a prince so taciturn and evasive.'

This evasiveness — his brother Provence was to remark that pinning him down was like trying to hold oiled billiard balls together — combined with the qualities of embarrassment and *retenue* to produce a fourth, special kind of silence. This was not just the silence which can be mistaken for stupidity, though it often was, but silence where the situation, or very often a direct question, required an answer but he found it convenient to hold his peace. His confessor set before him 'the example of Jesus, who warned his apostles that there were many things he would not say to them', but a more exact comparison, if one be sought, is with Jesus' silences to the direct questions of Pilate (who was only trying to help) and the high priest. This technique was occasionally employed by Louis XV as when, towards the end of the Seven Years War, the Foreign Minister asked him whether a particular avenue for peace should be explored; hoping to evade responsibility for either concluding an inglorious peace or prolonging a disastrous war, Louis gave no reply.[8] His grandson was to elevate this type of silence into a veritable instrument of government.

A youthful exercise which was continued throughout his reign was the celebrated diary, begun on 1 January 1766.[9] Its format, a cross between an engagement diary and a hunting record, partly explains the banality of some of the entries in this numbing catalogue of trivial achievement, such as that for 23 December 1780 after the death of his mother-in-law, the Empress Maria-Theresa: 'respects of 319 men in the morning and 256 women at six o'clock'. Whatever his reflections on the events of his times, he does not choose to confide them to his diary which, over a period of twenty years, contains only one display of feeling, or rather pique, the entry for 9 July 1786: 'The Queen gave birth to my second daughter . . . there were no congratulations, no firework display and no Te Deum.'

The format partly explains the banality, but Louis-Auguste himself chose it. Over half the space is devoted to the achievements of his hunt, a minute record not just of every deer or boar but of every swallow killed, and this follows the pattern of the hunting diaries traditionally kept by the kings. He also decided that it was worth making a retrospective fair copy of the list of his engagements, which incidentally explains the celebrated entries of *rien*, the *rien* for 14 July 1789, for example, corresponding to a blank in his original schedule as the storming of the Bastille was not an official engagement. Furthermore, he does sometimes depart from his chosen format to record personal details such as taking a bath, but these are always strictly factual, and although the number of entries increases with the years — the first use of 'nothing', implying that something usually happened, occurs on 10 July 1770 — the quality of entry when he is thirty-eight is the same as when he is twelve. This meticulous record not just of game killed but journeys made, masses celebrated, even medicine taken, reveals an obsession with facts and figures, the mind of an accountant.

The Dauphin did not live to see the completion of his son's education, dying of tuberculosis on 20 December 1765. The Duc de Berry became the new Dauphin at the age of eleven. Marie-Josèphe contracted the disease from her husband and on 13 March 1767 Louis-Auguste wrote baldly in his diary: 'Death of my mother at eight in the evening'.

The old Dauphin is generally considered to have exercised an empire over his son from the grave. Marie-Josèphe instituted a veritable cult of the dead, going into elaborate mourning, cutting off her blond hair, commissioning a mausoleum for her husband in the Cathedral at Sens, with a scale-model of it the chief ornament in her room. On 1 March 1766, after a solemn mass for the repose of the deceased, La Vauguyon stood Louis-Auguste in front of a portrait of his father and instructed him to return every day to 'meditate before his image' and 'propose . . . one of his virtues to imitate'.[10] Finally the Dauphin bequeathed his son a list of ministers to employ. The Dauphin's posthumous influence is also generally considered to have been exercised at the expense of Louis XV. Even so, the relationship between the three generations was more complicated. In the first place, the new Dauphin was only eleven when his father died, so the dominant influence was likely to become that of the King himself, especially as he began to take an interest in his heir. Secondly, the differences between the old Dauphin and the King were more apparent than real and were in any case bridged by the later policies of Louis XV as well as those of his grandson as king.

The death of the Dauphin brought Louis XV and his grandson together, and they wept in each other's arms. It also removed the impediment to what was to become a great shared pleasure, hunting. The old Dauphin had hated outdoor exercise and had ceased to hunt altogether after accidentally killing one of his grooms. This meant that Louis-Auguste did not have his first riding lesson until he was thirteen and did not ride to the hunt — as opposed to following in a specially constructed light open carriage known as a *calèche* — until he was fourteen. This event he notes in his diary: 'Tuesday 18 [July 1769]: First hunt of the stag on horseback'. Soon he was hunting up to five times a week. Hunting was a life-line to the young prince, a sickly, gangling youth who may have contracted tuberculosis when nursing his elder brother and remained subject to bouts of illness throughout his teens. These diminished as he grew in strength with the fresh air and exercise.

Louis-Auguste did not adopt the censorious tone of his own father towards the private life of the King and, whatever he thought of Madame du Barry, he took the initiative of asking La Vauguyon to get him invited to the hunting suppers over which she presided. The King appreciated the gesture and, shortly afterwards, wrote to the Duke of Parma: 'Destiny has given me another son who seems sure to be the happiness of my remaining days; and I love him with all my heart because he returns my love.'[11]

Louis XV associated his grandson in his arrangments for the parlements. He accompanied the King to the *lit de justice* on 7 December 1770 when he publicly congratulated the Chancellor on 'having put the crown back on the King's head', later saying 'that is the correct public law, I am absolutely delighted with M. le Chancelier'.[12] The growing closeness, in public and private, between the old king and his grandson gives the last four years of the reign a special quality. One might almost give it the name applied to the fine furniture of the Louis XV/XVI period, 'transitional'. The association of the old Dauphin's son in these events may almost be said to represent his benediction on them and surely that embittered prince would have rejoiced to see the essence of his policies being implemented by his protégés, now in the Ministry. What might have qualified his delight at Choiseul's discomfiture would have been the Austrian marriage for his son — the Dauphin had favoured a Saxon match — which that minister had engineered shortly before his precipitate fall and which was to cast some doubt upon the finality of that event.

On 16 May 1770 Louis-Auguste, Dauphin of France, married the Archduchess Maria-Antonia, youngest daughter of Maria-Theresa, Queen of Bohemia and Hungary, the last of the Habsburgs, and of the late Francis, Duke of Lorraine, who had been elected Holy Roman Emperor but had had to cede his patrimony of Lorraine to Stanislas Lesczinska prior to its incorporation into France. They had met two days before at the edge of the Forest of Compiègne where the Austrian envoys had handed the Archduchess over to Louis XV. Marie-Antoinette at fifteen appeared much as she does in the portraits of her as queen: blonde, with slightly pinched features, high cheek bones, mercifully escaping the Habsburg chin of her grandfather, the Emperor Charles VI. The Dauphin, slim, with gangling limbs, high forehead and long nose, did not resemble the familiar portraits of him as king, plump and kindly, but it was the face that was to appear on his coinage, unchanged until 1786, and thus the one that was known by the millions of his subjects who never saw him in the flesh.

At the time of her marriage, Marie-Antoinette had scarcely any education. In 1768, when she was thirteen, Maria-Theresa, realizing that she was virtually illiterate, gave her a new tutor, a French priest, the Abbé Vermond, who was to devote one hour of the day to teaching her 'religion, the history of France, . . . a knowledge of the great families and especially those who occupy positions at Court . . . and the French language and spelling'. After a year's tuition, however, she still wrote 'inexpressibly slowly'[13] and when signing her marriage contract she made two spelling mistakes in writing her Christian names. In intellect and in educational attainment, Louis-Auguste and Marie-Antoinette were not equally matched.

Nor, for several years, was their marriage consummated: Louis needed a minor operation — the cutting of a ligament — to enable him to have a proper erection. His brother-in-law, the Emperor Joseph II, during his visit to France in 1777, persuaded him to undergo the operation and on 20 December of that year Marie-Antoinette was able to write to Joseph: 'I had great hopes, my dear brother, of telling you this time that I was pregnant. My hopes have once again receded but I have great confidence that it will not be long, since the King is living with me in the fullest sense, especially since our return from Fontainebleau when he has hunted less.' She had not long to wait. On 19 June Louis was able to tell his cousin Charles IV of Spain that the Queen was pregnant, 'which fills me with joy'.[14] She gave birth to a daughter, which was unfortunate since not only did the Salic Law bar women from the throne but it was difficult to find a husband of suitable rank for a princess of France (hence the unmarried state of Louis's aunts and of his sister Madame Elizabeth). After the birth of her daughter Marie-Antoinette suffered a miscarriage and she did not finally produce a Dauphin until 1781; the Duc de Normandie followed in 1785 and the following year a girl who died in infancy.

In time, Louis was to grow to love Marie-Antoinette, and the fact that he never took a mistress enhanced her potential influence, but because from the start her relatives leaned heavily on her to intercede for them and because of the feeling that Austria had exploited France in the late war, Louis determined to exclude her from all major decisions. A letter to her favourite brother, Joseph, shows Marie-Antoinette's awareness of this: 'The King's natural distrust was confirmed in the first place by his governor before my marriage. M. de La Vauguyon had frightened him about the empire his wife would want to exercise over him and his black mind took a pleasure in frightening his pupil with all the bogies invented about the House of Austria.'[15]

The death of the King

On Wednesday, 27 April 1774, the Dauphin breakfasted with the King and Mme du Barry in the Petit Trianon, the charming villa in the grounds of Versailles designed by Gabriel and completed in 1768. This was the last occasion on which the Dauphin saw his grandfather; his diary notes: 'Thursday 28: King's illness. Friday 29: In the morning smallpox is diagnosed. 7 [May]: Last rites of the King at six in the morning. 10 [May]: Death of the King at two in the afternoon and departure for Choisy.'

When Louis XV died at the age of sixty-four, he was almost universally detested, his earlier sobriquet of *le bien-aimé* having become a mockery. A canon of Notre-Dame relates that when he fell ill at Metz in 1744 six thousand candles had been lit for his recovery; after the attempted assassination by Damiens in 1757, the number had been reduced to six hundred, whilst during his last illness it was only three. An age not noted for its prudery nevertheless judged his vices harshly whilst scarcely comprehending his gentler virtues, such as his hatred of warfare — he had declared on the field of Fontenoy that the victory had not been worth the carnage. Of his subjugation of the Parlement, Barnave was to write: 'Frenchmen combined such submissiveness with such contempt for their master that they seemed ready to suffer everything.'[16]

At the King's death Louis-Auguste was nineteen. We do not know what direct instruction he had received from his grandfather. He did not attend the Conseil d'État, but neither had his father the Dauphin until the birth of his eldest son when he was twenty-two. Perhaps Louis

XV gave his heir a grounding in kingship during the long hours they spent together in the saddle and the grandson's comments to Maupeou after the *lit de justice* imply some knowledge of his grandfather's policies. His general education and the qualities he had displayed in the course of it suggested that he was not ill-equipped for his task, with a cast of mind suited to regulating the complex but also concrete financial and judicial matters that lay at the heart of the administrative monarchy.

Even so, his timidity, reinforced by the stress on *retenue* in his education, would make it difficult for him to pay the gracious compliments by which Henri IV and Louis XIV had been able to win over adversaries. After nearly eight years on the throne, his valet-de-chambre, Thierry, still found it necessary to give a minister the advice: 'I am convinced that when you ask him to speak to naval officers, to those you want him to praise, he does nothing of the sort . . . he is seized by timidity and when he wants to say something obliging, the words stick in his throat and, with the best will in the world, nothing comes out. Try to give him a phrase ready-made, he won't take it amiss and he'll use it.'[17]

2

1774: The New King and The Old Parlement

Half-an-hour after the death of Louis XV, the new King received a note from the Duc de La Vrillière, Minister for the Maison du Roi, posing urgent questions and leaving half the page blank for the King's replies. He could not see the King in person because like all the ministers he was in quarantine, having attended Louis XV on his death-bed. The King replied that he would be known as Louis rather than Louis-Auguste; he would be Louis XVI; he would retain his grandfather's ministers and communicate with them by letter until the ten days of quarantine had elapsed; the military commandants of the provinces and the Intendants should be kept at Versailles until he had seen them.[1] How long they hung around Versailles is not known, but the King left for Choisy the same day and was not to return to Versailles for three months. Pestilence hung about the Palace. Louis XV had had the virulent 'black' strain of smallpox and there was no question of his lying in state: his corpse was rushed to Saint-Denis, the burial place of the kings, and his tomb bricked up to contain the infection.

Cut off from his ministers, Louis could turn to his family for advice. The more distant members, the Princes of the Blood, had, with the solitary exception of the Comte de la Marche, son of the Prince de Condé, ranged themselves among the opposition to Louis XV's last ministry. The most outspoken was the Prince de Conti, 'mon cousin l'avocat' as Louis XV called him, the patron of the Jansenist theoretican of parlementaire resistance, Le Paige. Louis was also obliged to exile Orléans and Chartres for refusing to recognize the Parlement Maupeou. This inaugurated the poor relations which were to subsist between the King and the House of Orléans. Because they were close to the throne, the King felt it necessary to deny them a role: he interrupted Chartres's promising naval career because he hoped to succeed his father-in-law, Penthièvre, as Grand Admiral of France.[2]

Louis's immediate family was more supportive, though Marie-Antoinette was inclined to favour the old Parlement, if only because of her personal dislike for d'Aiguillon and the association with Madame du Barry. Louis's second brother, the Comte de Provence, who of the three brothers had been the closest to their governor, La Vauguyon, was firmly in the *dévot* camp. The royal historiographer, Jacob Nicolas Moreau, the ideologist of this position, had a place on his Council. Inevitably denied an official role, such as a place on the Council, he became a *frondeur* and became known as the 'briseur des ministres', though, whatever his intentions, he only contributed to the fall of one.[3] The youngest brother, Artois, was only seventeen; he was more charismatic, less intelligent and more transparent than his elder brothers, and his political development was not yet complete. Moreau says that he favoured the recall of the Parlement,[4] but this probably represented the reaction of a young blade to the stuffiness of the *dévots* rather than a settled conviction. Indeed, Artois was later to prove the main supporter of traditional absolute monarchy.

The main family influence on the young King at this juncture, though, was that of his maiden aunts Adélaïde and Victoire, 'mesdames tantes'. They were instrumental in the choice he made of an adviser to compensate for his youthful inexperience, though the choice of Jean Frédéric Phélypeax, Comte de Maurepas, was a natural one. Maurepas had been Minister for the Maison at the age of seventeen, then Minister for the Marine from 1723 until his dismissal in 1749, allegedly for circulating some scurrilous verses about Madame de Pompadour. This could only have recommended him to the Dauphin, who included him on the list of ministers his son should appoint. Maurepas had himself been the patron of two of that son's tutors.

From Choisy Louis wrote to La Vrillière enclosing a letter for Maurepas, together with permission to return to Court. Maurepas had been living in exile on his estates at Pontchartrain for the past twenty-five years: internal exile, often coupled with a severe restriction as to visitors, was the invariable lot of the ex-minister, a measure designed to prevent them from maintaining the threads of a political faction and staging a come-back. 'It seemed', wrote one of his colleagues, 'that fortune had wished to mature him by experience and above all by disgrace.'[5] Another colleague added that despite his cold cynicism and frivolous wit — he was one of the most refined products of the Ancien Régime — 'deep down he believed that he was eternally damned and only accorded his confidence and what he called his friendship to those whose souls he believed to be in the same case'.[6]

The King's letter concluded with these words:

I am only twenty years of age. I do not think that I have acquired all the knowledge that is needed. What is more, I cannot see any of the ministers, for they were all closeted with the King during his illness. I have always heard your integrity spoken of as well as the reputation which your deep knowledge of affairs has so rightly won for you. It is this that induces me to beg you to be so kind as to help me with your advice and understanding. I would be grateful, Monsieur, if you would come as soon as you can to Choisy, where I shall look forward with the utmost pleasure to seeing you.[7]

In summoning an adviser, Louis was merely following the pattern set by his Bourbon predecessors, who had all acceded to the throne young, younger in fact than Louis XVI since they had all been minors, i.e., younger than thirteen. Nevertheless, whereas advisers to former kings, such as Cardinals Mazarin and Fleury, had effectively run the country, that was not what Louis XVI had in mind. What he did have in mind is not exactly clear, since he never defined the role of Maurepas, whose status was to remain ambiguous until his death. At their first meeting Maurepas began with generalities: 'I will be nothing in the eyes of the public. I will be for you alone: your ministers will work with you; I will never speak to them in your name and I will never undertake to speak to you on their behalf. Just defer decisions that are not of a routine nature. We will have a chat once or twice a week and if you have gone too quickly, I will tell you.' Duty compelled him, however, to observe that the reign of Louis XV had been happiest when Cardinal Fleury had been prime minister, as it was essential for there to be a 'centre', a prime minister: 'If you will not or cannot be it, you must necessarily choose one.' Maurepas hinted that he should be that man but received silence for an answer.[8] Many of the ills of the reign of Louis XVI before the Revolution stemmed from the fact that he failed to take this advice.

Not that Maurepas himself would necessarily have been the right choice, for as the summer wore on it became clear to the young King that his special adviser was tendering unpalatable advice: to dismiss the existing ministers and recall the old Parlement. Maurepas was moreover aware that such a decision would be, as he himself put it, 'against the principles of the King's education'.[9] Most people in the ministerial milieu took the view, on constitutional as well as moral grounds, that a king's (especially a young king's) deepest convictions should not be violated; that, in the jargon, a *simple prévention* could be overcome but not a *décision précise*. Nor could Maurepas's advice have been easily predicted: his antecedents seemed to place him firmly in the ranks of the Bourbon traditionalists who supported an anti-Austrian foreign policy, as well as defence of religion (though personally Maurepas professed none) and of the royal authority against the Parlement. He was uncle to the Duc d'Aiguillon, scion of the traditionalist Richelieu family, and his Phélypeaux cousin La Vrillière was Minister for the Maison, which enabled him to say, loftily, to the King at their first meeting: 'Concerning your present ministers, I shall say nothing: some are my close relatives, the others are known only to me by public repute.'[10]

Perhaps, however, it was Maurepas's very traditionalism which led him to envisage a traditional Parlement, neither the invasive one of the 1760s nor the puppet body that succeeded it, rather the moderate body he had handled 'with his legal knowledge, foresight and skill as a negotiator' in the golden age of Fleury.[11] Maurepas was a fossil from that age; no disrespect is meant by this, but his attitudes and information had become fossilized: internal exile was designed to keep people out of touch. Maurepas took three guiding principles from that vanished age. First, the need for a traditional Parlement: 'point de parlement point de monarchie'. A second idea also advanced by Miromesnil, Maurepas's 'ami de tout temps', with whom he wanted to replace Maupeou, was that divisions within the Parlement reflected divisions within the Ministry that had not existed in Fleury's time. To prevent this, Maurepas was determined to create a *ministère harmonieux* of his own appointees. Thirdly, Maurepas wanted to turn the tide of courtier invasion of the Ministry and return once more to the situation under Fleury of *robe* ministers: as Besenval put it, 'homme de robe' was a 'title which always had a claim on M. de Maurepas'.[12]

Maurepas and the coterie that formed round him, the Abbé de Véri, his confidant, the companion of his exile and chronicler of his second ministry, and Miromesnil, also believed that the Parlement was no threat because, as Véri put it, 'it had never had the slightest intention of gaining control of the troops which are the basis of real power'.[13] Miromesnil thought Louis XV's fears had been 'puerile', adding: 'How can one fear three or four thousand unarmed men in black robes?'[14] Maurepas told the *Lieutenant-général de police*, Lenoir, that the Parlement would be restored but that if 'disputes arose they were not to be treated as matters of State but as police matters' and, as a general principle, Lenoir was instructed that in order to prevent tension, 'it is necessary for the police to act often'.[15] Thus Maurepas was led to the paradoxical conclusion that by using force you could avoid the imputation of despotism which Louis XV had invited by suppressing the parlements without resorting to it. The first-resort use of what was believed to be the ultimate basis of power was to be a disturbing feature of the new reign.

A cynical motive for Maurepas's advice to the King on the Parlement comes to mind: the King would not appoint him prime minister, but he could perhaps become an unofficial one by assembling a ministry of like-minded protégés in place of his grandfather's formidable ministry, which could only be achieved by a major reversal of policy.

Though Maurepas expatiated to Lenoir on the philosophy behind the new order, its birth was by no means assured. For as yet Louis XVI had given him nothing that he did not already possess, the title of *ministre d'état* being given for life. Thus simply by ending his exile the King enabled Maurepas to resume his seat in the Council, blinking across the table at those 'close relatives' and strangers as though he had woken from a sleep of thirty years. But in that body, where it was the convention that the King should abide by majority decisions, Maurepas could be expected to be outvoted by Louis XV's old ministers, who retained their portfolios, Maurepas having none, and continued to run the country.

On 2 June the Duc d'Aiguillon resigned in anticipation of being dismissed from his two ministries of Foreign Affairs and War, an event neither hastened nor retarded by Maurepas, who told the King: 'I will only act as his relation in seeking to obtain from you some relaxation in the *traitements de rigueur*' (i.e. to moderate the depth and duration of his exile).[16] Maurepas, incidentally, who had himself suffered, thought that loss of office was a sufficient punishment for a disgraced minister without having to endure exile, but his hopes of winning round the new King were shortlived. The fall of d'Aiguillon resulted not from a change of policy but from the personal intervention of Marie-Antoinette, who detested him for his links with Madame du Barry. Maria-Theresa and the Austrian Ambassador, Mercy-Argenteau, were appalled alike at her intervention (d'Aiguillon had deplored but permitted the partition of Poland in 1772) and her lack of interest in influencing the appointment of d'Aiguillon's replacements.

These appointments worked to the advantage of the Chancellor. He had already benefited from the resignation of his rival d'Aiguillon, who had lately been gaining at his expense with his appointment to the War Ministry in January and had contemplated a partial restoration of the old Parlement. Public opinion designated the Duc de Nivernais, who had married Maurepas's sister, for the Foreign Office but he had been one of the twelve peers who had protested against the suppression of the old Parlement. Maurepas did not dare put forward the name of a man so compromised but waited for the King to raise the subject, but in vain, for the King's silent veto operated. Finally, the Comte de Vergennes was appointed, a career diplomat of modest origins within the administrative *robe* and a 'workaholic' who managed on four hours' sleep. It is not clear whether the dominant influence in his appointment was that of Maurepas, the King personally, or Maupeou, whose protection Vergennes had sought[17] after Choiseul had recalled him from the Embassy at Constantinople for contracting an unsuitable marriage with a local woman. Moreover, Maupeou probably assisted his appointment as Ambassador to Stockholm where, in 1772, he had advised Gustavus III on carrying out a coup analogous to Maupeou's own.[18] Whether or not he owed his appointment to him, Vergennes certainly defended his work in the Council.[19]

The other appointment, as Minister for War, was of an old soldier, the Comte du Muy, who was a *dévot*, a former *menin* and lifelong friend of Louis's father, and chose to be buried near his mausoleum at Sens. He had declined office under Louis XV because, only possessing one estate, which he detested, he dreaded exile. Now, 'counting on the coming moral reformation',[20] he accepted office under the son of his revered friend.

The appointment of Vergennes and du Muy seemed to strengthen the position of Maupeou, enabling the Duc de Croÿ to write of 'le début où le Chancelier domina'. At the beginning of July Veri thought that Maurepas should retire from the Ministry, 'unless he becomes its soul; having no portfolio, he cuts a ridiculous figure there'. But Maurepas had no intention of returning to Pontchartrain, developing instead a three-pronged counter-attack. The first part of this was to emphasize the distinction which the King already made between the achievements of his grandfather's ministry, particularly in the fields of the judiciary and finance, and their manner and agency which he found distasteful (a moral, even austere, tone being the main tangible difference between late-Louis XV policies and those which his grandson intended to pursue); the second concerned the King's residence; and the third the decision-making role of the Conseil d'État.

'Talented but disreputable' would summarize Louis XVI's view of his grandfather's Ministry, the latter quality being epitomized by their association with Madame du Barry, who had sat rather incongruously at the head of the *dévot* faction. He had been polite to her for the sake of the King, and 'out of consideration for the memory of the King' he now granted her a pension, but she had to spend it in a convent. Similarly with Maupeou. Nothing had caused him to revise his opinion of 1770 that the Chancellor had 'put the crown back on the King's head', but whereas Louis XV had been fond of his minister, calling him his 'little Seville orange' because of his sallow skin, the new King found him uncongenial.[21] Louis's sense of justice was affronted by the fact that the exiled parlementaires had not been given financial compensation for the loss of offices which were regarded as incorporeal property, whilst Maupeou had used the coup to work off old scores on his personal enemies in the Parlement. Maurepas was aided by the fact that Maupeou did not bother to defend his work before the King:

Maurepas asked the King whether Maupeou had discussed the question of the Parlement with him: 'Not a word,' the King replied smiling, 'he scarcely does me the honour of . . . noticing me, let alone speaking to me.'[22]

Terray, the *Contrôleur-général*, presented a contrast to the Chancellor both in physique, Terray being tall and gaunt, and in manner. For whereas Maupeou suggested the finality of his achievement by his very aloofness, Terray, by contrast, 'multiplied his contacts with the King in order to creep into his confidence'.[23] Many considered him servile and contemporary cartoons depict him bowing so low that his large, aquiline nose and clerical bands are seen from behind between his legs. His progress with the King was aided by the fact that Louis's boyhood interest in mathematics had developed into one for public finance, 'a field', he was later to tell the nation, 'which the King understands'.[24] He plied the King with memoranda on economy, working out the produce and consumption of each province, and on the need for a government budget. Nor was it easy to deny his talents: since his appointment in 1768 he had increased annual revenue by about eighty million livres and reduced the deficit to twenty-five. He instituted a minute parish by parish investigation or *vérification* into evasion of the *vingtième* by the nobility. It was slow work and over the next ten years only a quarter of the parishes had been covered, but revenue in these had been raised by fifty percent. Marcel Marion considered that his measures prolonged the life of the Ancien Régime by a generation. They had, however, been harsh, notably the 'bankruptcy' or forcible reduction on the rate of interest on *rentes* of 1770 and in 1771 the tax of one tenth on life-annuities and one fifteenth on *rentes*.

The King's residence at Versailles, which he preferred to any of his other palaces, worked to the disadvantage of Maurepas because of its formality, in that official ministers had the advantage over unofficial and the King, surrounded by ceremonial, was hard to closet. In the heat of the summer, when Versailles with its rudimentary sanitation became fairly unpleasant, it was customary for the kings to spend a month or two in the smaller royal châteaux such as Compiègne or Marly, and in the autumn they went to Fontainebleau for the hunting. In 1775, for example, Louis spent fifty-seven nights away from Versailles. In 1774 it was necessary for the Royal Family to decamp to Choisy to avoid infection and they remained there from 10 to 17 May, with Adélaïde and Victoire, who had been in contact with their father, living in a separate building. Then, however, instead of returning to Versailles, Louis proceeded to travel round his palaces until 1 September. We learn from his diary that his summer was spent as follows: Choisy: 10–17 May; La Muette: 17 May–16 June; Marly:

16 June–1 August; Compiègne: 1 August–1 September. September was spent at Versailles. Then the travelling resumes: Choisy (again) 5–10 October; Fontainebleau: 10 October–10 November; La Muette: 11–12 November.

Away from Versailles, ministers did not have automatic access to the King, apparently having to write for permission to see him.[25] Most of the major decisions of the reign of Louis XVI were taken in one of the smaller palaces, which also meant that most of them had to be taken in the summer or autumn. It is hard to resist the conclusion that Maurepas arranged this itinerary for his royal charge in 1774 to suit his political purposes. It must have seemed to Louis like an over-prolonged holiday, as when a child whose parents have been overtaken by calamity is whisked off by a caring relation on a long trip which soon breeds anxiety instead of excitement. No wonder Croÿ talks of 'this curious excursion [to Compiègne] so striking in events'.[26]

Maurepas's third stratagem was an institutional change: the transference of decision-making from the Conseil d'État to ad hoc comités, from which ministers who were hostile to Maurepas's policy as it unfolded could be excluded when it was a matter of general policy, or surrounded when it concerned their department. Under Louis XV, comités had prepared work for the Conseil but decisions had usually been taken there.[27] Maurepas also believed that it would be easier for the King to learn his craft in informal comités, as he explained in a circular designed to still the complaints of excluded ministers:

> The function which I have come here to perform has as its sole aim to teach the King to carry out his vocation. Nothing would give me greater delight than to be able to please all the ministers and still carry out this duty. But I do not see how I can teach a young man his craft of kingship in Councils of eight to ten people where everyone speaks in order of rank and often extempore. Comités are lost conversations . . . and it does not matter whether they lead to a conclusion or not. The King must be able to speak his mind without making law.
> . . . I do not claim that the comités decide everything. Their conclusions are often sent either to the Conseil d'État or the Conseil des Dépêches for their definitive form because I have no wish to deprive any member of the Ministry of the consideration which is his due.[28]

The system of comités had taken shape by the beginning of August and from July Maurepas began to take a stronger line with the King: on 20 July Turgot, the Intendant of Limoges who favoured a recall of the Parlement, replaced Bourgeois de Boynes at the Ministry of the Marine and Maurepas began to criticize Maupeou and Terray more openly. Terray continued to hold his ground with the King, to the extent that Véri thought they would have to buy him off by giving him Maupeou's job, to which Maurepas replied: 'But how can we place a man who has forfeited his honour at the head of the Judiciary?'[29] Maurepas made a cynical exception to the move towards more informal government by resurrecting the *Conseil royal des finances* to restrain Terray and it met for the first time in years on 19 July.[30] Rumour also came to Maurepas's aid, for in July the King received an anonymous letter accusing him of personally profiting from Terray's *régie des grains*. On 30 July he wrote to Maurepas: 'Whilst you are in Paris, try to get to the bottom of the so-called grain treaty — and find me a *Contrôleur-général*. Adieu and good-night till we meet at Compiègne.'[31]

Still the King deferred a final decision. Eventually, at ten on the morning of 23 August, his patience exhausted, Maurepas went to the King for his usual tête-à-tête working-session or *travail*:

'You don't have your portfolio,' said the King, 'do I conclude there is not much business?' 'I beg your pardon, Sire, but the matter about which I must talk to you has no need of papers. It is a question of your honour . . . if you do not want to keep your ministers, say so . . . and appoint their successors.' 'Yes, I have decided to change them,' said the King, 'it will be on Saturday, after the Conseil des Dépêches.' 'No, Sire,' the Minister replied with some petulance, 'that is not how to govern a state! I repeat: time is not a commodity with which you can dispose at pleasure. You have already lost too much for the good of affairs and I am not leaving until you have decided . . .'[32]

So, with a heavy heart and against his better judgement, Louis dismissed Maupeou and Terray. Apart from Maurepas's arguments, Louis was influenced by the state of public opinion. In his youthful *Réflexions*, he had written: 'I must always consult public opinion, it is never wrong.' Public opinion gave an appearance, perhaps illusory, of unity and 'it offered an abstract court of appeal to a monarchy anxious to put an end to several decades of political contestation'.[33] Public opinion required that the new king take an active decision on the question of the Parlement. An existential decision, a decision not to decide, would have suited Louis's temperament and his political beliefs; it would have been a decision in favour of the Maupeou settlement. As he deferred his decision, however, the immense popularity which greeted the start of his reign began to cool. At length, when the *dévot* faction stressed the perils of cancelling his grandfather's achievements, he is said to have replied: 'That may be true. It may be considered politically unwise, but it seems to me to be the general wish and I want to be loved.'[34]

Maupeou's carriage was stoned as he left Compiègne. He would not resign the office of Chancellor — even, it was said, for the promise of a dukedom — and by convention a Chancellor, as the last of the great medieval officers of state, could not be dismissed without being put on trial. Since Maupeou lived until 1792, he was the last Chancellor of France; he even made a point of leaving behind in the Chancellerie his effects, which in 1789 he was anxious to retrieve.[35] Meanwhile, his successor, Maurepas's candidate Miromesnil, had to content himself with the title Keeper of the Seals. Turgot became *Contrôleur-général*. When Terray went, Louis told Maurepas: 'I'm sorry; I would really like to have been able to keep him, but he is too great a knave. It's a pity, a pity!'[36] Knave or not, he had impressed on the young King that his measures had done no more than alleviate the desperate state of royal finances and on 19 October Louis circularized every *ordonnateur* (paymaster), requesting details of their projected spending for 1775, of what could be deferred 'until happier times' and of what economies could be made: 'otherwise I could not carry out my heartfelt desire to lighten the load [of taxation] on my peoples'.[37]

It was generally accepted that the common people could not pay any more, whilst the privileged groups would not pay any more without a say in how the money was to be spent. Again, though France's public debt was no larger than her rival England's, it required an additional two percent in interest payments to service. This was because it was a royal rather than a national debt and because there was a risk premium involved in the Bourbon's propensity to default on their debts: they would pay high rates of interest when credit was weak during a war and at the peace forcibly reduce them on the grounds that usurious rates of interest were proscribed by the Church. It was crude but effective and took only the greedy by surprise. On Turgot's appointment, Louis renounced all such 'bankruptcies' and this was the new framework within which all ministers had to work. Whether the new King was inspired by a sense of justice or the need to improve credit, he voluntarily surrendered an important weapon in his arsenal just as he was about to relinquish the constitutional gains his grandfather had made at the expense of the Parlement.

Government by comité was not abandoned after the fall of Maupeou, and Terray had removed its original raison d'être. It was considered necessary to re-educate the King on parlementaire affairs and to make him think that the recall of the Parlement had been his own decision because it would be more difficult to restrain the restored Parlement if the King's spirit had been broken. The process would involve hours of discussion and the Council was deemed unsuitable both because of the publicity and because Vergennes and du Muy were unsound on the parlementaire question: the presence at the Quai d'Orsay of memoranda advocating the retention of Maupeou's settlement even after the fall of the Chancellor suggests discreet activity on the part of the Foreign Secretary.[38] Accordingly a *comité restreint* of four ministers, Maurepas, Miromesnil, Turgot and Sartine (the Minister for the Marine), met in complete secrecy to discuss the question of the Parlement. Véri has left a detailed account of its aims and methods:

> The comité of four ministers has had frequent discussions before the King. The aim is to persuade this Prince that the result will be his own doing in order that he may bring to bear the degree of warmth and involvement necessary in all large-scale operations of this kind. The will of the master, known and reputed as constant, is the true means of ending internal troubles. It is essential to give him this in reality and not be content with the appearance.
>
> The method that has been adopted has been to place before his eyes all that has been said, written, thought and circulated, for and against, on this subject. The ministers wanted to know his opinion on everything and establish the most detailed discussion with him. . . . This method has had the desired effect, which was to make him regard the plan which has been determined as his own — and to be able to circulate this opinion among the public.
>
> Because, whatever the decision, the capital point is that it should come from his mind and not from the Council of his ministers. As this decision is different from the ideas he had before ascending the throne, he has himself confessed his astonishment: 'Who would have said, a few years back when I went to the *lit de justice* with my grandfather, that I would be holding the one I am about to hold?'[39]

This uninhibited account of the virtual 'brainwashing' of the twenty-year-old King tells us something of the dilemma facing the ministers of a king who was expected to rule personally. It would have been convenient if the ministers could simply have told themselves that they were forcing the King's hand in his own best interests, the conventional device employed in an explicitly constitutional monarchy. But the King's active co-operation was needed because the programme outlined in the *lit de justice* of 12 November (Louis had finally returned to Versailles that very day) was not a crude capitulation to the old Parlement, but a complicated system of checks and balances which would depend for its success on the spirit in which it was operated, which depended in turn on the King's spirit being left intact. Provision was made for a plenary court — consisting of the Princes and great dignitaries of state — to pronounce forfeiture against the Parlement if it broke certain conditions (if it went on judicial strike it would automatically be replaced by the Gran'Conseil) and only one further remonstrance was to be permitted after the enforced registration of an edict. These were only rules on paper, but the King's demeanour at the *lit de justice* seemed to the ministers of the comité to offer hope that the rules would be obeyed: 'We were astonished at the tone of firmness and personal will which the King brought to his speech. The ministers of the comité did not expect it. . . . [to achieve this firmness] he learned his speech by heart. As he repeated it to his ministers, one of them would mark time with his hand. "Too fast," he would tell him, "we didn't hear you properly!" '[40]

Maurepas and Véri accused the King of indecisiveness because it took him so long to decide the fate of Maupeou and Terray and that of the 'Parlement Maupeou'. Véri thought that if this 'spirit of indecision really took hold M. de Maurepas would be forced to usurp, so to speak, the function of prime minister for decisions'.[41] However, not only did Louis have to make the most imporant decision of his reign at its very outset, he also faced a structural dilemma: the man whom he had summoned to advise him was tendering advice with which he disagreed, whilst his official advisers, the Ministers, were tendering advice which contradicted that of his personal adviser. Moreover, his initial reaction, to maintain the Maupeou settlement, seems to us correct, and his subsequent concession to an ill-defined and fleeting public opinion appears to us as weakness rather than realism.

The evil Louis XV did lived after him; the good was bricked up at Saint-Denis. Any harm done by the Maupeou coup in 'underlining the need for . . . a reconstitution of the body politic'[42] was permanent, the benefits achieved by reversing it were transient: the disposition to criticize the Government continued, but the Government could no longer afford to disregard it. If the slavish maintenance of the status quo had been the objective, as it was for both Maurepas and Miromesnil, the restoration of the Parlement was probably necessary. Louis, however, in contrast with both men, was to show himself to be accessible to plans for reform, and in the long run the Ancien Régime could only be reformed over the dead bodies of the parlements.

3

Maurepas and Turgot

When he finally returned to Versailles, Louis set about making himself comfortable in his private apartments, the same that had been occupied by Louis XV: the furniture and décor were left untouched, an action of piety, perhaps, if not economy or just inertia. The staircase leading to the apartments was hung with Louis's hunting trophies as Dauphin. On the first floor was the drawing-room, hung with engravings of the French canals; above was the geography room, equipped with maps, globes and instruments, the table always covered with the map on which he was currently working. On the third floor, Louis housed his grandfather's collection of fine wood-working tools, with rose-wood and silver mounts, and on the fourth — Louis XV's games-room — Louis installed his library, which was to contain everything published in France during his reign. On the fifth floor was a smithy where Louis indulged his passion for locksmithing. An interest in the mechanical arts was quite usual for the period and was made fashionable by Rousseau's educational treatise *Émile*, in accordance with which, for example, Louis's young cousin, Louis-Philippe of Orléans, had dutifully to learn how to use a plane.[1] Right at the top of his wing of the Palace was a small turret just large enough to contain an armchair and a telescope through which Louis liked to watch arrivals and departures at Versailles.

Louis spent much of his time in the private apartments, often signified in his diary by the word *rien*. He had 'nothing' on in the way of public engagements, but was reading or seeing ministers or engaged in metalwork. A man of simple tastes, he attached little importance to representation or public display. Louis XIV, acting on the medieval notion that when a man was not at Court he was in rebellion, had enforced attendance. Louis XVI did not and stipulated that Court service was to be 'reduced to what is absolutely necessary'. The ceremonies of the *lever* and the *coucher* continued to be the focal point of the Court's day, whilst the King, who liked his food, served excellent

suppers in the private apartments to members of the *noblesse présentée*;
but there was no life in it.

Many ceased going to Court because with the King either inaccessible
or uncommunicative they could get nothing out of it. When Louis made
the Duc de Croÿ a Marshal of France, he remained totally silent 'as
ceremonies bore the King';[2] and Croÿ was one of the few courtiers who
liked Louis and respected his abilities. He was one of the few, moreover,
with whom the King could have a natural conversation based on a
common interest: in 1779, Croÿ notes, 'the King talked to me for a long
time about geography and he spoke well'.[3] Even so, he could find
nothing to say on the occasion of making a Marshal out of a man whose
fighting days were long over.

Above the King's apartments, crammed into the eaves of Versailles,
had been the cramped quarters of Madame du Barry, which were
connected to the King's by a 'secret' communicating passage. In an
act which seemed symbolic of the 'coming moral regeneration', Louis
replaced Madame du Barry with Maurepas and his wife, whom an
enchanted public christened Baucis and Philemon. These cramped
quarters, in which he was often further confined by gout, were to be
the centre of Maurepas's power for the next seven years. Necker, the
finance minister from 1776 to 1781, has left a graphic description of
them: 'I can still remember that dark, long staircase of M. de Maurepas
which I ascended in trepidation and heaviness of heart.... I can still
remember that entresol apartment, placed under the eaves of Versailles
but above the King's apartments which in its smallness and situation
seemed the very essence, the refined essence of all human vanity and
ambition.'[4]

The key to Maurepas's power was physical access to the King —
hence the importance of the communicating passage — but it seems
that, such was the King's thoughtlessness, Maurepas, despite his gout,
did not use this secret passage until 1775, when he was granted the
grandes entrées. Previously he had to hobble the long way round to see the
King. This formal approach to informality — dozens of people had
the *grandes entrées*, but Maurepas to whom they really would have given
the chance of casually dropping in on the King was denied them —
mattered because Louis denied Maurepas both the formal title of *premier
ministre*, which was available under the Ancien Régime, and the delega-
tion of authority which, for example, the young Louis XV had given
Cardinal Fleury in the following instruction: 'We order [such and such
a minister] to work with and despatch all affairs under the direction of
[Fleury] and to carry out his instructions as if they were our own.'[5]

Maurepas, in short, was never a viceroy and, in particular, the
King always retained the power of final decision: every decision of any

importance had to be thrashed out with him, a process which could take weeks or months or end inconclusively. In addition, whether through choice or necessity, Maurepas adhered to the promise he had made to the King in his first audience, that he would neither speak to the Ministers in the King's name, as Fleury, nor speak to the King in the name of the Ministers (as an English Prime Minister). Instead, just as his quarters, squeezed under the eaves, had been an afterthought in the construction of Versailles, so Maurepas's power had to be squeezed into the interstices of the political edifice. This meant that in the period 1774–6 Maurepas developed a complicated system which exploited his physical access to the King, the only concrete advantage Louis had given him, to regulate or filter all Louis's political encounters, the King consulting Maurepas before taking important decisions and the other ministers consulting Maurepas before bringing up important matters with the King. In practice this meant that Maurepas would descend his long staircase to sit in on a minister's weekly *travail* with the King or, as Maurepas's favour and gout increased, the minister and the King would venture up to Maurepas's apartments. The system quickly became institutionalized: in 1774 Louis XV's old ministers resented and contested it; by 1780, when Maurepas was on one occasion indisposed, he asked Necker to have his *travail* alone with the King and caused them both embarrassment.[6] The new arrangement of government by comité continued and was easily grafted into this scheme: thus, for example, a war cabinet might consist of Maurepas sitting in on the Foreign Secretary's *travail* with the King, while the relevant service minister was in attendance.

Maurepas, however, was under no illusions that this arrangement, with himself as 'at least the shadow of a focal point', compensated for Louis's failure to take his initial advice that if he could not be his own prime minister he must 'necessarily choose one', a failure which led to many of the ills of the reign: ministers constantly engaged in demarcation disputes, undermining each others' policies and spending money regardless of the total amount available since there was no one to fix a global budget and a *ministre ordonnateur* needed only the King's signature to spend any amount. The absence of a clearly defined prime minister also encouraged the political pretensions of the Queen or at least magnified the ministers' fears of danger from that quarter.

The Queen, Choiseul and the new ministry

Mercy-Argenteau wrote that the influence of a prime minister in France was always exercised at the expense of the Queen's,[7] and though

Maurepas was not a full-blooded prime minister, his position, based on physical access to the King, had a special relevance to Mercy's point, which was reinforced by the very lay-out of the royal apartments. For whereas Maurepas's apartments communicated directly with the King's, to get there from her own apartments the Queen had to pass either through a crowded room or the apartments of the King's hostile aunts, Adélaïde and Victoire. In 1775 Mercy arranged for the construction of a secret passage connecting the King's apartments to the Queen's, though he complained that she did not make sufficient use of it.[8] This passage was later to save her life.

In the struggle for the King's ear between Maurepas and Marie-Antoinette, the advantage lay almost entirely in favour of Maurepas. Such, however was his fear of her influence — a fear that 'bordered on the puerile'[9] — that he believed it was the Queen's ultimate intention to replace him with the Duc de Choiseul, and the other ministers with a 'shadow' ministry of Choiseulistes. He was wrong in this assumption. The Queen wished to display gratitude to the man who had arranged her marriage and she granted him a long audience at the time of the coronation at Rheims in June 1775 — on this occasion Louis confined himself to the observation that Choiseul had grown a lot balder at the front — but her main delight in this was in baiting Maurepas: 'I bet', she wrote, 'old Maurepas can't sleep in his bed tonight.'[10] Moreover, the advice coming to her from Austria was summed up in the words of the Chancellor, Kaunitz: 'Choiseul is the man least suited to our purposes.'[11]

The reality was that there was a group of ministerial aspirants who knew that Maurepas would block their careers — men such as the Marquis de Castries, a mildly successful general in the Seven Years War who believed that soldiers rather than lawyers should hold the service ministries; the Baron de Breteuil, the well-connected Ambassador to Vienna who wanted to be Foreign Secretary; and the Comte de Guines, an accomplished flautist (he commissioned a concerto from Mozart without paying for it) who was Ambassador to London. They had been associated with Choiseul when he had patronage at his disposal, but now, as Véri put it, 'if any of them became a minister, assuredly he would not work for Choiseul's return'.[12] Increasingly they looked for protection not to Choiseul but to the Queen herself and in the course of the reign they were transformed into what has been called a 'Queen's Party'.[13] But that was a long way off in 1774.

The chief reason why Maurepas's fears were groundless was that Louis had resolved that Choiseul should not return to power and that whilst the Queen could have a say in the disposal of Court patronage — military promotions became her forte — she should have none in the conduct of major affairs. Louis had come to accept the recall of the Parlement as a pacifying synthesis of the warring creeds which had rent his grandfather's kingdom, but to reappoint one of the protagonists, Choiseul, would upset the balance completely and represent a denial of everything that he and his father had stood for. Nor would Choiseul's aristocratic ridicule of Louis's new *robin* ministry, which made an impression on Marie-Antoinette,[14] have found favour. The 1760s had not just been a time of dependence on the Parlement but one when three of the six ministries had been occupied by grands seigneurs, who had quickly shed their old notions that such bureaucratic functions were degrading and now believed that they alone were competent to run at least the service ministries. They had a different conception of the monarchy from that of the kings, who had always relied on men trained up in the royal administration, and from Maurepas, who, for all his pride in his aristocratic connections, gloried in the ministerial traditions of his family and on whom '*homme de robe* was a title which always had claims'.[15] Maurepas's ministry, with only one soldier, du Muy, and five lawyers in the principal Departments, represented a temporary reversal of the trend of aristocratic incursion.

Louis now had a ministry of his choosing, if not exactly of his choice, one with which he was comfortable. Yet far from giving them open support, he even 'set the example of showing contempt for his ministers'.[16] This was perhaps product of resentment at the way he had been manœuvred over the recall of the Parlement, of his natural *brusquerie* — courtiers called him 'the butcher' — his impenetrability or that natural distrust of ministers and tendency to distance himself from their operations that he had inherited from his grandfather. Whatever its cause, Louis's failure to make explicit his basic support for his ministers fed Maurepas's neurosis and gave his enemies unwarranted hopes. It was in this unnecessarily charged atmosphere that the *Contrôleur-général*, Turgot, introduced his celebrated reform programme.

Turgot and the grain trade

Anne Robert Jacques Turgot, a bachelor of forty-seven from a family which tended to die young — hence, he would say, the urgency of his mission to reform — was loosely associated with the group of economists known as the Physiocrats, whose central tenet was that land was the basis of all wealth. From this it followed that to tax commerce and industry would be self-defeating since the tax would ultimately be paid by the land. Instead, a single land tax should be imposed, payable by noble and commoner alike, since the land was being taxed rather than its proprietors, and should be based on a survey or *cadastre* of all the land in France. Though the theoretical basis was new, these general aims had been accepted by several *Contrôleurs-généraux*, most recently Bertin. This explains why Louis, who had no more love of the Physiocrats, the political and economic wing of the Enlightenment, than of the Enlightenment in general, should support Turgot. Louis may have called Turgot 'bien schématique', but he realized that, beneath the jargon, his measures represented the orthodoxy of the reforming wing of the royal bureaucracy with which he aligned himself.

Physiocracy, literally 'rule of nature', implied free trade, especially of agricultural produce, and in September 1774, within a fortnight of becoming *Contrôleur-général*, Turgot abolished the elaborate regulations which governed the grain trade in France. These reflected the traditional view of the kings of France that the grain trade was a matter of police rather than economics, a means of avoiding riots over bread, the staple diet of most people. Accordingly the farmer was not allowed to sell his grain directly from his granary but was obliged to sell it all openly at market, where he had to serve private individuals before grain merchants and bakers. If he failed to sell his crop at three successive markets he had to take whatever price he could get. Limited free trade in grain had been introduced by legislation of 1763–4 which had been supported by Louis's father, the Dauphin, but Terray had re-imposed state controls and his contract to stock the markets had led to the allegations of a *pacte de famine*. The new King had set up a commission of inquiry to investigate the allegations that he personally had been profiting from the 'pacte' and, though this allayed his fears, he had been sufficiently shaken to be receptive to Turgot's proposals.[17]

Unfortunately free trade in grain was only workable in eighteenth-century France when the harvest was good, as it had been in the 1760s. The peasantry had an almost superstitious dread of allowing grain to leave their district, even if they had a glut and the grain was being sent to an area where there was a dearth. Moreover, until the completion of the Departmental railway network in the 1870s, there were insuperable problems of distribution and a national market did not exist. The harvest of 1774 was poor, the price of bread almost doubled and in April–May 1775 the King had to face riots. These, forming what was known as the Flour War, were more serious than any for half a century, causing him temporarily to lose control of the Île de France and four adjacent provinces.

The crisis was handled by Turgot and Louis personally, Maurepas staying in the background but at the same time feeling jealous. When the disturbances reached Versailles on 2 May, Turgot and Maurepas were at Paris, the latter at the opera. Louis took charge of the situation, displaying, in Véri's words, 'a presence of mind and a calm courage unexpected in a man of his age and peaceable disposition'. The rioters were dispersed 'like a flock of sheep'. The story that Louis harangued a crowd of 8,000 from the balcony and weakly ordered bread to be sold at the price demanded by the rioters is refuted by a note he scribbled to Turgot: 'M. de Beauveau [Captain of the Guards] interrupts me [as I write] to tell me of an act of folly which is to let them have bread at two sols [the livre].'[18]

When the disturbances reached Paris the next day, the situation was handled less effectively. Lenoir, the *lieutenant-général de police*, was by his own boast reluctant to use force; Louis dismissed him at Turgot's request, though after a period of disgrace he was reinstated. Véri thought he had been unlucky; his responsibility was only for Les Halles and in any case 'an *homme de robe*, new in his job, had a right to be anxious'. The prolongation of the riot was principally due to the Duc de Biron, Colonel of the French Guards, who was fearful of falling foul of the Parlement which disliked Turgot's measures as diminishing its jurisdiction over the grain trade. The general position of Biron, who remained in his post until his death in 1788, was that he would not take politically sensitive measures without both direct authorization from the King and a knowledge of the King's personal view of a situation.[19] Maurepas had only 'advised' Biron to act, but Véri told him: 'You should have ordered him, in the name of the King, and taken the consequences on your own head until the return of the courier you should have despatched to obtain the King's orders.'[20]

Once Louis and Turgot had taken control of the Flour War, it was put down firmly, even brutally. There was a massive concentration of troops; they fired on the crowd and the rebels were cleared from the markets and towns. There were two public executions in Paris. Lenoir drew a telling contrast between Louis XV and Maupeou, who carried out 'a major operation of state' without troops, and Louis XVI and Turgot, who staled the impact of this ultimate deterrent by its massive deployment to quell a bread riot.[21] Louis, for his part, had been angered by the whole affair, as appears in the letter he wrote to Gustavus III thanking him for sending grain to France:

The bad harvest and the wicked intentions of a few people whose manœuvres had [*sic*] been uncovered led some scoundrels to come and pillage the markets. The peasants, led on by them and by the false report — sedulously circulated — that the price of bread had been lowered, joined them and they had the insolence to pillage the markets of Versailles and Paris, which forced me to order in troops who restored perfect order without difficulty. After the extreme displeasure I felt at seeing what the people had done, I had the consolation of seeing that as soon as they had been undeceived, they restored what they had taken and were truly sorry for what they had done.[22]

Louis's phrase 'the wickedness of a few people' suggests that he shared the widespread belief that the Flour War was the result of a political conspiracy. He was inclined to blame the Parlement. He had neither forgiven nor forgotten their conduct in the 1760s and when he was angry with them 'his whole physiognomy altered'. The Parlement had taken no action during the early stages of the riots and by a *lit de justice* of 5 May the King deprived it of cognizance over all matters relating to the grain trade. For Maurepas, on the other hand, the conspiracy had been directed by Choiseul, backed by the Queen. Accordingly, when La Vrillière retired in June after fifty years at the Maison du Roi, Maurepas was determined that the Queen should have no say in the appointment of his successor: 'The capital point', he told Véri, 'is not to allow the Queen to choose ministers or direct major affairs.'[23] He need not have worried because, quite apart from the King's stance, her candidate, Sartine, whom she rather gauchely tried to adopt as a protégé, refused to move from the Marine to the Maison du Roi.

Maurepas too seemed to face insuperable obstacles in the way of his candidate, Malesherbes. Not only was the King displeased with Malesherbes for his opposition, however nuancé, to the Maupeou coup, but he had also uttered a 'décision précise' against him: 'He [Malesherbes] is too dangerous an encyclopedist — don't mention him for anything!'[24] Maurepas's fears should have been allayed by the fact that the King swallowed these words — Véri employs the euphemism 'the King has gone back on his misconceptions' — and appointed Malesherbes despite the fact that Malesherbes, who had no administrative ability and regarded his appointment as 'next to a fatal illness the worst thing that could befall me', only accepted office on the singular condition that he could raise the subject of his resignation from time to time.

Malesherbes was the archetypal 'absent-minded professor' (his family had to persuade him to sleep fully clothed because of his tendency to get up in the middle of the night to jot down an idea and catch cold) and it was unfortunate that he should have been appointed to a Department needing a grasp of administrative detail simply because that was where the hole in Maurepas's defences happened to have appeared. For in the long run Louis's grasp of detail would have complemented Malesherbes's breadth of vision but lack of focus, which

Maurepas perhaps realized when he said to the King: 'He is a man I am giving you to replace me and you will do well to place your confidence in him. . . . he will provide the link between policies and ministers. I must soon retire because of my age and, even more, because of the Queen's opposition . . .'[25]

Despite the reluctance of the one to appoint and the other to be appointed, Louis and Malesherbes got on well, each respecting the other's simplicity and basic integrity. On several occasions Louis gently tried to convert his minister: 'My dear Malesherbes, without religion there is no true happiness either for societies or individuals.'[26] Malesherbes in turn took time off from his thankless task of reforming the Maison du Roi and *lettres de cachet* to talk to the King about the more general aspects of government with his customary insight. In a letter to Maurepas he summarizes two memoranda he sent the King: 'One concerns the establishment of Provincial Assemblies which would present the King and the people with the advantages, without the disadvantages, of Provincial Estates and which would rid the King of the pressure which is beginning to be brought to bear upon him — and will, I foresee, for the rest of his reign — for Estates, be they provincial or General.'[27]

The next instalment of Turgot's reforms, the Six Edicts, revealed opposition at several levels, personal, ideological and political. At the personal level, Marie-Antoinette was so enraged by Turgot's tactless attack on her protégé Guines that she wanted Turgot thrown into the Bastille and Guines made a duke on the same day: the gods were to grant half her request, 'the rest consign to air'. At the ideological level, the Keeper of the Seals, Miromesnil, believed that Turgot's measures were subversive of the social order and undermined his own colleague in the Parlement. Turgot survived these two attacks but was finally undone by the political exasperation of Maurepas and, in the final analysis, the King, because Turgot was acting as a de facto prime minister, a role more properly belonging to Maurepas or to the King himself.

The Guines Affair

The Guines Affair, one of the most obscure causes célèbres of the Ancien Régime, 'owed its origins to the Falkland crisis of 1770 between France and England when the Comte de Guines, the French Ambassador to London, accused his secretary, Tort, of using his name to sell privileged diplomatic information to share speculators'.[28] A five-year lawsuit followed which became politicized. Guines was a friend of Choiseul, whose rival and successor, d'Aiguillon, accordingly favoured Tort. The new Maurepas Ministry attempted neutrality as part of its policy of distancing itself from the quarrels of the previous reign. Marie-Antoinette, however, hating d'Aiguillon and favouring Guines as an old protégé of Choiseul, accepted Guines's request to go direct to the police minister, Lenoir, asking for letters proving d'Aiguillon's bias in the case. Brave Lenoir sent the letters instead to the Foreign Secretary, Vergennes, which won the King's approval but failed to avert the wrath of the Ministry from Guines. Vergennes, for all his timidity — his *mésalliance* was to be the most reckless act of his life — wrote a strong letter to the King: 'I was absolutely amazed that [Guines] should have run to the Queen for something which I could have obtained for him without troubling Your Majesty.'[29]

Thereafter, Maurepas and Vergennes sought Guines's head on a plate as a means of working off their anxieties and frustrations, testing the extent of the Queen's power, and smoking the King out into open support for them. Guines played into their hands by assuring England, on his own initiative, that if she refrained from assisting her ally Portugal in her dispute with Spain over the boundaries of Brazil, France would not help Spain. The Spanish ambassador to England's angry despatch was shown to Vergennes; Vergennes read it out in the Conseil d'État; Louis collected it in at the end of the meeting and kept it (later Vergennes ceremoniously reminded the King that he had not 'favoured him with returning it'.[30] Finally the impetuous Turgot, secretly spurred on by Vergennes,[31] 'did not scruple to affront the Queen and importune the King'[32] until Guines was dismissed (31 January 1776).

At the end of February the Queen attempted to arrange a disputation between Guines and Vergennes before Their Majesties. Vergennes threatened resignation and starkly exposed the issues to the King:

> If Your Majesty deigns to recall that it was by his direct command that I informed M. le Comte de Guines of his recall, he will realize that the only explanation I can give him is to tell him quite frankly that he was dismissed because Your Majesty ordered me to dismiss him. There would be no harm in Your Majesty's informing the Queen of the reasons for your decision, but to submit them for discussion with M. le Comte de Guines would not so much compromise the character of your Ministry as undermine your supreme authority.[33]

In another memorandum Vergennes stressed that the retention of the King's ability to 'hire and fire' was at stake. The Ancien Régime had always distinguished between *officiers*, who had purchased their jobs and were difficult to dislodge, and *commissaires*, who had a revocable commission. It did not greatly matter if Maupeou's exile on his estates in Normandy was sweetend by the retention of his honorific title — the King even wanted him to witness royal births — but the King must be able to dispose of the key posts at will. Vergennes told the King:

> An embassy, Sire, is not a property, it is a trust confided in the recipient. I had, Sire, the misfortune to be recalled myself, and very brusquely at that. . . . I did not have the temerity to ask why. To conduct oneself differently would be to establish the principle or the practice that Your Majesty cannot recall an ambassador nor dismiss any of his ministers without explaining his reasons and consequently submitting them to the judgement of public opinion. This new doctrine, such an encroachment on the supreme authority, could become very pernicious at a time when . . . the hot-heads seem to acquire more activity and force with every passing day.[34]

Both the notion of a post as a property and the influence of public opinion were indeed to increase as the reign progressed;[35] meanwhile Louis told Vergennes: 'Your memoranda . . . gave me the greatest pleasure to read.'[36]

As a result, Guines was not reinstated and though Marie-Antoinette had him made a duke a year later, her attempt to meddle in high politics, such as it was, was abandoned for five years. No one thanked Turgot.

Miromesnil and the Six Edicts

Armand Thomas Hue de Miromesnil had spent fourteen years as *premier président* of the troublesome Parlement de Rouen. He had regarded his duty as that of representing the King's interests in the Parlement and the Parlement's with the King. This was not the usual conception of the job (the *premier président* was the agent of the King, from whom he held a revocable commission) and certainly not one which Louis XV was prepared to countenance. In 1760 the King had summoned him to Paris and administered a personal as well as an official rebuke: 'Monsieur le Premier Président, I am very displeased with you, personally displeased; you have not carried out my orders; do not let this happen again; give me your remonstrances.'[37] Miromesnil, who had contracted family alliances in the Parlement of Rouen, had thrown in his lot with his brethren when that body was suppressed in 1771.

Many considered that he was of insufficient calibre for the job of

Keeper of the Seals. In particular they thought that Malesherbes, whose father, the Chancellor, had started Miromesnil on his career, should have been preferred, an opinion not shared by Malesherbes himself, who wrote a memorandum 'demonstrating that the office of Chancellor should neither be given to him nor to any of his class':[38] they would lack the necessary objectivity in dealing with the Parlement, either fawning before or, as in the case of Maupeou, biting the hand that had fed them. Véri considered that Miromesnil, a short man, only 5′ 4″, with mousy hair, 'possessed a bourgeois figure, not at all that of the head of the Judiciary', which contrasted with Malesherbes's serene and noble countenance (the Lamoignon family claimed chevaleresque origins, though this was not accepted by Chérin, the Court genealogist). People were inclined to confuse mediocre birth with mediocre ability. Even so, Miromesnil, 'normand et rusé', was one of the subtlest players in the game, and whilst he may not have had Malesherbes's breadth of intellect, his political skills were of a higher order, as were his political apothegms, such as 'Time is my first secretary' and 'Consider [this to a *premier président*] that when you seek to harm a minister of the King it is to the King that you render that minister harmful.'[39] Asked in 1775 whether he would be embarrassed by Malesherbes's presence in the Ministry, Miromesnil replied that he would be only too delighted to give him the chance to demonstrate his incapacity for administration.

Miromesnil was dangerous not because he lacked ability but because he possessed it; his was the most disastrous appointment Louis ever made and he was the biggest single obstacle to reform; the architect of the 1774 settlement, he was ultimately destined to wreck it. His need to curry favour with parlementaires who despised him increased his natural tendency of complaisance towards them, first manifested when he 'conspired in the degradation of the Grand Conseil',[40] allowing the Parlement to contest its status as the supreme appellate court. The Grand Conseil had formed the nucleus of the Parlement Maupeou and, according to the provisions of the 1774 settlement, was automatically to assume the Parlement's functions if it resorted to a judicial strike. It was essential to maintain its prestige as a threat and as a resource.

To Miromesnil, Turgot's Six Edicts were naturally like a red rag to a bull. The two most controversial were that abolishing the *corvée* (forced peasant labour on the royal roads) and replacing it by a tax paid by everyone except the Clergy, and that abolishing the Parisian craft guilds. The commutation of the *corvée* marked a further encroachment on fiscal privilege, because the work that was being commuted had been performed by non-nobles. The abolition of the guilds was one step towards dismantling the 'corporate' nature of the *régime* whereby the State had relations with groups or *corps* rather than individuals. The scope of the reforms was limited, but Miromesnil fully realized that their implications were extensive. Later, he told Véri of his opposition to Turgot's measures: 'Yes, I was against him because my opinions were opposed to his. The privileges of the nobility and of the clergy are unjust in origin; agreed. The privileges of certain towns, of certain *corps*, are in the same case; agreed again. Very well, I think they must be respected because they are tied to all the rest.'[41]

In this classic statement of the conservative position, Miromesnil perceives that from Turgot's modest proposals to the destruction of the whole social order is but a short step. Reformist agenda had been circulating in the bureaux of the *Contrôle-générale* for decades: abolition of internal customs barriers and tax farming, the *cadastre* and, more recently, Provincial Assemblies. Turgot had been considering the abolition of tax farming but had been dissuaded by friends; plans for Provincial Assemblies were well advanced and he may even have been contemplating an attack on feudal dues. At this time there appeared a pamphlet entitled *Inconvénients des droits féodaux*, written by Turgot's secretary, Boncerf, and it was Turgot's practice to 'fly a kite' by patronizing works relating to impending legislation.[42] Thus one can understand Miromesnil's hostility.

The accusation against Miromesnil is not just that he combated Turgot's measures — in the ministerial *comité* which discussed them and the tactics of their presentation before the Parlement — but that he encouraged opposition in that body by informing it of his own opposition, Maurepas's vacillation and the 'silence' of other ministers. Malesherbes had no doubt that Miromesnil had 'hidden contacts among the parlementaires to undermine Turgot's operations', whilst Turgot, in a letter to the King, explicitly accused him of 'encouraging cabals' in the Parlement 'through his intrigues'.[43] Miromesnil hotly denied to Véri any suggestion of treachery, whilst conceding 'I do not deny that I let Turgot proceed with his Edicts even though I foresaw that they would cause his downfall.'[44]

Miromesnil, however, was wrong in this prediction. For Louis, having studied them in seclusion for three days, took personal charge of sending the Edicts through the Parlement, adopting a tougher procedure: instead of circulating paper copies privately among leading parlementaires (the usual practice), he presented the Edicts straight away in their final form on parchment.[45] The replies to the remonstrances of the Parlement were drafted by Miromesnil and thus contained aguments which Turgot perhaps lacked the sensitivity to furnish, but they were controlled and amended by the King. Thus, with the commutation of the *corvée*, Louis showed his appreciation that the nobility did not see taxation primarily in financial terms but felt humiliated at having to pay a tax hitherto paid only by *taillables*. The following passage has all the hallmarks of being written in Louis' own words and represents what was to be his consistent position on this important issue:

> I have no intention of blurring the distinctions between the Estates nor of depriving the nobility of my kingdom of the distinctions it has acquired by its services . . . which I shall always maintain.
>
> It is not a question here of a humiliating tax but of a simple contribution which everyone should take a pride in sharing, since I am myself setting the example by contributing in virtue of my domains.[46]

Nevertheless, despite Louis' reasoning, it was still necessary for him to register the Edicts by *lit de justice* on 12 March 1776.

The fall of Turgot

Louis XVI dismissed Turgot on 12 May, two months to the day after the *lit de justice*, and this long interval suggests that it was neither the Queen's personal hostility nor Miromesnil's ideological objections nor parlementaire opposition that brought about that event. The main political issue during this interval was Malesherbes's resignation and replacement at the Maison du Roi. Malesherbes had only accepted office on the understanding that he could raise the question of his resignation from time to time, nor did he find the taste of power addictive, which may partly explain why, when the time came, the King was as reluctant to let Malesherbes go as he had been to appoint him in the first place. Louis made it a rule never to see anyone who was about to leave the Ministry, whether to avoid embarrassment or the effects of persuasion; usually it was a matter of the King dismissing a minister. Resignations were rare and Louis treated them as cases of 'ingratitude'. In either case, the royal response was the same, inaccessibility, and poor Malesherbes was reduced to drafting the following letter to the King:

> I communicated to M. de Maurepas my intention to resign two months ago, so that he might notify Your Majesty and have the time to reflect on the choice [of a successor] he would propose to you. Your Majesty knows that for the last two months I have not been able to talk to you alone. Your Majesty has only allowed me to have one *travail* with you when you gave me to understand that you would find it disagreeable if I mentioned the subject [of my resignation]. The same prohibition on Your Majesty's

part has been reiterated since and I have been told that my retirement is to be deferred from Easter to Pentecost. It is thus the impossibility of speaking which has forced me to write . . .

What affects me most painfully is being forbidden to speak to Your Majesty in person. Allow me to observe that I do not believe that this has ever happened to any of your ministers. If I am unworthy to be heard by Your Majesty about my retirement and the Department with which I have been honoured, am I worthy to remain a single day in your Council?

Nothing is more humiliating for me than to be reduced to this silence and I do not think, Sire, that I have deserved these humiliations.[47]

When Malesherbes was finally allowed to go, Maurepas proposed as his successor Jean Antoine Amelot de Chaillou, the undistinguished scion of a ministerial dynasty. Turgot disagreed with the choice and in a remarkable series of letters to the King[48] he accused Amelot of being sold to Miromesnil, who in turn was sold to the Parlement. Instead he proposed Véri, both to supplement Maurepas's weakness and to implement Turgot's memorandum for economical reform of the Household. He accused the King of avoiding him 'to hide the fact that Your Majesty has decided to choose [Amelot]'. He also avoided Turgot because he was about to dismiss him, the reasons being supplied by Veri:

The personal inclinations of the King, which M. de Maurepas has reinforced but not produced, were the real cause of this event. . . . M. de Maurepas and M. de Malesherbes had sized up the young man better. . . . they had not taken his silence as evidence of conviction but of embarrassment.

If one adds to this the tenacity of this minister in wanting the assistance of his equals for the goal he saw clearly ahead, the advice he gave the King when his colleagues opposed him, and his desire to have colleagues who were of his opinion [all classic hallmarks of a prime minister], it is easy to see that the young man was bound to feel importuned in the end; which made him say: 'M. Turgot wants to be me and I don't want him to be me.'[49]

If Maurepas, the preponderant minister, felt that Turgot was usurping his role, how much more would the King feel this? In the vacuum resulting from the King's inability to appoint or be his own prime minister, Turgot was instinctively driven to make claims which would have effectively made him one — hence Louis's remark: 'M. Turgot wants to be me.'

One explanation of Louis's refusal to appoint a prime minister is that he distrusted his ministers. Neither of the protagonists, Miromesnil and Turgot, shared his conception of an absolute reforming monarchy. This is clearly so in the case of Miromesnil, who identified himself with the Parlement's obstinate defence of entrenched privilege, but, in his conscience-stricken way, it was no less true of Turgot, orthodox though the measures themselves were. The founding fathers of Physiocracy, Quesnay and the elder Mirabeau, had suppressed their Treatise on Monarchy because they had realized that the rule of nature was fundamentally incompatible with rule by an absolute monarch. Similarly, Turgot told Véri that he had not introduced Provincial Assemblies because they would diminish the King's authority, but added: 'As a citizen I would have been very happy: but acting as a minister of the King I made a scruple of abusing his confidence to diminish the extent of his authority. I intended to do it but I wanted to wait until the King was older and had more experience and maturity so that he could judge for himself and not through the eyes of another.'[50]

The conflict between a minister's sense of duty and his private inclinations was to be a powerful solvent of the *régime*. Louis must have seen the double irony of Turgot's observation 'on a thousand occasions the interests . . . of your ministers are diametrically opposed to your own' in the context of Turgot's observation that the Parlement, whose recall Turgot had advocated, was stronger in 1776 than before Maupeou's coup. As for Véri — whose lack of respect, let alone veneration, for the King comes across in his frequent use of the expression 'the young man' — he believed that France would be a republic within fifty years and did not seem to mind, and yet Turgot seriously proposed to the King that he should be made a minister.[51]

The rise of the Polignacs

The rise of the Queen's favourite, the Comtesse Jules de Polignac, is best explained by the supposition that her uncle, Maurepas, 'planted' her at Versailles in the hope that she would give Marie-Antoinette the companionship she was not getting from Louis and in return seek to neutralize the Queen's political influence which was necessarily exercised at his expense and which it was difficult within the conventions to deny. Mme de Polignac was a country-cousin of Maurepas, beautiful and suggestible but of a family which, though good, 'had never had a place at court and whose connections were not sufficient for it to shine at Versailles'.[52]

In 1775 Maurepas brought her to Court and launched her in the salon of the Princesse de Rohan-Guéménée. The Princesse was the daughter of the Maréchal-Duc de Soubise, whom the King, out of respect for the memory of the Duc's personal friend Louis XV, had allowed to continue attending the Conseil d'État. Maurepas allowed this touching eccentricity to pass: he had reduced the Conseil to a largely ceremonial status and he prided himself on his alliance with the Rohan. The Princesse had become *Gouvernante des Enfants de France* in succession to her aunt, Mme de Marsan, Louis's former Governess. Her only official duties concerned Louis's eleven-year-old sister, Madame Elizabeth, but her salon was one of the most brilliant and the Queen a frequent visitor.

There she encountered Madame de Polignac and a deep and lasting attachment formed between them. Around them grew the Queen's *société intime*, a tight-knit group which included Artois (who became the lover of Mme de Polignac's sister, Mme de Polastron), the Marquis de Vaudreuil, and the Comte d'Adhémar. Much has been made of the baleful influence of this group. Marie-Antoinette is blamed for ceasing to hold court in her state appartments and retreating with the Polignacs to the privacy of the Petit Trianon. At the same time, following the dismissal of her Dame d'honneur, the Comtesse de Noailles, *Madame l'étiquette*, she is blamed for becoming *too* accessible. Much also is made of their so-called monopolization of pensions and the resentment of those excluded. This, for example, has been presented as the motive of the d'Aiguillon faction in circulating damaging pamphlets depicting Louis as a cuckold and Marie-Antoinette as a harpy,[53] but surely the Queen's treatment of d'Aiguillon in 1774 is sufficient explanation.

In any case, before 1780 the Polignacs only enjoyed two Court offices.[54] In that year things improved: Mme de Polignac was made *Gouvernante des Enfants de France*, i.e. of Louis's daughter Madame Royale, born in 1778; M. de Polignac was made a Duc and *Directeur-général des postes*; and their daughter received a dowry of 800,000 livres. This was, however, as nothing compared with the 1,800,000 livres a year which the entirely parasitic Noailles were said to enjoy under Louis XV. Moreover, their expenses were considerable because 'the Queen and a part of the royal family had contracted the habit of eating and living with them every day'. The words are those of the austere d'Ormesson, Contrôleur in 1783, who was asked by the Duc de Polignac for a pension of 380,000 a year. Embarrassed, because he was much richer than the Duc and because 'ministers needed 300,000 a year to entertain less exalted members of the Court', d'Ormesson proposed to the King that the Duc be given 400,000.[55] Much misunderstanding concerning the level of expenditure on the Court (only six percent of the total) can be dispelled by reminding oneself that there were twenty-four livres to the pound sterling.

Moreover, what is completely ignored is that the Polignacs fulfilled the political purpose of their institution in a way which Maurepas could never have dared to expect. In 1776 Mme de Polignac told the Queen 'that it would be in her interest to persuade the King to nominate M. de Maurepas prime iminster', which prompted Mercy to say that she was 'manifestly . . . conducted by the Comte de Maurepas'[56] In that year also, she persuaded the Queen to end the exile of Maurepas's cousin d'Aiguillon.[57] With a solitary exception,[58] the Queen's *société* sided with Maurepas in all his disputes with the Queen. Nor were these services merely personal to Maurepas: he was, after all, the King's chief minister and the two men were in total agreement about the need to restrict the political influence of the Queen. After Maurepas's death, the Polignacs supported those ministers who continued this tradition, notably Vergennes and Calonne. In this way they held the ring and let the King and his ministers get on with governing. Initially the Polignacs may have regarded their sojourn at Court as little more than a smash-and-grab raid; increasingly, though, they identified themselves with the interests they were paid to serve and by the middle 1780s had acquired a set of political views similar to the King's. Louis in turn, always a shy man who did not participate in the social life of the Court, found it increasingly pleasant to relax in their company, forming, with a few servants, the audience of their amateur theatricals. They became his *société intime* as well as the Queen's.

4

The Price of Victory: Necker, 1776–81

The removal of Turgot in May 1776 revealed that he had been a rival centre of gravity to Maurepas within the Ministry. Almost immediately after his dismissal, the other ministers invited Maurepas to sit in on their weekly *travail* with the King on a regular basis. Shortly afterwards the King appointed him *Chef du Conseil royal des finances*. It was a purely decorative title — the *Conseil royal* hardly ever met — but so was the English First Lord of the Treasury: if the Ancien Régime had lasted longer, the title might have gathered to itself functions analogous to those of an English Prime Minister. At all events, it seemed that Maurepas would be able to see out the rest of his days in peace and preponderance. This was not to be the case, partly because Louis, whilst enhancing Maurepas's status, was not prepared to delegate to him any more power than he already possessed; partly also because the problem of royal finance was so central and so intractable that a finance minister of any talent, or even any character, was bound to exert a powerful influence. Turgot was succeeded by Clugny, who revoked his predecessor's reforms, Vergennes being most virulent in his criticism of his late colleague's 'metaphysical' Edicts: 'he wanted to create and did not know how to correct'.[1] Clugny, who installed his three sisters at the *Contrôle-générale* and reputedly lived incestuously with them, is otherwise remembered as the only *Contrôleur-général* of the century to die in office (18 October 1776). Clugny's sudden death led to the most unconventional of Louis's appointments, apparently a personal one, that of Jacques Necker as de facto finance minister on 22 October.

Necker was to weigh heavily on the remainder of Louis's reign, and his first ministry, which lasted until 1781, is the subject of this chapter: the obscure circumstances of his appointment, his reliance on loans rather than increased taxation, his tentative steps towards devolved government for the provinces, his demands of the King and his resignation shortly after publishing a misleadingly optimistic statement of royal revenue and expenditure.

Necker was, as the King put it, 'a foreigner, a republican [he had grown up in the Republic of Geneva] and a Protestant';[2] starting as a bank clerk, he was now, at forty-four, a banking millionaire. He had achieved a certain reputation by writing against free trade in grain but he had no place within the governmental establishment and had occupied none of the rungs of the cursus honorum. The appointment of such an outsider is attributable to Louis's personal interest in finance and the finance ministry, which he called 'the most sensitive position in the Kingdom',[3] and to the fact that he received advice and information from a variety of extra-ministerial sources in an attempt to discover the true state of 'public opinion', from which he was isolated by his counsellors and courtiers. Louis's chief source of such information, though it was not through him that Necker was appointed, was the Intendant des Postes, d'Ogny. He had a secret bureau of twelve clerks employed in opening intercepted letters and showed Louis extracts from these on Sundays, when he had a regular *travail* with the King. D'Ogny and his *cabinet noir* represented a major breach in Maurepas's system of controlling the information which Louis received; indeed, Maurepas's own wife dared not express herself freely in letters because she knew that d'Ogny read the King extracts from them.[4]

Apart from gaining information from intercepted letters, which Véri considered contributed to his indecisiveness, Louis, perhaps because of his physical inaccessibility, was inundated with letters from informers, cranks or men with projects, and it was by this epistolary means that Necker was worked into the Ministry. The agent of this manœuvre was a *littérateur* and former soldier called Masson. His father had been a naval contractor when Maurepas was minister for the Marine and Maurepas stood godfather to the boy who later fabricated for himself the title Marquis de Pezay. But, in Véri's words, 'he created for himself a sort of ministry by writing letters to the King and receiving replies', which admirably defines the essence of a ministerial relationship with the King and shows how easy it was to establish one.

It seems that Pezay recommended Necker to the King some time in 1776 and that Necker then sent memoranda both to the King and to Maurepas. A letter from Necker to Maurepas of August or September refers to 'the analysis of the financial situation which I have made and which the King has approved'.[5] The most likely explanation of the step from this 'approval' lies in the international situation. France was moving inexorably towards armed intervention in England's struggle with her American colonies: she provided them with material assistance from 1776 and formally recognized their independence in 1778. One reason why Vergennes had turned against Turgot had been the latter's reluctance to find the money for such a war.[6] Louis, however, accepted the verdict of both Terray and Turgot that the existing structure would not support additional taxation. He had also eschewed 'bankruptcy', Vergennes for example telling him that he dare not mention the prospect or even the word, 'Your Majesty, out of delicacy and equity, having proscribed the word from the very day of his accession'.[7]

These constraints meant that a future war would have to be financed by credit and Necker observed plausibly that this could more easily be obtained by an ex-banker than an ex-Intendant (the usual background of a *Contrôleur-général*). To preserve the forms, it was agreed that an ex-Intendant would be made nominal *Contrôleur-général*, but as the parlementaire Lefevre d'Amécourt noted, 'Le Roi, en même temps se réserve la Direction du Trésor royal et nomme, pour l'exercer sous ses ordres, le Sieur Necker, avec le titre conseiller des finances et Directeur-général du Trésor royal',[8] which suggests that Louis felt personally responsible for keeping an eye on his unconventional appointment.

On the choice of a *Contrôleur-général*, Necker mused to Maurepas: 'We have still got to find this man in whom I am looking only for very ordinary qualities and I have to say that I myself do not know a single *homme de robe* I can confidently suggest.'[9] Thus Necker questions the adequacy of the classical training of a minister under the Ancien Régime, i.e. presenting cases in the Conseil d'État as a *maître des requêtes* before administering a province as an Intendant and finally returning to Versailles as a minister. It was one of his most important contributions to the debate about government, raising an issue relevant to all periods and all *régimes*: the claims of the specialist, the technician, against those of the man with a good general training, such as the 'Greats man', but no directly relevant experience.

The straw-man chosen was Taboureau des Réaux, who soon felt that the humiliation of his position exceeded its prestige and resigned in June 1777, Necker becoming Director-General of Finances: as a Protestant he could not be given the title *Contrôleur-général*, nor a place in the Conseil d'État, nor countersign *arrêts*, so that Maurepas had to sit in on every *travail* of his with the King, however routine.

True to his word, Necker did not increase taxes to pay for a war which cost about four hundred million livres during his period in office. He did, however, prolong until 1790 the second *vingtième* which was due to expire at the end of 1780. The parlementaires were never to accept the permanency of the vingtièmes, regarding them as 'extraordinary revenues, momentary imposts' available largely for the pressing needs of war. Moreover, Necker declared that 'the revenues of the King must follow, at least at a certain distance, the growth of the value of lands'.

This doctrine was enunciated in the *arrêt* of November 1777, which announced that the rolls of the *vingtième* would be progressively updated.

The parlementaires' objections to 'permanent and permanently increasing taxation' were all the greater in that *arrêts* were executive decrees which did not require registration in the parlements. With war in the offing, however, and with Necker ostentatiously striving for economies at Court, the parlementaires were content at this stage to register disquiet rather than edicts.[10]

In any case, relatively small amounts were involved: Necker paid for the war by borrowing. First he raised eighty-five millions by lottery, for which the Crown contracted to pay out 105 millions in prize-money and repayments. Bad as this was, the sale of life-annuities by which he raised a further 260 million livres, contracting to repay a sum almost double, was crippling. Life-annuities were very popular because they were self-extinguishing and did not burden posterity, for which people in this period, Louis not excepted, were excessively solicitous. The going rate of interest for a life-annuity was 8 percent; Necker paid 10 percent (proportionately less if more than one life was being insured). Speculators had reduced investment in life-annuities to a fine art, as Necker himself admitted:

> I must point out that life-annuities have become more onerous to the King since people started buying them not just to increase their income during their lifetime but as a pure speculation. This novel usage originated in Geneva and has since been followed in other places. You choose about thirty people aged about seven, when life-expectancy is greatest; you take care to exclude anyone whose health seems at all precarious or who has not yet cleared the hurdle of smallpox; you even go as far as to choose the sex which, because of its sheltered life, seems less exposed to unforeseen accidents; in short you take all the precautions necessary to ensure the longevity of these thirty persons. The speculators [*capitalistes*] then place an agreed sum on each head and, since such contracts can be sold and transferred, one can see why there is every incentive to increase this kind of speculation.[11]

A general aim of Necker's was to replace the venal element in the administration of royal finances with salaried employees. The advantage of a man who had bought his office was that he was a man of substance who could lend money to the Crown when credit was difficult; the disadvantage was that he would tend to be more independent and, in the long run, would cost the King more. Necker abolished the powerful *Intendants des Finances*, whose Council assisted and limited the finance minister, and the Receivers-General, who collected the *taille*, a slow process, and, against this collateral, advanced money to the King. Recent Anglo-Saxon historians[12] have attached great importance to this modernization of royal finances but there is room to doubt the sufficiency of a technical solution to the problems of the Ancien Régime, which were essentially moral and political, centring as they did on the nature of consent to government in general and taxation in particular, though it is true that Necker did address this problem also, albeit in a very limited way, with his Provincial Administrations.

A pilot Administration — he did not call it 'Assembly' in case a resemblance to Turgot's project should frighten anyone — was set up in Berry in 1778. The main difference between Turgot's and Necker's bodies was that whereas Turgot's Assemblies would have been elected, in Necker's Administrations the King appointed a third of the members, who co-opted the rest. The Administration allocated the taxes owed by the Province — though the amount continued to be decided by the King — and supervised public works; but all its proceedings had to be shown to the Intendant and the Council. The impression given at the time was of cautious progress: people noted that Necker, the Protestant, had made the Archbishop of Bourges president of the Administration. Another was set up at Montauban in 1779 and two more were planned for Moulins and Grenoble.

When proposing the Provincial Administration of Berry, Necker had submitted a confidential memorandum to the King which succeeded in attacking both the Parlements and the Intendants, envisaging the eventual replacement of both by Provincial Administrations. In this memorandum, Necker bends over backwards to please the King: the Administrations, he argues, would strengthen the authority of the absolute monarchy, weaken the power of the parlements and the local Estates, and facilitate the raising of loans and taxes. Louis, however, who never fully trusted Necker and regarded his appointment as a regrettable necessity, resisted these blandisments and wrote some oracular marginal comments on this memorandum which call to mind the Marquis d'Argenson's observations about Louis XV: 'The King's pet hobby is wanting to remain enigmatic.'[13] When Necker observes that the parlements are increasingly taking it upon themselves to speak for the people, Louis replies, if that is the right word: 'Notice what the Estates of Brittany do from time to time.' This may mean that it has been possible for the Government to play off the Estates of Brittany against the Parlement of Rennes; or it might mean anything. When Necker says that the parlements should be confined to judicial matters, Louis muses: 'Is it more expedient to entrust the supervision of administrative matters to administrative bodies, or is it wiser to leave it with judicial ones?'

Elsewhere the King is more explicit but perversely critical of suggestions Necker had inserted to please him. To Necker's suggestion that the new Administrations would be useful in lending money to the Crown, Louis counters: 'All the corporate bodies [Estates, municipalities etc.] are heavily indebted; to create more simply to indebt them further is to overload Frenchmen as much as the English. Could there not be some other way?' Finally, when Necker suggests that the new bodies would grant taxes automatically and that the very term Free Gift employed by the Provincial Estates would disappear, Louis remarks: 'I do not think it would be prudent to abolish the words Free Gift. First because this phrase is ancient and appeals to those who are mindful of forms; secondly because it is perhaps as well to leave my successors with a phrase which teaches them that they should expect everything from the love of Frenchmen and not dispose of their properties militarily.'[14] Nevertheless, despite the King's distrust of Necker, the first four years of his ministry, with the finesse of Maurepas holding the ring for his operations, were the still-centre of the reign. Money flowed in, the war was fought without fuss, the Parlement was quiet. In 1780, however, things began to go wrong.

'Unless the King', Véri wrote in 1780, 'reduces Departmental expenditure to a sum inferior to the revenue, the post of *Contrôleur-général* is untenable for long.' Louis's failure to do this, serious enough in time of peace, became critical during the war because of the large sums of money involved. The problem was expressed in terms of a clash between Necker and Sartine, who, as Minister for the Marine, was the biggest paymaster during an overseas war. 'No minister', observed the naval Intendant, Malouet, 'had as many ships constructed or provisioned the ports better.' But he did this regardless of expense: there is a pleasant cartoon of him bending down by the shore skimming silver écus across the sea. Necker was not alone in attributing Sartine's extravagance to the 'attention to detail of the *homme de plume*' and thinking that a military man, which meant a *grand seigneur*, would be cheaper because of his expert knowledge[15] — a conclusion which was never devoid of paradox and would soon be filled with irony: Sartine's seigneurial successor would bankrupt the monarchy.

In 1779 Necker allocated Sartine 120 million livres for the naval campaign of 1780; judging this to be inadequate Sartine, without consulting Necker, ordered the Treasurer of the Marine to issue notes to the value of twenty million livres. Necker was understandably furious and complained to the King. In 1780 Necker again allocated Sartine 120 million livres and Sartine posed his dilemma neatly: the King had eighty ships-of-the-line, but for the money Sartine could only put sixty to sea. It was a policy decision the King would have to make. Necker in turn threatened to resign unless Sartine were dismissed.

The crisis found the lines of communication between the King and

Maurepas cut as Maurepas was confined to bed in Paris with a particularly bad attack of gout — in a secretary's hand he told Louis, 'I do not have the strength to hold a pen'[16] — and Necker was able to have his *travail* alone with the King, whom Sartine, ominously, found it impossible to see. Louis wrote Maurepas one of his most characteristic notes: 'Shall we dismiss Necker, or shall we dismiss Sartine? I am not displeased with the latter. I think Necker is more useful to us.' This cynical and graceless communication makes no attempt either to impose a policy decision or reconcile the two ministers. Necker had the audacity to demand that Maurepas show him the King's note and Maurepas the weakness to comply; thus Necker temporarily reversed the tables on Maurepas, screening the King's contact with his own leading minister![17]

Before Maurepas recovered his health, Necker, with some support from the Queen, persuaded Louis on 13 October 1780 to dismiss Sartine and replace him with Necker's friend the Marquis de Castries, a former protégé of Choiseul and fellow director with Necker in the Compagnie des Indes, who agreed to hand over to Necker the Treasury of the Marine. Maurepas consoled himself by telling the King that they could always dismiss Necker as soon as the war was over, and Sartine by delivering himself of a bitter indictment of Louis:

> You will not find any class of citizen in public affairs for whom the King and his family display the slightest affection. They will let the various groups fight each other, if they so desire, and the King will in turn sacrifice them one to the others, beginning with the ministers of whatsoever party. Everyone has now had time to judge the King. The statement by the ministers that a measure represents the King's volition is no longer an efficacious weapon in their hands. The measure is regarded as representing merely the ministers' personal policy, to be contested with every confidence.[18]

In December, Necker and the Queen followed up their advantage by persuading the King to replace Maurepas's cousin, Montbarey, the Minister for War, with the Marquis de Ségur (Louis consoled Montbarey with a treasured letter stating that it was only at the Minister's 'reiterated request that he had consented to his resignation'). Maurepas's chagrin was increased by the fact that not only had he lost control over ministerial appointments but that, for the first time, the Queen had played a role in this field, albeit one that was only contributory and was exaggerated by contemporaries.[19]

By no stretch of the imagination could Montbarey's tenure of the War Ministry be described as distinguished, though he did have the integrity to oppose entering the American war in spite of the fact that it would 'quadruple' his influence.[20] A prince of the Holy Roman Empire and a grandee of Spain, in France his consideration depended largely on the kinship and protection of Maurepas. Nevertheless, two episodes in his career exemplify a minister's relationship with Louis XVI. Montbarey had thought that his age (he was forty-eight in 1780), 'although double that of His Majesty, being much closer than that of his other ministers, spoke in his favour'. Perhaps for this reason he decided to tell not only Maurepas but also the King of his decison not to take a conventional mistress (who would take up too much time, demand favours and embarrass his wife) but to ask Lenoir to procure him a prostitute and arrange for her to be spied upon to prevent her causing trouble. Louis, 'without exactly approving, agreed with me that this course of action was the least subject to drawbacks'.

On another occasion, Louis smoothed Montbarey's path with the Queen, whose interference in military promotions was a source of frequent disputes. After one of these, he ran to the King's apartments, trusting that his superior speed would outweigh the Queen's advantage of the secret passage. Outstripping her, he was the recipient of elaborate advice from the King:

> No one knows better than I... what you have gone through; calm yourself; I will take it on myself to speak to the Queen of the matter. But for some time avoid seeing her; and as for the matters of which you are accustomed to give her an account, I will undertake them, and I will tell you when you may and when you ought to present yourself before her. For this await my positive orders. Moreover, rest assured about the possible consequences of this affair; I will take you under my protection and you have nothing to fear.

It was six weeks before Louis judged it right for Montbarey to see the Queen. Montbarey told Maurepas of his quarrel with the Queen, but not, at first, of his audience with the King.

The following year, 1781, Necker received two kinds of publicity, one sought, the other unsought. In February he published his *Compte rendu au Roi*, which purported to be a statement of royal revenue and expenditure and was designed to facilitate another loan by raising Necker's own stature. In this work, which became a best-seller and fashionable reading for ladies at their toilet, Necker claimed that despite four years of war with no extra taxation, annual revenue exceeded expenditure by 10,200,000 livres. In reality there was an annual deficit of about seventy millions. An attempt has been made recently to rehabilitate the *Compte rendu*,[21] but the most we can say is that Necker was providing figures for a typical rather than an actual year (a distinction Louis was himself later to employ)[22] and that the state of war, though common, was not typical. Thus expenditure was put at about 254 million, whereas in 1780 it had been 677 million. Most, though not all, people were taken in, because they wanted to be and because, hitherto, royal finances had been shrouded in mystery, being regarded as strictly arcane.

In April, the confidential and highly controversial memorandum on Provincial Adminstrations was leaked and published through the treachery of the King's malicious second brother, Monsieur, Comte de Provence. It enraged both the parlementaires and the Intendants and revealed an identity of interest between them. For whereas the parlementaires increasingly championed the social and economic privileges of the nobility to which they belonged, they did not want the nobility in general to interfere in administration and politics. That should be left to the *noblesse de robe*, whether members of a parlement or of the King's direct administration.[23] Of the Intendants, Necker, in a famous passage, wrote: 'One can scarcely give the name administration to this arbitrary volition of a single man who, whether present or absent, informed or incompetent, is obliged to run the most important aspects of the public service, for which he is necessarily unsuited, having devoted his entire life previously to the appellate functions of the Council.'[24]

A lively war of pamphlets ensued, the best, *Les Comments* and the *Lettre du Marquis de Caraccioli à M. d'Alembert*, being written, anonymously, by the powerful and well-connected, and second highest paid, Intendant[25] — of Flanders — Charles Alexandre de Calonne. The *Lettre à d'Alembert* was a reply both to the *Compte rendu* — Calonne wanted to be *Contrôleur-général* and knew that the *Compte rendu* would make it difficult for the Crown to plead poverty — and, from an Intendant, to the memorandum on Provincial Administrations. The *Lettre* is brilliantly written and has many witty sallies: 'to lacerate the Intendants and their administration . . . is of no political consequence and is just firing on your own troops'. It also reveals what was to be an abiding obsession with Calonne: his hatred of the Clergy, 'sold to anyone who extends its power'. He also notices Necker's symbiotic relationship with the 'liberal' grands seigneurs at Court, epitomized by his introduction into the Ministry of the two military aristocrats Castries and Ségur: 'Ever since places in the Ministry have been given to grands seigneurs — who are all equally entitled to believe that they have the same degree of aptitude to fill any of them — they all devour these places with their eyes and have been seized with ministerial mania.'[26]

Here Calonne stands on its head Necker's argument in favour of specialists rather than generalists by saying that soldiers are not trained in government and that there is no logical reason why they should restrict their designs to the service ministries; they might even covet the finance ministry, that furthest removed from their competence, provided the seigneurial title of *Surintendant des finances*, suppressed by Louis XIV to deter them, were revived.

Necker's views called into question the composition of Maurepas's ministry, which was based on the idea of the lawyer trained in the royal administration, and his actions had altered it. Moreover, although Necker was a commoner — it is ironical that he had quarrelled with Sartine, the only other born commoner in the Ministry — his political sympathies were very similar to those of the ministers, particularly Castries, whom he had introduced into the Ministry: they all favoured a 'liberal' aristocratic constitution such as England's. This was far from the position of the King, who in May asked Vergennes, to whom he was increasingly turning, to give him his written opinion of the *Compte rendu* less from a financial point of view than from that of Necker's basic loyalty. Vergennes, who apparently believed that Necker had secret relations with the English for the profit of his bank and to bring the war to a close, leapt at the opportunity, replying that Necker was undermining the traditional French monarchy and basing his conduct 'on the example of England, which publishes its accounts, an example for which Your Majesty's predecessors have shown such considerable and justified aversion'.[27]

Thus Louis was not inclined to be receptive to Necker when, taking the opportunity of closeting the King when the Court removed to Marly in May, he presented a list of marks of royal confidence he required to buttress his position, shaken by the pamphlet war against him and the leaking of his memorandum. Accounts vary as to what Necker demanded and what he was offered. According to his friend Castries, Louis offered him the *grandes entrées* and the registration, by *lit de justice* if necessary, of the Edicts creating more Provincial Administrations. Necker, however, wanted admission to the Conseil d'État and direct control, for the duration of the war, of the treasury of the Ministry of War. These Louis refused, despite support for Necker from Marie-Antoinette, whose mother and brother Joseph were admirers of Necker.[28] When Maurepas informed Necker of the King's refusal, he was so thunder-struck that he could not open the door, so that Maurepas had to summon a valet, telling him with barely contained relish: 'See M. Necker out!' Necker resigned and was ill for weeks afterwards.

Of Necker's subsequent conduct, d'Angiviller, Director-General of Royal Buildings, a former *menin* of the King's who remained close to him, wrote: 'Hitherto a disgraced minister, ... so far from meddling in affairs, made it a duty to remain aloof from them, to live in retirement, even to abstain for a while from seeing those of his friends who were so involved and seemed to desire to make himself forgotten [a paraphrase of the instructions usually given to the disgraced minister by the Minister of the Maison].'[29] Necker, however, forgetting or probably not even aware of the convention that the King never admitted a mistake by reappointing an ex-minister to his old job, schemed tirelessly for precisely that, obliging the King to tell Castries in 1783: 'Considering the generous way I treated M. Necker and the way in which he left me voluntarily, he must think no more of returning to office.'[30] It was a *décision précise*.

Necker's resignation was an error of judgement: Maurepas's health was clearly failing and his death, at the height of an expensive war, would have made Necker impregnable. Nevertheless, his proud nature had been strained by years of paying court to Maurepas, of 'ascending that dark and long staircase' which, did he but realize it, represented for him the 'refined essence of human vanity' just as much as his cramped quarters did for Maurepas.

The *Compte rendu* made it harder for future governments to plead poverty and to educate the parlements about the financial needs of a modern state. The *Compte* and Necker's loans, through their dependence on publicity, also permanently altered the nature of royal finance and even, as Vergennes implied, the government of France. Necker had increased the power of public opinion, to which Louis himself already paid great attention: 'Your Majesty has had the goodness to show me several times that he busies himself with reading this mass of literature.' The *Compte rendu* was, of course, an account rendered less to the King than to the public. As such, it inverted a basic principle of absolutism, that the king was the only public persona, the only one to be addressed;[31] it made a mockery of the King's claim that the parlements should not publish their remonstrances.

Moreover, Vergennes argued, even given that the monarchy should be governed by opinion, that opinion needed to be defined. Why should it necessarily be 'the public opinion of M. Necker'?

He finds this opinion in the spirit of innovation of the times, in the society of men of letters, of the *philosophes* ... or again in the plaudits given him by a section of the English Parliament ...; finally in the ideas of reform and humanity which he himself propagates. ... Your Majesty has already made very considerable sacrifices to this spirit of innovation ... which increases its demands and pretensions with every new favour.

Such, Sire, is the nature of the public opinion which M. Necker calls to

his assistance and which becomes his strength . . . since he has been
deprived by the nature of his operations of the support of the true public
opinion of this monarchy.

If 'the opinion of M. Necker' finally wins the day, if English and
Genevan principles are introduced into our administration, Your Majesty
can expect to see the portion of his subjects which now obeys in command, and the portion which presently governs take or share its place.[32]

Vergennes is not objecting, as an earlier absolutist might have done,
to the force of public opinion as such, but to the wrong sort of public
opinion, and he had always taken pains to help the right sort, 'the
true public opinion of this monarchy', to prevail through his own
counter-manipulation of the press. Until 1789 there were underground
polemical pamphlets but no regular political journals in France. The
gap was filled by illegally imported French-language periodicals, such as
the *Gazette de Leyde*, published in Holland, and the *Courrier de l'Europe*,
published in London. Not only did Vergennes turn a blind eye to their
introduction, but also most of their information came from a semi-
official news bureau run by Pascal-Boyer under his own direction. It
served the purpose of the non-attributable briefing. Vergennes's views
coincided with those of the *Gazette de Leyde* over the American War and
it was the recipient of privileged information, but the *Gazette* supported
Necker. Accordingly Vergennes starved the *Gazette* of all information
relating to the events leading to Necker's fall and there was a virtual
'news blackout' concerning France from 1781–3.[33] As regards the
Courrier, Vergennes went further. Having ignored the French censor
by admitting the journal, Vergennes himself censored the actual pro-
duction, informing the editor of his wishes in an unattributable way by
employing the word *on* to refer to himself (Brissot, one of the correspondents, cracked this device). The editor was severely rebuked for
an encomium on Necker, which was not repeated.[34]

Necker was succeeded by the sour and ailing *Conseiller d'État* Joly
de Fleury who, it was said, resembled neither of his names. In July
the Keeper of the Royal Treasury, Bourgade, presented him with a
memorandum which established that the *Compte rendu* was erroneous.
Bourgade's two main conclusions were, first, that even discounting the
extraordinary expenditure incurred as a result of the war, there was an
underlying deficit on the 'ordinary' account of fifteen million livres
instead of Necker's surplus of ten; secondly, assuming the King wanted
to repay the debt over a period of ten years from the conclusion of
peace, the annual deficit for that period would be fifty-two million
livres.[35] Joly believed that on Bourgade's death in 1784 this memorandum or a copy passed to his nephew and heir, Calonne.[36]

The departure of Necker was a ray of winter sunshine for Maurepas in the last months of his life. His last year had been darkened by his losing control of ministerial nominations: to add to his mortification, the Queen had played at least some part in the appointment of Castries and Ségur and she encouraged them to think of themselves as 'her' ministers. Even so, she had not wanted to provoke Maurepas into resigning until her position had been sufficiently strengthened by the birth of a Dauphin for her to suggest that her nominee, Loménie de Brienne, Archbishop of Toulouse, should succeed him. On 22 October 1781 she at last gave birth to a Dauphin. In his joy the King bursts the narrow confines allotted for the day in his diary with minute details of the confinement. On 21 November Louis notes in his diary: 'Nothing. Death of M. de Maurepas at eleven-thirty in the evening'.

As Maurepas lay on his death-bed news reached Versailles that the Franco-American troops had won a great victory at Yorktown which might end the war. Louis sent the Duc de Lauzun to go and tell Maurepas. Lauzun ran through the list of prisoners, cannon, standards taken. After each item Maurepas repeated 'Good, good', but then, turning to Lauzun, he said: 'I am dying and I don't know whom I have the honour of addressing.' Maurepas's body was allowed to remain in the palace until his funeral on the 23rd — 'a high favour', as Castries notes, adding: 'The King seems really affected — or should one perhaps rather say embarrassed.'[37] Maurepas's monument was to be the future conduct of the King he had trained and of the Parlement he had recalled. In his lifetime Maurepas had, in Lenoir's words, 'despite his lack of energy, known how to contain [the Parlement]' and at his death Joly de Fleury 'lamented that the King no longer had the man who directed [it]'.[38]

Shortly after Maurepas's death the Queen, at the instigation of her *lecteur*, the Abbé de Vermond, proposed that Toulouse should enter the Conseil as a preliminary to his becoming chief minister. This was trebly displeasing to the King: he had no intention of replacing Maurepas in any case, still less by a nominee of the Queen's and least of all by a political priest who, following precedent, would acquire the added prestige of being made a cardinal. Lenoir was in the apartments of the King's aunt, Mme Sophie, when the King burst in 'in a towering rage' and declared that 'the one must be confined to his diocese, and have his revenues confiscated and the other [Vermond] must be sent away from the Queen'.[39] Louis's rage subsided but, though thwarted, the ambitions of Toulouse did not.

5

The Last Years of The Ancien Régime, 1781–6

The day after Maurepas's death on 21 November 1781, Castries notes in his diary: 'The King assembled a comité where he spoke more than usual, as one saying to himself: "I want to reign."'[1] Louis was now twenty-seven and he did not appoint a successor to Maurepas, who in truth had abandoned any ideas he may have had of preparing one. A portion of his mantle fell to Vergennes, who in February 1783 was made *Chef du Conseil*. The Queen's influence increased somewhat, and there was a further drift towards what Vergennes himself described as 'this kind of anarchy in the Ministry'.[2] He tried to bring order out of chaos — though the struggle, according to Mercy, at times 'consumed his whole attention'[3] — as we must in attempting to describe it, but the picture of these years will perhaps always be blurred.

The essence of ministerial politics in the period between the death of Maurepas and the meeting of the Assembly of Notables in February 1787 which effectively brought the Ancien Régime to an end was a division into two groups. On the one hand there were Maurepas's old *robin* protégés, Vergennes and Miromesnil plus the current Finance Minister; on the other, the ministers who fell loosely under the Queen's protection — military aristocrats like the Service ministers Castries and Ségur and the ex-Ambassador to Vienna, the Baron de Breteuil, who became Minister for the Maison du Roi in November 1783. The King naturally supported the former group and since, particularly after the conclusion of peace in 1783, they occupied the key ministries, they formed, under his chairmanship, what was sometimes called the *Comité de gouvernement*. This was not the same thing as ministerial unity: the other ministers were simply overridden or excluded from important decisions. This did not make for stable government or stable decisions, since the other ministers were present in the Ministry because they represented important interests, such as the Queen, the Court nobility and the Armed Services. Maurepas had not been able to prevent the appointment of Castries and Ségur any more than Vergennes that of Breteuil. Unity at the price of exclusion is ultimately illusory but contributed to the illusion of well-being which envelops the last years of the Ancien Régime.

Part of that illusion had been created by the *Compte rendu*, because the critical state of the royal finances resulting from the war, which cost 850,000 livres or roughly two years of revenue, was the central dilemma throughout the period and the division in the Ministry was expressed in terms of it. In the period 1781–3 the struggle centred on the attempt to end the financial independence of the Service ministers, particularly the profligate Castries; it culminated in the *Comité des finances* of 1783, an attempt formally to reduce the Service ministers and the Minister for the Maison to secondary status by ending their direct relationship with the King in financial matters. The period 1784–6 saw Breteuil, excluded from major decisions of government, mount a dangerous challenge to the ruling comité in the Parlement.

The *Comité des finances*

Joly de Fleury may have demonstrated the falsity of the *Compte rendu* to his own and to the King's satisfaction but he could not demonstrate it to the public because the King had authorized its publication. Necker's reliance on loans meant that the very idea of new taxation had to be re-won: the King himself was reluctant to impose any. This comes over in the different responses of Vergennes and Joly de Fleury to the French naval defeat at the Battle of the Saints in 1782. Whereas Vergennes assured the King that 'the reverse to Your Majesty's arms ... does not change the fundamental situation',[4] Joly seized on the news with alacrity as providing his best chance to impose new taxation. On 23 June he wrote to the King that the disaster 'had already prepared public opinion for this tax [a third *vingtième*] and to allow it time to cool off would be fatal'. After convening a comité of himself, Miromesnil and Joly, Louis consented. Moreover, this argument was calculated to appeal to the Parlement and it is likely that Joly supplied them with it. Lefevre d'Amécourt, the *rapporteur du roi*, who was responsible for presenting the case for royal legislation and was a close friend of Joly's, assured his colleagues: 'Without attempting to fathom the causes of our military reverses, we know we have sustained them, and that at the very time when peace seemed imminent, when our enemies desired peace. [The King can only] ... impose peace on our adversaries by showing them the immensity and the inexhaustibility of our resources.'[5]

D'Amécourt, a handsome, convivial man with ministerial aspirations, was a pillar of what was known as *le parti ministériel*, a group of parlementaires who in return for royal patronage or the hope of ministerial preferment, had managed the Parlement for the Crown since the beginning of the reign. These were headed by the *premier président*, d'Aligre, a chronic invalid who nevertheless 'constantly assured himself of majority support in his court'. D'Aligre was given 80,000 livres by Louis XV on his appointment whilst Louis XVI gave him a pension of 20,000 livres in 1775 and his wife 8,000 in 1779. Perhaps to maintain a hold on him, the Government turned a blind eye to two considerable debts of his to the Crown: 50,000 livres for the *charge* of *conseiller au Parlement* for his son and 200,000 livres, the capital on a life-annuity from the loan of 1781.[6] D'Aligre was already a very rich man. D'Aligre's deputy, the *président* Louis d'Ormesson, famous like all his family for his absolute integrity, had long enjoyed a pension of 15,000. Joly de Fleury's brother, Président Jean Omer, enjoyed three pensions totalling 17,000 livres. The Solicitor-General (another Joly de Fleury) and the two Attorneys-General also formed part of the *parti ministériel*; other recipients of patronage will be mentioned later in connection with the Diamond Necklace Affair as an example of the working of the system. Patronage was dispensed by the *Contrôleur-général*: the posthumous publication of Turgot's papers embarrassed those magistrates who had been in his pay. Miromesnil claimed that this was no job for a Keeper; he had never bought votes, though he had sometimes given money to magistrates 'on account of domestic misfortunes'.[7] The third *vingtième*, which was to last for the duration of the war and three years thereafter, was discussed at a meeting between Joly, Vergennes and Miromesnil for the Government and d'Aligre and d'Amécourt for the Parlement. Afterwards, Louis made a special effort with d'Aligre, addressing him kindly in his cabinet and bringing tears to the old magistrate's eyes, but Miromesnil was still worried that the King would lose his temper unless the Edicts were registered 'purely and simply' with any *remontrances* following.[8] This proved to be the case, but to secure this, the last new tax of the Ancien Régime, the King had to concede that the existing rolls for the *vingtième* would be used. He did not specifically promise that *vérification* would never be resumed, but this proved in fact to be the case.[9]

The slender resource of the third *vingtième* did not prevent Joly from being 'terrified at the prospect of peace'[10] when facts would have to be faced, the principal one being Louis's refusal to countenance bankruptcy. This made the situation graver, when peace preliminaries between France and England were signed on 20 January 1783, than at the Peace of Utrecht in 1713 (when the debt had been higher) or at the Peace of Paris in 1763 (when it had been similar). On 23 February the King rewarded Vergennes with the title of *Chef du Conseil royal des finances* and, with Joly's encouragement, Vergennes decided to make some use of it: on the 26th a *Comité des finances* was instituted, presided over by the King and consisting of the Chef, the Finance Minister and the Keeper of the Seals, before which all ministers had to submit their regular accounts as well as plans for future expenditure. It was an elaborate response to what Louis could not or would not do himself, impose a budget.

Nor was Louis totally master in the Comité. Joly had originally proposed that the members of the Comité thrash out their differences adversarially before the King, who would make an informed decision (the theoretical procedure in the Conseil d'État). In practice the members had preliminary discussions and presented a united front, Louis invariably adopting their conclusions. Vergennes and Miromesnil justified this on the grounds that it was 'unseemly' to have dissensions in the King's presence — a novel and decidedly English point of view.[11] For, like his grandfather before him, the King had found that ministerial disunity, though weakening the Government, strengthened his position within it.

Dissension enough came from those who were summoned to appear before the Comité, which above all represented the revenge of Maurepas's robin protégés against the grands seigneurs who had been foisted on them in 1780, a 'war to the knife', as Ségur picturesquely put it, 'between the *hommes de robe* and gentlemen like us'.[12] Even so, it ran deeper than social and personal antagonisms, though Joly, in particular, cordially loathed Castries. The latter, who quarrelled violently with Vergennes over France's modest gains at the Peace of Paris, would have liked to continue the war and, in any case, planned to maintain the Navy on a wartime footing in readiness for a follow-up war with England which France could not possibly afford. Joly vented his feelings to Véri: 'He never mentioned the sums involved but by his gestures and his eyes indicated that they were enormous.' Castries was in fact planning to spend 100 million livres during the first six months of 1783 (Sartine had been broken for wanting to spend 120 for the whole of 1781); in addition, with the conclusion of peace, letters of exchange issued by the treasurer of the Marine — after Necker's fall, once again independent — came flooding back to Paris for redemption. On 23 February, with the King's backing, Joly suspended their repayment, though the King insisted on paying interest on them at 5 percent. Joly had hoped by this action to force Castries to resign; when the Queen persuaded him to stay on, Joly himself resigned.[13]

Finally, the Comité was able to insist that both Castries and Ségur submit their accounts, thereby making them subordinate ministers and ignoring Castries's claim that there should be no intermediary between a Secretary of State and the King and that the two men alone could decide the budget of his Department. When Ségur presented his accounts on 31 May, Louis employed silence to deliver him a calculated insult. Véri's account, which is corroborated by that of Castries, runs:

> When the Minister [Ségur] had finished his *travail*, without any warning, he saw the three members of the *Comité des finances* file into the King's *cabinet*. When they had taken their places, the King told M. de Ségur to show him his accounts. In his exposition, he showed that he had spent four or five millions less than the original estimate. When he had finished, he remained seated. No one broke the silence and the King got up, went to pick up M. de Ségur's portfolio himself and, handing it to him, indicated by this gesture that he could go. It was only after he had left that the members of the Comité praised his administration, afterwards continuing the session for another hour.
>
> Nothing could give a greater impression of subordination, and this whole rigmarole has only served to humiliate the Minister for War in the eyes of the public.

Naturally, the two ministers wanted to resign, which infuriated Louis, who let Castries know through Mme de Polignac that he considered him ungrateful and that, if he resigned, he would block his son's career.[14]

Having with great difficulty achieved its primary purpose of subordinating the Service ministers and establishing a budget, the Comité was ultimately destroyed by internal dissensions and an attempt to reform the collection of the indirect taxes. Both centred on Joly's successor as Finance Minister, Henri François-de-Paule Lefevre d'Ormesson, the scion of a rich and powerful Robe family which shared with the King the distinction of being descended from a saint, though only collaterally: in the sixteenth century they had married into the family of Saint François-de-Paule. One branch of the family was distinguished in the Parlement: Henri's branch, as Intendants des Finances, had run the *vingtième* since its introduction in 1748. For some years d'Ormesson, as Intendant of the charitable foundation of Saint-Cyr, had had a *travail* alone with the King and in addition had been giving him a 'résumé of the state of his finances ... every six months' — presumably for some years also. D'Ormesson, at thirty-one the only minister remotely the King's own age, was Louis's personal appointment, part of an attempt by him to set a limit to Vergennes's power by blocking the appointment of his cousin de Crosne to succeed Joly de Fleury.[15] In addition, the proverbial integrity of the d'Ormesson family — *probe comme d'Ormesson*

— was in contrast with Vergennes's cupidity, which Louis found distressing; but Maurepas had been fond of observing that only a fool or a knave could possibly want to be *Contrôleur-général* and this witticism had passed into governmental thinking, Miromesnil, for example, reminding the King of the rare conjunction of 'probity' and 'talent'.[16] Consequently, d'Ormesson acquired and has retained an unmerited reputation for dullness — his brief Ministry and his projects were anything but — and was abused by the King on that account.

D'Ormesson was miserable in the Ministry. He had to promise the King that he would never resign and he declined the honour of being made a *ministre d'état* in the hope that by refusing this lifetime appointment he would avoid exile should he be dismissed. Louis's diary refers to neither his appointment nor his dismissal; d'Ormesson's to 'the indifference with which he treated me and all too often public affairs'.[17] In their *travail* together, Louis refused to talk about anything but the current state of the royal treasury or to allow d'Ormesson to strike up a general conversation. Once, d'Ormesson having apologized for a hurriedly prepared *travail* because he had been up all night nursing his dying son, Louis replied brutally: 'C'est fâcheux!' — leaving it in doubt whether he was referring to the lack of preparation or the boy's plight. 'Une réponse brusque du Roi', d'Ormesson writes in the margin. Louis's own elder son was to prove a sickly child. Perhaps in an attempt to break out of the conversational strait-jacket imposed by the King, in August d'Ormesson drafted a radical memorandum which, looking beyond the usual hand-to-mouth measures, focused on 1787, presented by d'Ormesson as a time both of crisis and of opportunity:

> Happily the approaching expiry of the last lease of the General Farm and of the third *vingtième*, which both occur in 1786, allow us to prepare, by this not too distant date, a better internal order as well by changing or modifying the consumption taxes, presently farmed out, which may be harmful to agriculture and commerce, as by finally enabling Your Majesty to know the respective wealth of his various provinces, still unknown, by means of a better assessment of the two *vingtièmes*, the only tax which is uniform throughout the whole Kingdom and consequently the only one susceptible of establishing a fair basis of comparison between the various provinces.[18]

He mentioned tax farming because in the early summer he and Vergennes had decided to take advantage of the removal of the Court to Fontainebleau in October to propose to the King its abolition.[19] Farming the indirect taxes, i.e. the Crown making their produce over to the Farmers in return for an advance, was one of the most characteristic institutions of the Ancien Régime; it was also one of the most entrenched, with vested interests not just in traditional high finance but at Versailles, where courtiers had stakes or croupes in the various syndicates of Farmers. It was a fashionable way of being associated with money.

The idea of abolishing the Farm may well have come from Vergennes, who had become both more knowledgeable and more radical in financial matters since his intemperate criticism of Turgot's proposals. His immediate concern was that the Farmers, by sending their agents aboard American ships in connection with tobacco, salt and other duties, were driving them into English ports.

The proposal was to convert the last three years of the Farmers' contract into a *régie intéressée* (i.e. the Farmers would be paid a fixed salary plus a proportion of the amount collected over an agreed figure) with effect from 1 January. The existing Farmers would become the *régisseurs* and their profits would remain the same, because the money that they had advanced to the King against them could not be repaid but the exercise would make for an easy transition to a rational system of indirect taxation in 1787.

D'Ormesson duly presented his proposals to the King in the *Comité des finances* on Friday 23 October. Louis, who normally accepted the Comité's proposals automatically, on this occasion 'hesitated for an instant' before ordering the Farmers' lease to be rescinded. During d'Ormesson's *travail* the following Sunday, the King complained of the rapidity with which the decision had been embodied in an *arrêt du Conseil* and published on the Saturday. Though Louis can be taken to have supported such a reform, he had been shaken by a run on the Discount Bank the previous September* and perhaps thought that the timing was bad.

There followed an outcry from the financiers but, since the Farmers' promissory notes had the same backing after the *arrêt* as before, one is inclined to believe d'Ormesson's allegation that their dramatic depreciation was engineered by the Farmers themselves to give them a pretext to demand the impossible repayment of their advance. The Farmers sent a deputation to the King at Fontainebleau, headed by d'Harvélai, the *garde du trésor royal*. On 1 November, just before the deputation was due to arrive, Louis sent Vergennes a note similar, except in its length, to the one he had sent Maurepas on the eve of Sartine's dismissal:

---

* This was a technical crisis resulting from a faulty ratio between what the Bank paid for gold and for silver, resulting in a dearth of gold coins: piastres had to be hurriedly and expensively imported from Spain.

I received your letter last night, Monsieur, and the papers of *M. le Contrôleur-général* on the General Farm and the Discount Bank; since the Farmers want an accommodation, we shall have to agree to treat with them; it would be extremely annoying to give the impression of yielding to them; it was M. d'Harvélai's letter yesterday which terrified [*fort effrayé*] me; you will be seeing him today and you will inform me before the Council [meets] of all that he said to you and of all the ideas you have been able to muster on the present crisis. I do not doubt M. d'Ormesson's zeal for my service but should credit run out, his good intentions will be no substitute. Inform him along these lines until I have made a final decision.[20]

Louis's 'final decision' was, naturally, that d'Ormesson would have to go. Vergennes gave him no support — a characteristic action in any case, but one additionally prompted by his anger at D'Ormesson's refusal to countenance the sale to the Crown, at an exorbitant price, of the regalian rights belonging to his estate of Fravenberg in Lorraine. Louis, who hated ministers making money on the side, was deeply disturbed when he heard of Vergennes's scheme and Vergennes wrote desperate letters to the King: 'My misfortune is extreme because I have caused Your Majesty a moment of pain' and 'I will go into retirement consumed by the misery of having lost the esteem of a master to whom I have always referred everything'.[21] But when d'Ormesson, who still had his *travail* with the King as Intendant of Saint-Cyr, planned to denounce Vergennes on 4 December, Louis thwarted him by the simple expedient of having all the doors to his *cabinet* kept open so that d'Ormesson would have to make his accusations before the courtiers. At Vergennes's request, Louis appointed a commission to investigate the matter and at the end of December professed to accept the exoneration of his minister. Nevertheless, Vergennes's attempt to be a prime minister was over.

Calonne

D'Ormesson had been destroyed by an alliance between high finance and the Queen's *société intime*, the Polignac group and the King's youngest brother, the Comte d'Artois. They had, wrongly, called the Comité des finances 'le tombeau des grâces'. This same combination also secured the appointment of Calonne as *Contrôleur-général*. On 3 November, Louis wrote to Vergennes: 'You have only to summon M. de Calonne to Fontainebleau and explain our plans for him and report back when you have seen him. I do not know whether he is at Paris or in Flanders. I am returning the papers you gave me yesterday. So something good can be salvaged from the work of the Farms; but the main thing we must concentrate on is the support of credit, to assure the funds for the rest of the year but without taking any precipitate measures.'[22]

Louis need not have wondered about Calonne's whereabouts: he had observed every recent change at the Finance Ministry at close quarters. His appointment, perhaps the most decisive of the reign, had a quality of inevitability about it suggested by the King's slightly cryptic remark to d'Angiviller: 'There's one arrived safely against wind and tide.'[23] A contemporary has left a striking picture of him: '[He possessed] the vivacity of a young colonel; the elegance of a man of means; a coquettishness ridiculous in anyone but a pretty woman; the pedantry of the magistrate; some of the gaucheness of the provincial.'[24]

For all his ease of manner in Court society, Calonne was a relative parvenu: his father had been ennobled.[25] And for all his airs of the grand seigneur, he was a dedicated Crown lawyer. In 1781 he had attacked the courtier-minister, the power of the Clergy and the *Compte rendu*, whilst his early career was marked by two episodes which made him desperate with the parlements. In the first, in 1766, he had been the principal draftsman[26] of the speech in which Louis XV claimed that 'le pouvoir législatif m'appartient sans dépendance et sans partage' and so lacerated the Parlement that it came to be known as the *séance de flagellation*. In the second episode, Calonne was accused of abusing the confidence of La Chalotais, the *procureur-général* of the Parlement of Rennes, to obtain proof that he had been writing poison-pen letters to the King.

These were his antecedents, but his immediate priorities were dictated by the circumstances of his appointment. Whilst maintaining the same medium-term perspective as the *Comité des finances* (which he disbanded), he had to rely heavily on his contacts with traditional finance to fulfil the King's imperative: 'the support of credit'. He then sought to work out the size of the debt and to 'constitute' it, i.e. to arrange for it to be serviced in a regular way and spare the King the buffets of surprise demands for repayment. For this purpose, loans of some 100 million livres were registered each year in the Parlement.

Calonne also paid his debts to the Polignac group, that is he paid their debts, notably those of Artois, who became his staunchest supporter. In 1784, he increased the Polignac family's income by 100,000 livres, which was not a large sum considering that they had to entertain the Queen and divert her political ambitions. Vergennes, who formed a close alliance with Calonne, further secured their support by making one of their number, the Comte d'Adhémar, Ambassador to London, a candidacy the Queen had refused to encourage.[27]

In the country at large, with France adopting the new technology developed in England and rapidly industrializing, Calonne promoted a boom, inaugurating a vast programme of public works, beautification of cities, the creation of a great naval fortress at Cherbourg, and aid for the armaments industry.

Breteuil

After the failure of the *Comité des finances*, Castries continued with his programme of naval armament unchecked. But peace removed him from the centre of the stage and the main threat to the *Comité de gouvernement* came from Amelot's successor at the Maison du Roi, the Baron de Breteuil, previously Ambassador to Vienna and a former protégé of Choiseul's. Vergennes, at the height of his power, had been unable to prevent his appointment, through the Queen's influence, first as a minister without portfolio (July) then on 27 November as Minister for the Maison. Breteuil was the Queen's man in a sense that Castries and Ségur never were and he intended 'faire régner la Reine'.[28] The Ministry for the Maison had a mixture of functions, not rationally assembled — it became the Ministry for the Interior in the Revolution — but its colloquial title Ministry of Paris gives the clue to Breteuil's activities: the King and the *Comité de gouvernement* could exclude him from decision-making at Versailles but he would then seek an outlet for his undoubted energies in the Capital.

Miromesnil thought that Breteuil's capacity for harm was limited, 'now that we [i.e. Miromesnil, Vergennes and Calonne] have enough credit with the Master to prevent his errors or at least correct them',[29] and on at least three occasions Louis rebuffed Breteuil in front of the other ministers, notably over his support of a rival syndicate to that favoured by Calonne for increasing the water supply to Paris, when the King slapped Breteuil down 'assez nettement et assez durement'.[30] But in three episodes Breteuil inflicted decisive if not mortal damage on the monarchy: the purchase of Saint-Cloud for the Queen, his conduct in the Diamond Necklace Affair, and his undermining of Calonne's operations in the Parlement.

The purchase of Saint-Cloud

Breteuil's purchase of the palace of Saint-Cloud from the Duc d'Orléans in October 1784 seems to have formed part of his plan 'faire régner la reine' and he may himself have dreamed of becoming its governor.[31] It was unusual for a palace to be purchased directly for the Queen — rather than for the Dauphin — and the impropriety was intensified by the Queen's insistence that the servants wear her personal livery and that orders be issued 'by the Queen's command'. It was also unusual for a minister to buy an expensive palace without consulting the Finance Minister. Calonne's anger with Breteuil was uncontained; nor did he bother to contain his anger with Marie-Antoinette. It was the beginning of an implacable enmity between them.

The Diamond Necklace Affair

Towards the end of the last reign, the Court Jeweller, Böhmer, commissioned a necklace consisting of 579 large diamonds of perfect colour, valued at 1,600,000 livres, in the hope that Louis XV would present it to Mme du Barry. The King, who had already given her the beautiful château of Louveciennes, declined the bait and Böhmer was left with expensive stock on his hands, which made him credulous when a chance came to dispose of it.

In 1785, a gang of confidence tricksters headed by Jeanne de Valois, Comtesse de la Motte, the destitute descendant of an illegitimate son of Henri II, conceived of a plan for obtaining the necklace. The plan centred on persuading Prince Louis de Rohan, Cardinal-Archbishop of Strasbourg and Grand Almoner of France, that Marie-Antoinette wanted him to purchase the necklace on her behalf without telling the King. Rohan, in turn, was rendered credulous by his need to placate the Queen's enmity towards him. The origin of this enmity remains obscure; it may have stemmed from some disparaging remarks he had allegedly made about her mother, the Empress Maria-Theresa, when he had been Ambassador to Vienna. Also he owed his appointment to this post to the ministerial changes in 1770: he, the ally of d'Aiguillon, had displaced Breteuil, the protégé of Choiseul. Marie-Antoinette's antipathies had been based on flimsier foundations. Rohan was doubly desperate because his family, the proudest in France, had been ruined and disgraced by the bankruptcy of his cousin, the Prince de Rohan-Guéménée. The Princesse de Guéménée had been obliged to tender her resignation as Governess to the royal children, thereby depriving Rohan of a channel of communication to the Queen. When Breteuil formed a dynastic alliance with the new Gouvernante, the Duchesse de Polignac, Rohan felt that an 'iron ring' had been placed about the Queen. He became 'obsessed by the threat posed to his political existence . . . by Breteuil'.[32]

Securing the necklace presented the best chance of penetrating the iron ring and capturing the Queen's favour. Mme de la Motte arranged a midnight assignation in the gardens of Versailles between Rohan and a Paris prostitute impersonating the Queen. The gang also forged the Queen's signature as third party to the Cardinal's promissory notes to Böhmer, though Rohan should have known that the Queen did not place 'de France' after 'Marie-Antoinette' any more than the King did after 'Louis'. Rohan obtained the necklace and handed it over to Mme de la Motte, who bought a vast château whilst her husband crossed over to England to dispose of the diamonds.

After several anxious months, on 9 August 1785, Böhmer, believing Marie-Antoinette's signature to be genuine, presented the Cardinal's promissory notes to the Queen for payment, and the affair was out. On seeing her signature next to Rohan's, the Queen flew into a rage and persuaded Louis to take precipitate action, the details of which she gives in a letter of 22 August to her brother Joseph:

> Everything has been concerted between the King and me; the ministers knew nothing about it until the moment when the King summoned the Cardinal [just as he was about to celebrate mass in his full pontificals] and interrogated him in the presence of the Keeper of the Seals and the Baron de Breteuil. I was also there and I was genuinely touched by the reason and force employed by the King in this arduous session. The Cardinal begged not to be arrested but the King replied that he could not consent to this either as King or husband.

The Queen and Breteuil, whose Department happened to be the relevant one, had persuaded Louis to arrest Rohan without making sufficient preliminary enquiries into the affair. Lenoir asked his succesor as Lieutenant de Police, de Crosne, why he had not taken steps to arrest La Motte and seize the diamonds in order to discover whether Rohan were a dupe or an accomplice. Lenoir was told that de Crosne's superior, Breteuil, had not wanted the police bureaux to have anything to do with the affair but had personally given his orders to the senior police officers and the Governor of the Bastille where Rohan was imprisoned.[33] That Louis believed that Rohan was an accomplice is clear from his letter of 16 August to Vergennes: 'You will surely have learned, Monsieur, that yesterday I had Cardinal Rohan arrested; from what he confessed and from the papers found on him, it is proved only too well that he has used the Queen's name by means of forged signatures to obtain from a jeweller diamonds to the value of 1,600,000 livres. . . . It is the saddest and most horrible affair I have ever seen.'[34]

Vergennes's first reaction was also that Rohan could not have been 'assez franchement dupe' as he claimed.[35] His instinct, however, was always to defuse crises and had he been consulted, he would undoubtedly have advised that the whole affair be hushed up. There was also the danger, which Lenoir pointed out to Miromesnil, that the King, by seeming personally to accuse Rohan, was flouting a tenet of the un-written constitution or Fundamental Laws that the King should not dispense justice in person. Miromesnil agreed, claiming that he had warned the King that he must distinguish between his role as king and judge and that of husband.[36] Marie-Antoinette was able to insist, on this one personal issue, that the ministers only speak to the King in her presence — which made her, in effect, a prime minister for the conduct of the Diamond Necklace Affair — and, as she told Joseph, 'they have not been able to budge him an inch'. The bad decision to arrest Rohan was compounded by that concerning the venue for the trial. On 25 August a comité had met to decide the issue. Vergennes and Castries, in a moment of rare agreement, had voted for sending Rohan before a special tribunal. Breteuil, however, argued that Rohan's request to be tried by the Parlement be accepted and Louis adopted this view. This apparently magnanimous gesture can be explained by the fact that Breteuil, in whose office the *lettres patentes* sending Rohan before the Parlement were drafted,[37] had managed to win over the leaders of the *parti ministériel* in the Parlement, the *rapporteur du roi* d'Amécourt being particularly close to him. Breteuil clearly believed that he could sufficiently manage the Parlement in what was always going to be a political trial to secure Rohan's conviction.

Breteuil's stance was enough in itself to ensure that Calonne and Vergennes would take the opposite side, even against the interests of the King, who had staked his reputation on securing Rohan's conviction and the Queen's reputation on demonstrating that it was implausible that she would have a midnight assignation with Rohan to discuss the purchase of costly jewels without the King's knowledge. Apart from his detestation of Breteuil, Calonne worked for Rohan's acquittal because he believed Breteuil could not survive it, enabling him to move to the Maison before the expected financial crisis of 1787.[38] We know from a list of the votes supplied by d'Aligre to Mercy-Argenteau at the conclusion of the trial that seven judges had been directly influenced by Calonne, who had a hold on four of them through suspending payment of their debts to the Crown. The seven were Présidents de Gilbert, Rosambo and Lamoignon, and Conseillers Oursin, Pasquier, Delpêche and Barillon. In addition, Pilleur followed Barillon and Lepeletier de Saint-Fargeau, Saron and Glatigny followed Lamoignon. Lamoignon, who was Calonne's *âme damné*, had split the Parlement in 1783 over his attempt to reform criminal procedure and to rationalize the *épices* or tips which litigants had to give the parlementaires. The King had supported

Lamoignon's reforms but had been dissuaded by Miromesnil on the grounds that they would need the support of the senior judges for 'important pending legislation'. Vergennes and Calonne had then apparently attempted to displace Miromesnil in Lamoignon's favour but had encountered the King's general satisfaction with Miromesnil's handling of the Parlement over the previous ten years.[39]

There is no evidence that Calonne wasted any sympathy on the plight of the House of Rohan. Vergennes, however, who had many links with it, did. He played some part in the proceedings in the Parlement and a number of the judges paid fulsome tributes to him.[40] His main contribution towards thwarting the King, however, was performed with such subtlety that the King seems not to have suspected him or at least not to have borne him any resentment, though the Queen did both: Vergennes ensured that the witnesses who could prove Rohan's innocence were available.[41] There is some evidence that Breteuil allowed some of Mme de la Motte's accomplices to escape; there is ample evidence that Vergennes was prepared to go to any length, including the bending of extradition laws, to bring them back.[42] A key move was the extradition from Geneva of the man who had forged the Queen's signature.

Vergennes was, however, less anxious to have La Motte himself brought back from England, because his best defence would be to attempt to inculpate Rohan. On this matter of personal importance to the Queen, he differed with his political allies, her *société intime*, and his own nominee to the English Embassy, d'Adhémar, who now wrote to him: 'Do not forget, I beg you, Monsieur, that the Queen ardently desires that the Sieur de La Motte can be heard before the judgment.'[43] Needless to say, La Motte arrived too late.

As a result of Calonne and Vergennes's tireless pursuit of justice, Mme de La Motte and her accomplices were found guilty in May 1786 and given varying sentences: she was to be branded V for *voleuse* and imprisoned for life, though she escaped; the Cardinal was acquitted by twenty-six votes to twenty-three. With what his biographer is compelled to call 'breath-taking hypocrisy', Vergennes informed Adhémar: 'People are generally surprised, and no one more than I.'[44] The Queen, well aware of Vergennes's role, tried to have him dismissed and she compromised her dignity by treating him as if he were about to be when there was never a chance of its happening. For the King, whatever his suspicions, found that — as in 1783 — he could not dispense with Vergennes's services. He used the Polignacs to unwind Marie-Antoinette.[45]

The King's reaction to the verdict was to strip Rohan of all his decorations and dignities and to exile him to the Abbey of Chaise-Dieu high in the mountains of the Auvergne. The King's letter of dismisal from his post of Grand-Almoner crossed with the Cardinal's letter of resignation. The King extended his displeasure to the whole Rohan clan: the aged Maréchal de Soubise, whose redundant presence at the Conseil d'État Louis had tolerated out of respect for the memory of Louis XV, was now told he was no longer welcome there.[46]

There were no winners in the Diamond Necklace Affair, which mercilessly exposed the weaknesses of each of the players: Böhmer's greed, Rohan's despair, Marie-Antoinette's vengefulness, Breteuil's clumsy arrogance. The King was betrayed by his two most trusted ministers but he had failed to consult them and had acted — rare for him — unadvisedly and unjustly. Rohan, after all, was innocent. People asked what further punishment he could have suffered had he been found guilty. The question of civil liberty was raised in many a pamphlet. Moreover, this could not be passed off as 'ministerial despotism': Vergennes had supplied the *Gazette de Leyde* with copious details of his search for witnesses.[47] This was naked royal despotism.

The wags noted that Breteuil sat uneasily on his seat at the opera, a reference both to his haemorrhoids (an affliction he shared with his king) and his shaky political position. But he survived, thereby attesting to the security of the Ministry of the Maison. Miromesnil, the head of the Judiciary, observed everything and said nothing. In a sense, however, he was the biggest loser of all: the *parti ministériel*, which he had nursed with infinite care for over ten years, was ranged against the *Comité de gouvernement* and he did not know where to place himself.

The Affair marked a decisive stage in the development of Marie-Antoinette's unpopularity. The gutter press poured out a stream of political pornography against her, one *libelle*, for example, claiming that she had contracted venereal disease from Rohan and proceeded to infect half of the Court, and others that her second son, the Duc de Normandie, born in 1785, was illegitimate. One might have thought that such libels were too gross and palpable to be credible, but Vergennes took them seriously, writing in 1782–3 'as many letters to England about the need to suppress a smut factory run by émigré French *libellistes*' as about the peace preliminaries. The police minister, Lenoir, thought 'the Parisians had more of a propensity to believe the malicious rumours and *libelles* that circulated clandestinely' than offical information. He added that his effort to suppress these writings 'was undercut by courtiers who had scandalous works printed and protected the printers' — the revenge, perhaps, of those affronted by her rudeness and their exclusion from the magic circle of the Polignacs.[48] Some of the mud must have stuck and a popular stereotype of Marie-Antoinette arose that was the opposite of the truth: she was regarded as extravagant and lascivious, whereas she was parsimonious and, from personal predilection as much as from the imperatives of the Salic Law, chaste.

Breteuil versus Calonne in the Parlement

Just as Calonne had hoped that Rohan's acquittal by the Parlement would bring about the fall of Breteuil, so the main objective of Breteuil's alliance with the *parti ministériel* was to bring down Calonne. And, to defend himself, Calonne was to attempt to destroy the *parti ministériel* through which the Government had managed the Parlement since its restoration in 1774. D'Amécourt had no need of prompting from Breteuil. He hated Calonne for his youthful attacks on the Parlement and his high conception of the royal authority, accusing him of 'despotism'; the section on Calonne in his manuscript 'Ministres de Louis XVI' is headed 'M. de Calonne, sa despotisme'. D'Amécourt also accused Calonne of venality — 'under Calonne no contract was given without enormous bribes' — and made the preposterous assertion that 'in three years and four months he and the courtiers consumed more than three billion livres besides the ordinary revenues'.[49] Ironically d'Amécourt, who had himself hoped to replace d'Ormesson as *Contrôleur-général*, shared many characteristics with Calonne. They were both good-looking, both fine and lucid speakers; both were relative parvenus yet both had social grace; both gave and received lavish entertainments. Finally, both had a reputation for being 'smooth and ambitious'.[50]

In December 1785, the Parlement registered Calonne's annual loan, but with such difficulty that he never risked another. There had been the usual preliminary meetings between Calonne, Miromesnil, d'Aligre, d'Amécourt and senior parlementaires, after which d'Amécourt borrowed Calonne's memorandum to use as the basis of an attack on the minister. Calonne sent the former Contrôleur-général Bertin to tackle d'Amécourt, accusing him of (1) asserting to parlementaires that he had ascertained the falsity of various items of expenditure and (2) 'treating the very enunciatory principles of the preamble with sarcasm', which d'Amécourt denied to Bertin but confessed to his diary.[51]

In 1785 Calonne carried out a re-coinage. The ratio between gold and silver — fixed in 1726 at 14·4:1 — had become too low, with the result that gold coins were being exported. This had underlain the crisis at the Discount Bank in 1783. Calonne raised the ratio to 15·5:1 and consequently reduced the weight of the gold coinage by one sixteenth, which had the desired effect. For d'Amécourt and his ilk, however, the King or Calonne personally was simply pocketing the difference. The

Parlement remonstrated and made its remonstrances public. The King, who was known to respect confidences and require the same of others,[52] was furious and on 23 December intervened with the weight of his authority by *lit de justice*. This session has not achieved the celebrity of Louis XV's *séance de flagellation*, precisely because his grandson regarded it as a private matter, but from the King's exasperation parlementaires should have read the signs that ten years of fine weather were breaking up. D'Amecourt, its principal object, has left an eye-witness account of the King's concentrated anger. He began by accusing the Parlement of publicizing

'things which ought to remain in the secrecy of the intimate relations I permit it to have with me'. [He accepted the practice of remonstrances]

'But I do not accept that [the Parlement] should abuse my kindness to the point of constituting itself at all times and in all places the critic of my administration.

'I am going to annihilate an *arrêt* whose rashness is equalled only by its lack of respect (here the King personally scored out a portion of the *arrêt*) . . . [criticizing Calonne's loan].

'For the rest, I want you to know that I am satisfied with my Contrôleur-général.'

Then the King gave the Baron de Breteuil a piece of paper he had taken from his pocket and told him to have the Greffier-en-chef inscribe on the register all that he had just said: 'Let there be no misunderstanding: the *arrêt* must be printed exactly as it now stands.'

As the Parlement was withdrawing, the King called back M. Le Premier Président and said to him: 'I no longer want M. Dammécourt [*sic*] as the *rapporteur* of my affairs. You will suggest another to the Keeper of the Seals who will report to me.'

We were a long time without a *rapporteur de la Cour*.[53]

In March 1786 Calonne followed up this advantage by having the Conseiller d'État, Foulon, Breteuil's candidate for the Contrôle-générale, exiled and in August 1786 he attempted the more ambitious step of breaking the *premier président* d'Aligre. Calonne had a hold over the *premier président* through turning a blind eye to his unpaid debts of his to the Crown; he now resurrected them, Louis was scandalized and d'Aligre, dishonoured, genuinely wanted to resign. At this point, however, Miromesnil, who had acquiesced in the removal of d'Amécourt, conceding to the King that he was treacherous,[54] demurred. He persuaded d'Aligre to fight and sent the King an elaborate letter, a monument to his subtlety, which included the bogus constitutional doctrine that it was impossible to dismiss a *premier président* unless he were first 'put on trial'.[55] The post of *premier président* was in fact a revocable commission and needed to be if the King were to retain any control over the Parlement. When the Keeper of the Seals formally advised the King of France that the head of the Parlement was 'permanently disposed to undermine the measures' of the Finance Minister but could not be dismissed, the classic system of the Ancien Régime had reached an impasse.

The impasse had been accelerated by the destruction of Maurepas's *ministère harmonieux*, whose existence had enabled Miromesnil to tell Véri (in 1782): 'the magistrature has not made a fuss since I have been in office'. In the same conversation Miromesnil had attributed the Parlement's strength under Louis XV to inter-ministerial rivalries.[56] He was therefore in a good position to observe what had gone wrong. The alignment during the Diamond Necklace Affair, ranging the King, the Queen, Breteuil and the *parti ministériel* against Vergennes, Calonne and their adherents in the Parlement, may have been a transient configuration, though none the less damaging for that. As it was, the rift between Calonne and Breteuil made it impossible for the Government to preserve a majority in the Parlement and forced the King and Calonne to contemplate alternative arrangements. Since day-to-day government had in any case become impossible, wholesale reform held fewer terrors: the convocation of the Assembly of Notables did not create the crisis; it was the King's response to an already existing one.

6

Foreign Policy, 1774–87

The métier of a king of France was pre-eminently to conduct foreign policy. In a theoretically absolute monarchy internal politics was deemed not to exist — the Foreign Secretary, Vergennes, always apologizes to Louis for mentioning it[1] — and *la politique* is translated as 'foreign policy'. Louis reckoned to understand foreign policy; unlike Louis XV, he read the intercepted correspondence between the foreign powers first before passing it on to Vergennes[2] and he worked hard, though not as hard as Vergennes, who worked a twelve-hour day. Since, together with Miromesnil, Vergennes was Louis's longest serving minister and one of only four to die in office and since their correspondence was the most extensive of the King's to have survived, and almost certainly ever to have existed,[3] it may be worth making some preliminary remarks about the minister and his relationship with his king.

Charles Gravier, Chevalier then Comte de Vergennes, was the second son of a Conseiller in the Chambre des Comtes of Dijon. His undistinguished birth raised obstacles, which his marriage had seemed to render insuperable, to his advancement to the higher reaches of the diplomatic service. When, with the protection of Maupeou and at the insistence of the Comte de Broglie, head of the *secret du roi*, Louis XV had recalled him from disgrace and appointed him to the prestigious Stockholm Embassy, it was under protest: 'I disapprove of the choice of M. de Vergennes; it is you who are forcing me; but I forbid him to take his base wife (*vilaine femme*) with him.'[4] Marie-Antoinette was, in turn, to make difficulties about receiving Mme de Vergennes at Court. Vergennes thus had a numerous family to advance and none to support him.

For Louis XVI, however, this very freedom from family alliances and from the socio-political assumptions of the high aristocracy made him attractive as a loyal servant of the Crown. Louis let him push his relatives, his cousin Le Clerc de Juigné becoming Archbishop of Paris, whilst embassies and Intendancies came the way of the family also. He scandalized the courtiers and his colleague d'Ormesson[5] by obtaining the post of Captain-Colonel of the French Guards for his eldest son, a post to which the powerful Colbert family possessed the *survivance* or reversion. The King, however, distinguished between greed for office, which was understandable, and greed for money, which was not. As early as September 1775 Véri notes 'a few instances of petty greed for money', adding: 'The King has noticed them and the esteem which his work has won for him suffers from these peccadillos. A man is always coloured by his beginnings.'[6] In 1783 this attitude had seriously damaged him in the King's esteem.

Relations between Louis XVI and his ministers were never easy and all who have left a record of their personal dealings with him — in particular Maurepas, Malsesherbes, Sartine, Castries and d'Ormesson — were constantly being hurt. Vergennes was no exception and there were several occasions when even a minister with such *consistance* thought, however mistakenly, that he was in danger of losing the King's favour. During the Guines affair in 1775/6 the King and Vergennes exchanged several letters characterized by nervous tension on both sides. Those of Vergennes in particular are punctuated with such expressions as 'It might seem that the Minister was seeking to hide [from the Queen] behind his Master'.[7] Vergennes was also on tenter-hooks in 1781 and 1785. In 1785 he tells Louis that rumours of a change in the Ministry are damaging France's effectiveness abroad and in 1781 that similar rumours are undermining his ability to concentrate on his work:

Sire, When the heart is grievously afflicted, the mind cannot retain the freedom and activity necessary to sustain unremitting labour. My heart, Sire, is a prey to profound melancholy. Various indications make me only too aware that Your Majesty's kindness towards me is no longer the same. I seek in vain to know what can have deprived me of it; I have nothing with which to reproach my conscience and I cannot imagine that Your Majesty accepts the sinister bias that the Choiseul faction is seeking to spread around.[8]

The neurasthenic quality of these letters is reminiscent of the similar relationship between Louis XIII and Richelieu (whose policies Vergennes sought to emulate) and raises the question whether it was a Bourbon characteristic to exploit the constructive tensions within a ministerial relationship.[9]

At the same time, Louis's letters to Vergennes can exhibit genuine kindness, solicitude for his health and even a desire to manage his susceptibilities, as when in May 1776, knowing Vergennes's paranoid fear of being supplanted by the Ambassador to Vienna, Breteuil, Louis explains that a personal letter he had written to Breteuil contained nothing more sinister than the travel arrangements for Maria Theresa's projected visit to Brussels. 'I tell you this', Louis concludes, 'to dissipate your fears (if you ever could have had any) and to demonstrate my confidence in you.'[10] Elsewhere, he shows gentle concern: 'Having worked so hard, it is right that you should rest and I gladly grant your request to be excused seeing the Ambassadors on Tuesday, whether I go hunting or not.'[11]

On 30 November 1784, Vergennes received one of the most unaffected letters Louis ever wrote: 'If you are not tired today and would like to come and talk to me this evening, come at half-past-six, otherwise come tomorrow at the same hour.' There is no standing on ceremony here, just the utter simplicity of a man enjoying his relations with a colleague. The King, alone at his desk, forgot ceremony, shyness and awkwardness — he even made a rough joke about 'Mme Potemkin' (Catherine the Great) being at 'forty-five, a fine old age to be having a child'. Once, on 5 January 1785, he does not bother to conceal from Vergennes that he had been unable to concentrate (this was possibly a foretaste of the bouts of depression that were from 1787 to afflict him): 'You did well to remind me of the courier; I had not forgotten it but for two days now I have not been in a fit state to apply myself.'[12]

Thus the two men quickly established a working pattern which was to last until Vergennes's death. Each would send the other the material he had received first with comments; Louis, in particular, who read English fluently, avidly followed parliamentary debates, seeking clues to changes of policy and pressures on the British Government. Vergennes would generally draft Louis's letters to foreign rulers, the King making modifications which he designated as either essential or optional. They would sometimes discuss the general situation by letter, but this was generally saved for their chats in the early evening. Finally they would decide when to use the Conseil d'État, the supreme council for the elaboration of foreign policy, and what to show it and, during the American War, make arrangements for the comités with the Service ministers. From the growing understanding between these two men was born a successful foreign policy, a brilliant if insubstantial edifice, a curious product of two sound rather than brilliant minds.

The bridge between the foreign policy of Louis XV and that of his grandson was Louis XV's personal diplomacy, *le secret du roi*, yet the new King ordered it to be burned. In their discussions together in the saddle, Louis XV had never mentioned the Secret, so that it came as a complete surprise when its head, the Comte de Broglie, hoping for a dukedom, told an incredulous Louis XVI of 'the enormous volume of papers . . . dispersed in several depots in the well-founded fear that the Duc d'Aiguillon [the official Foreign Secretary] would surprise an order from the late King['s religion] to seize [the papers] from M. Dubois-Martin, their custodian'.[13] Louis told Broglie to burn the lot,[14] though he relented to the extent of accepting Broglie's request that the new Foreign Secretary, Vergennes, who happened to have been the second-in-command of the Secret and the Minister for War du Muy (friend of the Dauphin who, had he known of the Secret, would more easily have understood his father), examine the matter. Vergennes's report was naturally favourable; nevertheless, Louis repeated his order to burn the papers, Vergennes managing to salvage only a plan for an invasion of England which was to be resurrected in 1779 under Broglie's direction. But as Vergennes dutifully fed the ministerial grate with his life's work, the firelight glinting on his magnificent ormolu *chenets*, he must have smiled at the thought that from the ashes of that conflagration would arise the phoenix of the young King's foreign policy: the man had been saved, indeed promoted, what did it matter now if the book were burned? And at least there would be no betrayal of the young King's basic beliefs (something he could not guarantee as, simultaneously, he began his rear-guard defence of Maupeou's work).

On 9 June 1774, Broglie wrote to the new King to explain the purpose of the Secret:

> It consisted in preserving in Europe the equilibrium established by the Treaties of Westphalia [which in 1648 established the diplomatic frame-work of Europe for the next 150 years]; in protecting the liberties of the Germanic Federation, of which France was the guarantor in terms of the treaties; in binding together, by another perpetual treaty, Turkey, Poland, Sweden and Prussia, through the mediation and ultimately the accession of France; and finally in thus separating the House of Austria from Russia, confining the latter to her vast deserts.[15]

Broglie claimed, in a memorandum to Vergennes, that 'it was not dictated by a spirit of antipathy towards the established system of alliances [with Austria] but solely by the desire of conforming with the principles and intentions of the late King relative to that great object'.[16]

This distinction may seem sophistical, but it was just such a delicate balancing act that Louis XVI and Vergennes were destined to perform: to prevent Austria from either exploiting France or reverting to her traditional, perhaps natural, alliance with England. As the King put it in a letter to Vergennes in 1778 which inhabits the same thought-world as the Secret: 'We have an alliance which unites us very closely with

Austria, but it does not oblige us to enter into their ambitious and unjust schemes. Yet again, we have to maintain the reputation of France in Germany which has been only too considerably undermined for some time and, as you put it so well, the guarantee of the Peace of Westphalia is inherent in the Crown.'[17]

The King had to prevent the mistakes of the last reign from being repeated in his own. The general situation was not dissimilar. Austria, having lost the rich industrial province of Silesia to Prussia, felt she needed to gain an equivalent (Bavaria) to survive as a major Germanic Power. In America, there was little chance of France's regaining Canada, but England was facing growing unrest from her colonies as she tried to make them contribute to the cost of defending them in the recent war. The thirteen states were to declare their independence in 1776 and there was a chance for France to regain the prestige to which she was entitled by her resources and vast population of 25 million. There was no logical connection between the two conflicts, but since the other Powers could not afford to fight each other unless they obtained a subsidy from France or England — the point of Frederic II of Prussia's observation that they were the only Great Powers — they tried to entangle them in Europe. It was in the interests of neither France nor England to be so entangled unless the one could ensure that the other would be entangled much more deeply, as France had been in the Seven Years War. Louis's analysis of the situation is given in a letter of 19 June 1776 to his Bourbon cousin and ally, Charles III of Spain: 'I think the time has now come to concentrate exclusively on taking the measures most appropriate to humiliating this Power [England] which is our national enemy and the rival of our House. I am all the more free to concentrate entirely on this matter in that I have adopted the resolution, of which Your Majesty will surely approve, of not interfering, except by my good offices, in the quarrel which has arisen in Germany.'[18]

In addition to this approach — legacy of the Secret, legacy of the Dauphin or just plain common sense — Louis XVI brought a new element: the 'coming moral reformation' to which du Muy had referred when taking office should also extend to foreign policy. Louis believed that there had been a breakdown of international morality in the previous generation. It had begun with Frederic II's 'rape of Silesia' in 1740, but Louis considered that his brother-in-law Joseph II shared Frederic's belief 'in the law of the strongest'.[19] Above all, there had been the partition of Poland between Austria, Prussia and Russia in 1772 — 'the tragedy of the North', as Broglie characterized it — negating as it did the original purpose of the Secret to place a French prince on the Polish throne. Louis XV, in the midst of Maupeou's reforms, had been unable to restrain his Austrian ally. Louis XVI despised the three former enemies for shelving their quarrels to conclude a shabby deal, as he wrote to Vergennes in 1775: 'I have absolutely no faith in the new accord of the co-partitioners; I believe them to be rather observing each other with mutual distrust.'[20]

Louis's philosophy is summed up by his instruction to Vergennes of 12 April 1775: 'Honesty and restraint must be our watchwords.'[21] By 'honesty' Louis meant, above all, observance of treaties; by 'restraint' he meant restraint in annexing territory. Louis set great store by the observance of treaties, and in his first Edict he mentioned this quality in a eulogy of his grandfather — 'a Prince noted for his observance of treaties'. The Treaty of Westphalia assumes the almost mystical quality of being 'inherent' in his 'Crown', whilst he even scrupled about giving the Young Pretender a pension because he 'believed that the Treaty of Aix-la-Chapelle forbids our having any dealings with him'.[22] Louis's views on annexation are epitomized by his comment that Joseph II would confer greater benefits on his peoples by persuading Turkey to open the Black Sea to his shipping than by forcing her to cede Bukovinia[23] and find an echo in Vergennes's observation that France should 'rather dread than seek territorial aggrandisement'.[24]

France and the War of American Independence

Brooding, during the Revolution, on the financial consequences of France's involvement in the American war, Louis was to say that he regretted the decision to enter and that his ministers had 'taken advantage of his youth'.[25] Nevertheless, he was fully informed of all the steps which inexorably led to war with England: supplying the colonists with money, provisions, arms and volunteers and, in 1778, formally recognizing their independence. On 2 May 1776 Vergennes 'had the honour of placing at the feet of Your Majesty the paper authorizing me to furnish a million livres for the service of the English colonists, providing Your Majesty deigns to affix his *approuve*'.[26] Thereafter, Louis's letters to Vergennes show him taking personal direction of Beaumarchais's subsidy arrangements with the colonists. Véri even claims that the King had asked Beaumarchais to negotiate with the Americans without consulting his ministers, 'or if he did consult them, they are denying it now'.[27]

Vergennes even goes as far as to suggest, probably exaggerating to shift the responsibility, that Louis had taken the decisive role in the crucial step of signing a treaty of alliance with the Americans without first having secured the participation of Spain. Vergennes told

Montmorin, the Ambassador to Spain, that he had been very worried
— 'I could even say ill' — but the King had 'given courage to us all':

> M. le Marquis d'Ossun [the former ambassador to Spain] can tell you
> with what care this matter has been weighed and discussed. First of all
> we [Ossun and Vergennes] talked it over together and then with M. le
> Comte de Maurepas. Next the King heard my personal report, kept
> the documents and examined the arguments for and against. Since
> [Maurepas] had an attack of gout at this juncture, His Majesty went to
> his apartments yesterday, M. d'Ossun and myself being also present.
> The matter was discussed again afresh and minutely debated etc.[28]

All in all, the decision to enter the war has all the hallmarks of one of
those protracted, set-piece decisions, like that to recall the Parlement,
which were so characteristic of the reign.

The fortunes of the war were mixed, but the Franco-American forces
won the decisive battle, that of Yorktown, when a British army,
blockaded by a French fleet, was forced to capitulate. France's gains at
the peace were modest and were criticized as such, but they almost
exactly fulfilled the original war-aims which Vergennes had outlined
to Spain in 1778 in connection with the combined operations to be
concerted between the two countries:

> If the King had only to consult his own requirements this plan would be
> simple ... as His Majesty desires no greater advantages than to ensure,
> by the separation of its colonies from the metropolis, the enfeeblement of
> the most inveterate enemy of his Crown, of that of Spain and of the whole
> House of Bourbon. Neither the expulsion of the English commissioner
> resident at Dunkirk [to ensure that the port was not fortified] nor a little
> less restriction in fishing off Newfoundland, nor the recovery of the little
> islands of Dominique and Grenada were great enough reasons for us to
> go to war and yet these are the only objectives which the King would
> propose after a successful war.

The guidelines had been laid down by the King in a letter to Vergennes
of 18 October 1776: 'If we are forced to make war on England, it must
be for the defence of our possessions and the abasement of her power,
not with any idea of territorial aggrandisement on our part, aiming solely to ruin
their commerce and sap their strength by supporting the revolt and
secession of the colonies, despite the axiom of M. de Grimaldi [Spanish
Foreign Secretary] that one only fights wars for aggrandisement.'[29]

The real prize of the war was the recovery of diplomatic prestige, that indefinable commodity which determines whether a country should have more or less influence than its physical resources would suggest, and its first-fruits the Franco-Dutch alliance of 1785. The Dutch, jealous of England's naval predominance and angered at her insistence on searching neutral vessels trading with her rebellious colonies, had entered the war against England. The peacetime treaty was a tour de force for France because Anglo-Dutch solidarity and hostility towards France had been a permanent feature of European diplomacy for over a century. Though the Dutch were not the force they had been in the previous century, Vergennes could write to the King: 'Of all the alliances, that with the [Dutch] Republic is the most advantageous and the least subject to drawbacks'[30] — in marked contrast, he might have added, to the Austrian.

The Austrian alliance

There was a structural imbalance in the Franco-Austrian alliance, between a satisfied Power and a hungry one, and between a unified one with extensive overseas interests and a multi-national land empire held together only by personal, dynastic links. These problems had been inherent from the start; indeed, the main damage, the partition of Poland and the loss of Canada, had been done in the previous reign. Louis and Vergennes, however, adopted the line, which was a useful, self-deceptive fiction, that as Joseph II, characterized by Louis as 'ambitious and despotic', took over the running of Austria, as emperor and co-ruler from 1765 and as sole ruler on Maria-Theresa's death in 1780, so, *pari passu*, the alliance degenerated from its original principles: 'He must have positively hypnotized his mother', Louis told Vergennes, 'because all these usurpations are positively not to her taste.' In fact, the difference between Joseph and his mother was one of degree not of kind. In 1774, however, Vergennes was thrown into consternation by the false rumour that Maria-Theresa was dying, Louis acting to calm him whilst conceding that the death of the Empress 'would effect a change in the political system of Europe'.[31] Even so, whether Maria-Theresa lived or died, the most important new ingredient in 1774 was her daughter, Marie-Antoinette.

Although by temperament Marie-Antoinette was disinclined to be bothered with affairs, pressure from her relatives ensured that foreign policy was the one field in which she took more than a passing interest. Nevertheless, in order to prevent the Austrian alliance from getting out of control, Louis had to exclude her more rigorously from foreign policy than from any other field, employing a combination of obstinacy, silence and guile. Marie-Antoinette describes this process in a letter to Joseph of 22 September 1784:

> ... one has to know him to realize the few opportunities afforded me by his character and prejudices. He is naturally taciturn and it often happens that he does not talk to me about matters of state even when he has no desire to hide them from me. He replies when I bring the subject up but he never volunteers anything and when I have learned a quarter of some matter I have to ... get the ministers to tell me the rest by letting them think that he has told me everything. When I reproach the King with not having spoken to me about certain matters, he is not upset, he appears a little embarrassed and sometimes he replies naturally that he never thought of it. I tell you straight that matters of foreign policy are those on which I have the least hold. The King's natural distrust was confirmed originally by his governor before my marriage.... M. de Maurepas, though with less perseverance and malice, thought it would help his influence to continue the King in the same ideas. M. de Vergennes follows the same plan and perhaps uses the foreign correspondence to support falseness and lies. I have spoken openly to the King about it and more than once. Sometimes he has replied angrily and since he is incapable of discussion I have been unable to persuade him that his minister has been deceived or is deceiving him. I have no illusions about my influence; I know that, especially in foreign policy, I do not have an ascendancy over the King's mind. Would it be advisable for me to have scenes with his minister over matters in which it is almost certain that the King will not support me?
>
> ... I allow the public to think I have more influence than I really have because if people thought I was without it I should have even less.
>
> These confessions, my dear brother, are not flattering to my self-esteem but I want to hide nothing from you in order that you may judge me as fairly as possible, given the appalling distance placed between us by fate.

Austrian pressure on the Queen focussed on Joseph II's overriding ambition to acquire Bavaria in order to round off his territories, to increase his weight in Germany and to give his lands something of the homogeneity which he noted with envy during his visit to France in 1777. The Bavarian branch of the Wittelsbachs became extinct in 1777, the Palatine branch was likely to follow suit, leaving the Duke of Zweibrucken as heir. Joseph exploited this situation to make two attempts to gain Bavaria, in 1777–8 on the basis of medieval titles which Louis in common with most other rulers considered spurious, and in 1784–5 by trying to persuade the Wittelsbachs to renounce their claim in return for being put in sovereign possession of most of the Austrian Netherlands.

In the first Bavarian crisis Joseph mobilized, as did Frederic the Great, who was not prepared to countenance an increase in Austrian strength, and there was a 'stand off' between the two German Powers. Joseph asked for support from his ally, even promising a portion of Belgium in return for armed assistance. Louis declined the offer (since the acquisition of Belgium had been the central objective of French foreign policy for three hundred years, to renounce Belgium was in effect to renounce all annexation) and made it clear to Vergennes that he did not regard Joseph's claims as constituting a *casus foederis*.[32] At the same time he praised Vergennes's handling of the Prussian Ambassador, 'dispelling the notion of our detaching ourselves from the alliance with Vienna whilst not seeming to approve its usurpation'.[33]

It was a tense time between Louis and Marie-Antoinette. The King confided to Vergennes — 'this is for you alone' — that the Queen had just had a letter from his mother-in-law Maria-Theresa saying that she had been 'abandoned by her allies' and that 'having had glory all her life it had been reserved for her old age to know humiliation'.[34]

Maurepas too was worked up to fever pitch. There was no need for 'secrecy' in his dislike of Austria: when he had left the Ministry in 1749, France had just finished fighting a successful war against her. In addition he distrusted all alliances, especially long-standing ones such as those with Austria or Spain — 'everyone's friend, no one's ally', he was fond of saying — and believed that 'France should be self-sufficient and limit itself to what it can achieve on its own'.[35] He stated quite simply that if the Queen pressed for intervention in Germany he would resign and was driven to a final elaboration of his system of regulating the King's contacts. He could hardly insist that the Queen only talk to the King in his presence but he did insist that the Queen only talk to him, Maurepas, in the King's presence, which apart from being humiliating was also insulting to the Queen because its sole purpose could have been to prevent her from pretending to Louis that Maurepas had made her concessions.[36]

In the end, French and Russian mediation settled the first Bavarian crisis at the Congress of Teschen in 1779, the Emperor receiving a small, face-saving slice of Bavaria. The French plenipotentiary was the Baron de Breteuil, who was to retain a strong impression of what a congress could achieve. Joseph in turn was later to make a gratuitous offer of mediation in the American war, concerted, Louis thought, with speeches in the Commons extolling the virtues of an Austrian alliance.[37]

In 1784 Joseph decided to improve his Belgian territories by opening the Scheldt to shipping. Dutch pressure had inserted the clause closing the Scheldt in the Westphalian treaties to prevent Antwerp from becoming a rival to Amsterdam, and Vergennes even believed that Austria had picked a quarrel with the Dutch deliberately to embarrass France and (at the last minute) prevent her alliance with the Republic from being signed. Be that as it may, on 8 October an Austrian ship, the *Louis*, set off from Antwerp amidst applause, intending to sail down the Scheldt and buy wine in France. It was soon intercepted by Dutch frigates, one of which fired across her bows and forced her to head back. Joseph II demanded reparations for the insult to his flag, the cession of the key fortress of Maastricht, and asked what help his French ally proposed to give. Meanwhile he assembled his troops for an invasion of Holland.

Marie-Antoinette also mobilized. By 1784, she could not simply be ignored; the mother of the Dauphin, she now also had her protégés in the Ministry, notably the Baron de Breteuil. When Joseph announced that he would drop his claims against the Dutch provided the French would allow the Bavarian exchange to proceed, Marie-Antoinette thought she had squared Louis, writing to her brother on 2 December:

> As soon as I received your letters I went together with M. de Mercy to show the King one of your two letters and the plan for the exchange. Whether he did not want to commit himself on the spur of the moment or whether, because of a very confused recollection of what had been said to him about the exchange at the time of the Peace of Teschen, he did not at first take to this proposal, I have to say that before he had seen M. de Vergennes, further thought had already brought him round to it.

In fact Louis had devised an elaborate way of outflanking her: he would bolster himself with the authority of the Conseil d'Etat which, partly for reasons of secrecy, had languished during the American war. He told Vergennes: 'You will do well to communicate your important note on the present crisis to each of the other ministers in order to have their advice, as we did last year.'[38] Thus we have the written opinions of each of the ministers.[39] That of Vergennes is most favourable to the exchange; indeed he makes out an excellent case for letting it go through, arguing that if the Low Countries were no longer in the possession of a Great Power, France would no longer need to maintain an expensive army along the northern frontier. To Breteuil, the Queen's protégé but himself a senior member of the former Secret, is reserved the role of attacking the exchange outright, including a scathing personal attack on Joseph: 'He seems to think that the man who annexes the most territory will go down as the greatest prince in history.'[40] On 31 December Marie-Antoinette writes to Joseph: 'M. de Vergennes has communicated to all the minsters of the Council his report on the proposals for the exchange. I do not know whether this is a new trick on his part but, according to what the King told me afterwards, his report is more conciliatory than the opinion of several other ministers.'

The Council decided that the King should write the Emperor a letter in which 'without for the moment dwelling on its conformity with my interests' he said he would consider only the effects of the proposed exchange on the German Empire and in particular on the King of Prussia — a cynical manœuvre in view of the predictability of Prussia's response. Vergennes wrote the first draft of this letter, Louis making three amendments. Two Vergennes accepted, but he held out against the third: 'It was with the hope of binding the Emperor more tightly that, whilst applauding his intention of lending himself to a suspension of arms [against the Dutch], I inserted the word "immediately"; but as this adverb is not to be found in the Emperor's letter, there is no harm in omitting it.'[41] Louis must have thought that Vergennes was pressing the Emperor too far, because the adverb in question does not appear in the final draft.[42]

Frederic blocked the exchange as expected; Joseph resurrected his grievances against the Dutch but was induced to settle for the payment of six million florins, some of it provided by France herself, an expedient in which the hand of Calonne can perhaps be detected. The Franco-Dutch alliance, on which he as well as Vergennes had set his heart,[43] went ahead. The Dutch Ambassador presented Calonne with the star of the Order of the Saint-Esprit, of which he was *grand trésorier*, set in diamonds.

The Franco-Dutch alliance, signed at Fontainebleau in November 1785, was arguably the zenith of the reign of Louis XVI. France had success-fully mediated between Austria and Prussia, and twice between Russia and Turkey. By her consistent backing for Sweden, culminating in the close alliance of 1784, she had prevented that country from sharing the fate of Poland. She had won the goodwill of nearly every country — even England signed a commercial treaty in 1786 — except Austria, whose empty alliance provided a façade behind which France could effectively operate. Commercial treaties were also signed with Sweden (1784), Spain (1786) and finally with Russia on 11 January 1787. It all seemed a fulfilment of the passage in Louis's *Réflexions*: 'A King of France, provided he is always just, will always be the leading *and the most powerful* of the sovereigns of Europe *and may easily become the arbiter between them.*'[44]

France, however, was not allowed to enjoy the fruits of the Dutch alliance for long. It had been concluded not with William V, the Stadholder, who represented the monarchical element in the mixed constitution of the Dutch Republic, but with the Patriots, a revolutionary group who had taken over from the traditional opposition party in the States General. It was an unstable situation and one of Louis's last letters to Vergennes, dated Compiègne 11 September 1786, betrays his anxiety:

> I do not understand how the Stadholder could have employed the degree of violence he has; I can well believe that M. Harris [English Ambassador] is urging the most violent measures on him but this in itself will not be sufficient: England is delighted to see dissension sown in Holland but she will not lend the Stadholder effective aid; it is necessary that the latter should believe that he has the effective support of the new King of Prussia [Frederic William II, whose sister was married to the Stadholder].[45]

Louis's concern was all the greater because he was about to embark on his greatest initiative in home affairs, 'la grande affaire du dedans', as he characterized it to Vergennes,[46] the Convocation of the Assembly of Notables. The English delegates were surprised to see the pace of the negotiations for the commercial treaty accelerate to a successful conclusion (26 September). On this occasion Vergennes, knowing how easily his king became tongue-tied, especially if he had to say something gracious, wrote: 'As the commercial treaty with England could be signed within the day, I beseech Your Majesty to be so good as to treat Mr Eden with kindness and to let him know that Your Majesty lends himself with pleasure and interest to everything which can establish bonds of friendship between himself and the King of England and between their respective peoples. I beg Your Majesty's pardon for this request but these few words will create an excellent impression.'[47]

Whatever impression the King's words created, it did not last long. Taking advantage of the pre-Revolutionary crisis in France, in the Summer of 1787 a Prussian army, backed up by an English fleet, marched into Holland to restore the power of the Stadholder. Castries, the Minister for the Marine, produced a plan for the defence of Holland which would have been feasible if he had not himself helped to exhaust the treasury.[48] France allowed the Patriots to be defeated and the Prussian invasion was followed by a triple alliance between England, Prussia and Holland. Louis's diplomacy, like many a diplomatic edifice, collapsed like a house of cards, under the weight not of intrinsic defects but of financial and political disarray. For two years France turned in on herself, haunted by the unjustified fear that England would take advantage of France's internal weakness to renew the colonial war.[49] Later she was too divided to have a diplomatic persona.

PART II

Defeat, 1787–9

7

The Convocation of the Assembly of Notables

The French Revolution did not begin as an attack on a prison or a palace but as a programme of reform submitted to the King by one of the most devoted and orthodox servants the monarchy ever possessed, the *Contrôleur-général*, Calonne. The importance of the programme lay not only in its comprehensiveness and audacity, but in the enthusiasm with which the King embraced it and made it his own.

Hitherto, outside the field of foreign affairs, Louis had not exhibited a distinctive, personal policy beyond seeking to establish a new moral tone in public affairs, symbolized by his rejection of bankruptcy. He had taken a detached view of the operations of many of his ministers, even, Véri wrote in 1783, 'himself setting the example of showing contempt' for them.[1] For their part, ministers had sometimes sought to shift direct responsibility on to the King, as Maurepas had done during the Flour War, and this was a tendency which was to increase with the regime's difficulties. Calonne, however, achieved such an ascendancy over Louis — based partly on the intellectual satisfaction the King derived from his Minister's attractive presentation of financial matters but also on a shared dislike of parlementaires and political priests, and on a shared belief in the continuing viability of the administrative monarchy — that Louis's personal identification with his minister came to be as much of a constitutional embarrassment as had been his previous detachment.

On 20 August 1786 Calonne presented the King with a memorandum which, under the unassuming title *Précis d'un plan d'amélioration des finances*, announced an administrative and fiscal revolution. The measures were to be endorsed by an Assembly of Notables before being sent to the parlements for immediate registration by *lit de justice*. Calonne, who had mentioned his project to the King 'a few times' previously, had been working on it throughout the summer with the assistance of a few trusted subordinates and of the young Abbé de Talleyrand-Périgord, soon to be Bishop of Autun and later Napoleon's Foreign Minister, and the Comte de Mirabeau, a political adventurer and pamphleteer who wrote to the Minister on 13 June concerning 'the great and truly sublime object you have pondered with such genius and patriotism'.[2]

Assemblies of Notables were nominated by the King from fixed categories of people, whereas Estates-General were elected by the three Orders of the Kingdom, Clergy, Nobility and Third Estate. The last Assembly of Notables had met in 1626 and represented an attempt by Richelieu to outflank opposition in the parlements. This was again the motive, as Calonne told the King: 'Assemblies of Notables . . . though without the inconveniences of the Estates General . . . possess like them the advantage of sparing government the protests of the Sovereign Courts [parlements etc.] and of denying them the pretext of treating everything that does not meet with their immediate approval as surprises to the King's religion.'[3]

Calonne writes as if Assemblies of Notables had a fixed place in the political firmament, but though there had been some pressure for a meeting of the Estates-General since the Maupeou coup, there was none for the 'unwonted apparatus' of an Assembly of Notables: many people, accustomed as they were to a sense of prosperity at home and abroad, assumed that the convocation meant 'either a great disorder in the finances or incapacity on the part of the King'. There are two not necessarily contradictory views as to why Calonne should have dropped this bolt from a seemingly cloudless summer sky.

One view, the narrower, sees the monarchy in general and Calonne in particular as being in a tight corner in 1786. There was little chance that the Parlement would extend the life of the third *vingtième*, due to expire at the end of the year, or even endorse another annual loan in December, particularly after Calonne's unsuccessful attempt in August to break d'Aligre. This view, one commonly held at the time, suggests that if Calonne had managed to move to a more sheltered ministry, taking over the Maison du Roi from Breteuil after he had failed to have Rohan convicted, nothing more would have been heard of the Assembly of Notables. Furthermore, since Calonne's quarrel with the Parlement was essentially a personal one, he should have resigned with or without another ministry to go to; he had had three years as *Contrôleur-général* (the average for the reign being fifteen months) and although he would have to endure a period of 'internal exile' on his estates in Lorraine, it would be sweetened with the pension of a *ministre*.

Such a view ignores the fact that if an exemplary servant of the Crown is embattled with the Parlement because of his very services, his fate cannot be merely personal. It also disregards the ambiguity of human motivation: that Calonne would have switched to a safer ministry if he could does not diminish his sincerity in telling the King 'I would indeed have no regrets if I were the victim of the enterprise'.

Nor was the enterprise merely a desperate improvisation. The convocation of the Notables can be seen as the culmination of the work of the *Comité de gouvernement* through which Louis had ruled since the death of Maurepas in 1781. The period 1781–7 possesses a unity symbolized by Vergennes, the *Chef du Conseil royal des finances*, who, Calonne suggests, was behind the convocation of the Notables.[4] Minds had been concentrated by Joly de Fleury's report to the King in July 1781 on the falsity of Necker's *Compte rendu*, whilst a perspective on 1787 had been opened by d'Ormesson's memorandum of August 1783 which presented the simultaneous expiry of the third *vingtième* and the lease of the General Farm as a chance to reorganize the direct taxes in such a way that the King would be able to ascertain the relative taxable capacity of the various provinces and the indirect by abolishing customs barriers between provinces. This was the essence of Calonne's proposals. Indeed, d'Ormesson provides a link between Calonne's reforms and the period of reforming zeal at the start of the reign: a bundle of his papers is entitled 'Mémoires et projet d'édit pour l'établissement d'une subvention territoriale dressés en 1775 par M. d'Ormesson à la demande de M. Turgot'.[5]

The centre-piece of Calonne's measures also was an *impôt territoriale* (Land Tax) which would replace the two remaining *vingtièmes* and be payable by all landowners without exception, thus yielding more than the three *vingtièmes* put together and answering the King's imperative that the poor should not pay any extra. It was to be paid in produce rather than money and as a percentage of the crop rather than a fixed amount, which would prevent its yield from being eroded by inflation. The only variation admitted was between richer and poorer agricultural districts, land being divided into four categories on the basis of its rental value. This classification was to be carried out, in the provinces which had not retained their Estates, by a three-tier system of assembly at the parish, district and provincial levels.

Calonne felt that if the Provincial Assemblies were composed of the three Orders sitting distinctly, as in the Provincial Estates, they would be dominated by the Clergy and Nobility, who would rig the assessment. This, he told the King, was a weakness in Necker's Provincial Administrations, which were presided over by a bishop. Therefore in the proposed assemblies the sole criterion for membership would be the possession of land. In the parish assemblies there would be one vote for each six hundred livres of landed income, whilst the president of the Provincial Assembly would not be the man with the highest social rank but the delegate of the district which contributed the most taxation. In earlier drafts, half the seats were to be reserved for the Clergy and Nobility; in the memorandum presented to the Assembly of Notables this concession was omitted.

In the Third Estate, including many non-noble landowners, merchants, lawyers and so on, Calonne saw a vast untapped source of support for royal authority, as he told the King in November: 'If there is a clamour from vested interests, it will be drowned by the voice of the people which must necessarily prevail, particularly when, by the creation of the assemblies, . . . the government has acquired the support of that national interest which at the moment is powerless and which, well-directed, can smooth over all difficulties.'[6] Calonne envisaged that the Provincial Assemblies would gradually take over the political and administrative role of the parlements.

The Church was also threatened by his proposals. Not only were the Clergy to pay the Land Tax at the same rate and in the same manner as everyone else (they had forced Louis XV to allow them to pay a self-assessed *don gratuit* instead of the *vingtième*), but the King sought to undermine the independence of the Church by assisting it to pay off its debt. Since the whole machinery of the Gallican Church existed largely to service the clerical debt, its redemption would cause the separate administrative existence of the Church — a veritable *imperium in imperio* — to wither away unbidden. It also seems likely that Calonne envisaged some kind of dissolution of the monasteries.[7]

In addition to these measures, Calonne proposed the abolition of internal customs barriers and the free circulation and, with certain safeguards, export of corn. The *corvée* was commuted and the *gabelle* (salt tax) and *taille* (poll tax paid by non-noble country dwellers) were reduced as a prelude to their eventual replacement by the new kind of tax.

Finally, Calonne planned to consolidate the various departmental treasuries into one. This was more than an essential administrative reform: it presupposed the emergence of a co-ordinating first minister which, if the measures succeeded, Calonne would inevitably become.[8]

In sum, Calonne's proposals, exemplified by the following passage from his memorandum on the Land Tax, amount to a rejection of the spirit and mechanism of the Ancien Régime:

The most glaring anomalies vitiate the tax system. . . .

There are towns which have bought exemption, those which have settled for a lump sum; some provinces have their taxes farmed out, others collect them through their own Estates; whilst yet others have bought exemption.

One cannot take a step in this vast kingdom without encountering different laws, conflicting customs, privileges, exemptions . . . rights and claims of all kinds; and this dissonance, worthy of the barbarian centuries or those of anarchy, complicates administration, clogs its wheels . . . and everywhere multiplies expense and disorder . . .

Turgot's actual measures had been the tip of an iceberg; Calonne's, though without the full Physiocratic rhetoric, revealed its full mass. Even so, they were not original, being, as he put it, the product of the best minds within the royal administration over the century, and in this lay their appeal to Louis's unspeculative cast of mind. If they were revolutionary, it was the Revolution of Napoleon (to whom Calonne was to offer his services in 1800) rather than of the Rights of Man: the hand of equality was extended, that of liberty withheld. This was to lead his opponents to accuse him of 'ministerial despotism', for the Ancien Régime's conception of individual or corporate liberty was anchored in that very variety which Calonne so eloquently denounced. It is not clear how far Calonne or Louis realized the power that would be unleashed, the power of the modern state, by the destruction of the *pouvoirs intermédiaires*, the manipulation by government of public opinion through the Provincial Assemblies and permanent taxation. In view of his analysis of the subsequent phase of the Revolution, it is likely that it was grasped by Calonne's collaborator, Mirabeau.

Having intimated his plans to the King, Calonne pressed for speedy action: he wanted everything to be concluded before the expiry of the third *vingtième* lest he appear before the Notables merely as a beggar, which would devalue his measures. He asked the King to finalize the memoranda to be submitted to the Notables during the Court's autumn sojourn at Fontainebleau (9 October–15 November), which suggests that the King himself was aware that decisions were reached more quickly away from Versailles. But despite the enthusiastic reception Louis gave to the proposals, Calonne insisted that they be exhaustively examined by the *Comité de gouvernement* — Vergennes, the Contrôleur and Miromesnil. He had to carry at least this comité with him as he intended to exclude the other ministers and the Council from the deliberations.

Vergennes's support was assured; the problem was Miromesnil, concerning whom Louis was later to make a curious remark to Malesherbes: 'It was not those two [Calonne and Vergennes] who most influenced my decision but M. de Miromesnil, who disavowed this advice throughout the meeting of the Assembly; that is what determined me to part company with him.'[9] Clearly Louis does not mean that convoking the Notables was Miromesnil's idea but rather that Calonne and Vergennes had an identity of views with his own because they were among the last ministers to serve him who believed in the continuing viability of the classical administrative monarchy — Calonne was to call Vergennes 'the last minister truly devoted to him [the King]'.[10] Their views therefore were merely reflections of his own and added no light or power to them: they were in the Ministry because the King trusted them, not because they represented a group he had to accommodate. The King of France, however, was now not the only power in the State and did not, of himself, have the ability to implement a programme of the magnitude of that presented by Calonne, who admitted as much when he lamented to Castries in December: 'There is no one in France strong enough to carry through all that is necessary.'[11] Miromesnil was in the Ministry as the representative of the Parlement with whom Louis, at the beginning of his reign, had been prevailed upon to govern. If Miromesnil endorsed the programme, it might succeed.

It was disingenuous of Louis to say that Miromesnil had endorsed it. Rather, over a period of three months, Louis attempted to browbeat Miromesnil in the *Comité de gouvernement*, where he was in a minority of one. In using a comité in this way, the King showed that he had absorbed the lesson of Maurepas in 1774, though this had not been part of Maurepas's formal course of instruction since one of those thus isolated had been the King himself. Yet however much Louis may have deceived himself, Miromesnil remained totally unconvinced: witness the lengthy and anguished letters which he wrote to the King and which constituted his only means of free expression.[12] In particular, whereas Calonne wanted a puppet assembly, Miromesnil thought there was no point summoning one at all unless it were allowed to make 'de très humbles représentations' — a phrase suggestive of parlementaire resistance. An Assembly of Notables armed with the powers and staffed with the personnel suggested by Miromesnil could, by a perversion, become an instrument of aristocratic revolt against the royal initiative at reform.

The fundamental divide between Miromesnil and Calonne is clearest in the former's discussion of the proposed Land Tax. He tells the King that their comité had dealt with this 'only very superficially' and has left out of the discussion the whole variety of regional variations to be accommodated. This was not, however, 'superficiality' on Calonne's part, as a man of Miromesnil's infinite subtlety must have realized: the disparate nature of the regime, making general legislation for the whole country impossible, was precisely what Calonne was trying to end. The passage from Calonne's Memorandum on the Land Tax is at total variance with Miromesnil's considerations:

How to raise the Land Tax throughout your States [plural]. The difficulties it may encounter when applied to Brittany and Languedoc, bearing in mind that you have just allowed these two provinces to settle for a lump sum [*abonnement*]. The measures to be taken in respect of Burgundy and Navarre and the little Estates of the provinces adjoining Navarre such as Bigorre. Provence, which has its own individual régime, Flanders, Artois, the Cambrésis, in short all those of your provinces which have Estates or their equivalent.[13]

Miromesnil sought reinforcements. Knowing that the other Secretaries of State (Castries, Ségur and Breteuil) would support his conservative gloss on the Constitution, on 28 December he asked the King to include them in the discussions, thereby acknowledging the demise of the Comité de gouvernement. Louis, however, ignored this request and the very next day convened the Conseil des Dépêches to rubber-stamp the convocation of the Notables. That night the King could not sleep but, as he confided to Calonne, it was for joy.

Castries felt his exclusion as keenly as Miromesnil his intimidation: 'Your Majesty has determined the most important event of his reign without deigning to test my loyalty.' Louis replied, with lame and technical rectitude, that they were dealing 'only with the arrangements to be made for the assessment of taxation which had absolutely nothing to do with anything but finance'. Castries talked of his loyalty, but he did not really have any — except of the kind that delights in purveying unpalatable 'truths' — either to the King personally (whom he called an 'implacable master') or to the absolute monarchy (taking a leaf out of the *Compte rendu* of his friend Necker, he concluded his letter with the reflection that 'at least he would be able to give an account to the Nation of the functions with which Your Majesty has deigned to honour me'). Castries and Breteuil favoured an aristocratic, constitutional monarchy.[14]

Aristocratic attitudes challenged the King's attempts, in the interests of efficiency and fairness, to equalize taxation. They also sought devolution of power to bodies such as Provincial Estates and, increasingly, Estates-General, which they hoped to dominate. The process of aristocratic infiltration into the Ministry, denounced by Calonne in 1781, had seemed harmless as long as the King was pursuing socially and politically neutral policies. In the period 1781–6 he had been able simply to ignore the new ministers in the making of general policy, attempting to contain their higher departmental extravagance through the *Comité des finances*. When, however, the King was putting forward a programme like Calonne's, he could hardly expect men such as Castries to transcend the limitations of their class.

Castries said of his exclusion: 'The King prefers unanimity (which allows him to sleep peacefully) rather than resistance leading to a better course of action.'[15] He was right in saying that the King had created an artificial and temporary ministerial unity by exclusion and pressure. Nevertheless, the King's dilemma was insoluble: if he had consulted the other ministers, they would have tried to block the measures; excluded they were to intrigue with the Notables against them. If all the ministers and the interests they represented had supported the proposals, he would not have needed to turn to an Assembly of Notables in the first place.

As it was, if Louis had any doubts as to the necessity of the step he was about to take, two incidents in December must have served to dispel them. Even on the brink of the abyss, Breteuil continued his intrigues in the Parlement, planning to bring about Calonne's fall by having him denounced for leaving his loans open after they had been fully subscribed, thereby exceeding the amount stipulated in the Edicts (the *rentes* of the loan were backed by the Hôtel de Ville and, as Minister for Paris, Breteuil had access to the certificates). This was too much even for Miromesnil, who informed the King but insidiously added that if Calonne had indeed exceeded the amounts, it was a betrayal of faith to a public already cynical towards the Ministers — though again this was a matter for the King, not the Parlement. He suggested that

> It would be desirable for Your Majesty to ask M. de Calonne next Sunday whether the sums . . . have been exceeded and to tell him to give you the statements. It would also be necessary for Your Majesty to tell M. le Baron de Breteuil that he would like to have these statements checked secretly and to ask him whether he does not have people in the Bureau de la Ville who could obtain secret insights for him, at the same time recommending the greatest discretion.
>
> M. le Baron de Breteuil, flattered by such a confidence and happy to enlighten Your Majesty's 'religion' himself, will in all likelihood prevent M. d'Amécourt and his emissaries from acting.[16]

Presumably this complicated manœuvre succeeded, for no more is heard of the denunciation in the Parlement, but Miromesnil's second piece of advice concerning the Parlement was less fortunate.

When Calonne had realized that he would not get his measures passed in 1786, he had fallen back on the rather forlorn hope of detaching two of them — one to extend the stamp-duty, the other to alienate the Crown lands — and getting the Parlement to register them in December. Miromesnil advised the King — and Louis was never to forgive him for this advice[17] — that there was no hope of getting these measures through the Parlement and the attempt was not made. Miromesnil was right, but his advice hammered home to the King that the ruling partnership between the monarch and the Parlement, the cornerstone of the Ancien Régime, was at an end.

These developments in the Parlement at the end of 1786 specifically refute the view advanced by Doyle that 'the crisis began in 1787 because Calonne thought the consent of the parlements would not be enough to win general confidence for his proposals'.[18] It began because a situation had been reached in which the Keeper of the Seals, the minister responsible for getting royal legislation through the Parlement, had to advise the King that there was no point even attempting to get just two of Calonne's measures through. Calonne advocated an Assembly of Notables, as he had told the King, 'to spare the government the objections of the sovereign courts', couched as ever in the paradoxical language of hyper-loyalty. Paradox, however, was no longer a basis for government.

In choosing the Notables, Calonne had warned the King that since the parlementaires and clergy would be inclined to oppose the projects, the number of the nobility (he thought the Court nobility would be favourable or at least susceptible to patronage) and the Third Estate 'must be large enough for the wishes of the King to prevail'.[19] In the end, perhaps under Miromesnil's influence, Louis decided to follow precedent rather than attempt to pack the Assembly. Thus of the 144 members only a handful were commoners, whilst all the *premiers présidents* and *procureurs-généraux* of the parlements were summoned, to a total of thirty-seven. Even so, a cartoon depicted the Notables as turkeys with the caption: 'With what sauce would you like to be eaten?'

The opening of the Assembly was postponed from 29 January to 7 then 14 and finally 22 February. Calonne had fallen ill through overwork and Vergennes was dying of it. Louis's last letter to him, written some time in January, runs:

> I was very grieved to learn that you were worse yesterday. I am afraid that despite everything I have said to you, you are still working too hard. I exhort you even more strongly to look after yourself. I ask it selfishly because you know how much the good of my service depends on you. You have M. de Rayneval [the *premier commis*], who has your confidence, for the Foreign side; as for the great internal matter [the Notables], I will hold all the comités religiously so there will be no delay.[20]

On 6 February, he seemed to rally and the *Correspondance secrète* notes touchingly that he was going to retire, but 'would not leave the King and would accept M. de Maurepas's *appartements*', which, tenanted and divided as they were, still retained their symbolic signifigance.[21] On the 13th, however, he died, affirming that he saw the whole heavens opening before his eyes.

Louis did not attend Vergennes on his death-bed, though he put off the day's hunting and gave orders that all the ministers were to go to the funeral. Even the Queen felt obliged to cancel her concert. The loss of Vergennes to the King and Calonne at this juncture was incalculable. In the following July Calonne wrote to his fried d'Angiviller, the minister for royal buildings: 'What would he say today, that worthy and much-lamented friend whose last and only too prophetic words I shall never forget? Would that he himself had been able to execute the commission he bequeathed me! He would have spoken better than me; perhaps the plots he had run to earth would not have materialized had he lived; or in any case if the King had kept him he would not have been deprived of all the ministers who were truly loyal to him (*vraiment à lui*).'[22] By the last clause, Calonne meant that, apart from himself, Vergennes was the last minister to share Louis's conception of the absolute monarchy and that none was to give wholehearted support to the programme he was to lay before the Notables in the King's name.

Vergennes was succeeded as Foreign Secretary by the Comte de Montmorin, who had been Ambassador to Spain and was a former *menin* and personal friend of the King's. After no more than a decent interval Castries asked the King for Vergennes's post of *Chef du Conseil royal des finances*; the King's refusal can hardly have surprised him, but it enabled him to give a warning: 'If you give the post to M. de Calonne it will be to the detriment of the interests of the State.' Earlier, Castries had told his patron the Queen:

> that he had heard the Contrôleur-général say that the King was saving the post of Chef du Conseil des finances for the retirement of one of his ministers, giving it to be understood that this was his price if his plans for the Notables did not succeed. The Queen replied disdainfully: 'if he succeeds he will have no need of that since he will be staying and if he fails I can hardly imagine that the King will grant such a generous *retraite*.[23]

It would be good to think that Calonne was teasing Castries (there was certainly no precedent for a Chef du Conseil *in absentia*). Either way, the King's hopes and fears were accompanied by the more complicated feelings of cynicism, defeatism and dissension among his entourage.

8

The Assembly of Notables

The Assembly, housed at Versailles in a specially constructed hall in the Hôtel des menus plaisirs, was opened by the King amid great pomp on 22 February 1787. Seated on a throne covered in purple velvet covered with gold fleurs-de-lys, beneath a canopy of purple satin, both feet resting on cushions, he was flanked on the dais by his brothers, Provence and Artois, and the Princes of the Blood, but was not accompanied by the Queen, who found this way of distancing herself from the proceedings.[1] At a quarter to twelve the King doffed and replaced his hat and delivered himself of a short speech:

> Gentlemen, I have chosen you from among the different Orders of the State and I have gathered you around me to intimate my plans to you.
>
> This is a usage which has been employed by several of my predecessors and notably by the first of my branch (Henri IV), whose name has remained dear to all Frenchmen and whose example I shall always take a pride in following.
>
> The plans which will be communicated to you in my name are great and important. On the one hand they [aim at] improving the revenue of the State and assuring a stable surplus by a more equitable assessment of taxation; on the other, at freeing commerce from the various impediments which restrict its circulation, and so far as circumstances permit me, in alleviating the poorest section of my subjects. Such, Gentlemen, are the measures which have exercised me and which I have decided upon after a thorough examination. As they all tend to the common weal and as I know the zeal for my service of you all, I have no fear in consulting you about their implementation; I shall listen to and examine your observations carefully. I trust that your opinions, all tending towards the same goal, will easily harmonize and that no sectional interest will stand out against the general.[2]

Miromesnil, kneeling, took the King's orders and gave a short and ambiguous speech. It was customary for the Keeper of the Seals to 'develop the King's thoughts more fully', but on this occasion the task was performed by Calonne in a speech lasting an hour and six minutes. There was a résumé of his proposals but the Notables were most struck by his treatment of the deficit and by his very opening words: 'The measures which His Majesty has ordered me to present ... to you have become entirely his own through the extremely close scrutiny His Majesty has brought to bear on each before adopting them.' This intrusion of the King's personality, like that of an author, was an embarrassment, angering and frustrating his opponents by blocking the constitutional escape-route of the 'surprise to the King's religion'. Calonne said that the deficit had existed for centuries: when Terray had taken over the finances it had stood at seventy-four million livres, and at forty when he had left office; when Necker took over it had been thirty-seven, and on Calonne's appointment it had been eighty. Mindful that Necker's supporters were present in strength in the Assembly and were represented by Castries in the Ministry, Calonne had, in so far as possible, heeded the Genevan's request not to criticize the *Compte rendu*, though to reveal the size of the deficit without criticizing Necker's denial of its existence was like trying to square the circle. After Calonne's speech, the session was quickly concluded and the King left at half past one. On his way out, he was heard to say: 'This is my work and I will see it through.'[3]

At the following day's plenary session, Calonne read out the six memoranda of the first of the four sections or Divisions which comprised his work. The Notables were then to meet next day in seven working committees, each presided over by a Prince of the Blood, and to have a week in which to discuss the memoranda of the first Division. But from the start the Clergy, the parlementaires and Necker's supporters made a dead-set at Calonne, 'falling on him', as Castries puts it, 'like a quarry they wanted to devour', and seemed likely to mangle the Provincial Assemblies beyond recognition and reject the Land Tax outright. Calonne described to d'Angiviller the opposition he encountered: 'A combination of every kind of obstacle, a coming together of all the vested interests; the baneful preponderance of the Clergy; the manœuvres of a fanatical sect [Necker's supporters]; the perfidy of my main collaborator [Miromesnil]; the best intentions denigrated; a war of word-splitting; unseemly railing against the Minister; . . .'[4]

The Clergy, who had most to lose from Calonne's proposals, led the attack, the Queen's protégé, Loménie de Brienne, Archbishop of Toulouse, acting almost as a Leader of the Opposition. Men of his ilk, prelate-administrators like Boisgelin, Archbishop of Aix (who hoped at least to get the blue ribbon of the Order of the Saint-Esprit out of the business), set the tone for a revamped defence of clerical and other privilege. When one old duke got up to rehearse the argument that since the Church lands had been given to God by pious benefactors they should not be subject to taxation, a clerical deputy lent forward and whispered to him: 'We don't say that any more.' The casuistry and word-splitting bemoaned by Calonne was the product of the clerical mind, Brienne, for example, finding it possible to distinguish between 'equality', which he accepted, and 'uniformity' which he abhorred.[5]

The parlementaires realized that their political role had been called into question. Castries notes: 'The Parlement, uneasy and resentful, says that the intention is to deprive it of its right of registration and that this step will lead to the Estates-General.' There was an unsuccessful attempt to give their representatives in the Notables a binding mandate and many provincial parlementaires stressed that the opinions they gave in the Notables in no way bound their parlements or even the way they personally would vote when the proposed laws were sent for registration.[6] Miromesnil is reported to have held secret meetings with the parlementaires in the Notables to concert opposition, each *premier président* also sending his local parlement information about decisions taken so that when the edicts came to be registered, opposition would be uniform.[7]

The Notables' objections to the Provincial Assemblies were first that the 'confusion of ranks' was humiliating to the first two Orders who, according to Brienne, 'would not attend if they risked being presided over or even preceded by citizens of an inferior Order and that then the Assemblies would become tumultuous'; secondly, the Assemblies were too dependent on the Intendant: 'democracy or despotism'.[8]

Their objections to the Land Tax occasionally followed an old path: that the priest should give the King his prayers, the nobleman his blood and the commoner his money.[9] Generally, however, the Notables shifted the ground from the basis of assessment (with which it was difficult to quarrel without seeming to favour the 'sectional interests' which the King had denounced) to the very nature of the tax. They objected that the Land Tax was 'unconstitutional' because instead of its being related to a specific need, its duration and amount were open-ended. Their underlying objection was based on the concept of 'no taxation without representation' which had been enunciated by the American colonists. Not only were the nobility and clergy being asked to surrender their fiscal privileges but even the 'simulated' consent provided by the parlements was being diluted by the prospect of a perpetual, inflation-proof tax, whilst the proposed Provincial Assemblies threatened to give the King formidable new powers and influence. A sense of disquiet at the prospect of fundamental change comes over in

Brienne's phrase 'democracy or despotism' and the 'republicanism and despotism' used by one of his colleagues. The selfish exercise of their privileges blocked the exercise of central power, which, unfortunately for the King, was widely if temporarily unpopular.

Many of these contradictions and paradoxes, summarized by the phrase 'aristocratic constitutionalism', come together in the person of General Marie Jean Paul Motier, Marquis de Lafayette, a member like Brienne of the Bureau presided over by Artois, whose minutes have survived. His exploits in the American War had given him a taste for fame; in short the King, according to Castries, had wanted to exclude him from the Notables as being too independent. He started from the position that 'we should not lightly tamper with a constitution under which France has existed so gloriously for nearly eight hundred years' (1787 was actually the 800th anniversary of the election of Hughes Capet, the founder of the dynasty). He quickly realized, however, that the King was in difficulties and that the attempt to increase his power would lead to its diminution, concluding that he should not be allowed to escape until the country had acquired a new constitution. In his Bureau he observed that the second *vingtième* was due to expire in 1791 and added: 'It strikes me that we ought to beseech His Majesty to determine here-and-now the convocation of a truly national assembly for that time.' Artois, blunt but displaying far more intelligence in the Assembly than he is credited with, when he became King, having to battle long hours, often-single handed, for Calonne's measures, stepped in and 'asked whether . . . it was the convocation of the Estates-General he was requesting. He [Lafayette] replied that this was precisely the object of his request.'[10]

None of these arguments impressed the King, as he made clear to Castries, taking the Notables' part, on 28 February:

Castries: All the Orders of the State summoned to hear the projects of your Contrôleur-général are all, unanimously going to bring their disapproval to the Foot of the Throne; all privileges have been overturned . . . ruin and disorder [brought] to every part of the Kingdom . . .

Does Your Majesty want to constrain the parlements? If so, he must destroy them. Does he want to arm 100,000 men, does he want to leave a stain on his reputation? Your monarchy is absolute but not despotic.

Louis: Hah! you know perfectly well that I do not intend to govern like a despot but I disagree with you and I have thought about it a lot: the Land Tax is the most just and the least onerous of taxes.

Castries: Perhaps in the State of Nature you would be right, Sire. But so many agreements, rights, abuses even, have arisen that what would then have been justice would not be so today. The collection of a tax in kind would be impossible and would cost a quarter of its yield.

Louis: But I assure you, you are absolutely wrong on all of this.

Another matter of disagreement between the King and the Notables was the question of the deficit. The Bishop of Langres, among many, observed that in 1781 a minister of the Crown had published a detailed statement showing that there was a surplus, to which Artois had to reply:

'The *compte* of M. de Calonne is in print as well as that of M. Necker and it benefits from an approval on the part of the King which is the fruit of a long [elsewhere he says 'six-month'] scrutiny.'

Langres: One of them is false.

Artois: Yes, certainly one of the two and today's strikes me as safer than the other."

Calonne had told Necker that he had 'only said what he had been forced to say and had made no specific mention of the *Compte rendu* of 1781',[12] but on receiving Calonne's letter Necker had 'turned pale and trembled' (with anger). He also sent Louis a letter for which Castries was hauled over the coals on 11 March. Louis said in an animated voice as soon as he saw Castries: 'M. Necker has just sent me the most extraordinary letter, have you seen it? I find its tone extremely singular . . . I forbid him to make any public justification or to print anything. . . . He seems to think that M. de Calonne's figures are wrong but I have seen them and I am sure they are right.' The King wanted Castries to bring him Necker's evidence, but Castries refused unless his friend were present.

In the face of this rapidly deteriorating situation, Calonne wrote a very anxious letter to the King on 26 or 27 February:

I have learned much more than I knew when I had the honour of seeing Your Majesty last night. I can now no longer doubt that the clergy and all the disaffected deputies think that the Land Tax is sure to be rejected unanimously. They are wrong, but it is greatly to be feared that they have carried the vast majority with them: all the Princes think so, as do the members of the Council, and they need to be enlightened. It seems necessary that Your Majesty's views on the matter under discussion [the Land Tax] should be made known in order to prevent this move which, quite typically, has been decided on even before the examination [of the memorandum]. I have said this to all the Princes but they want the instructions in writing and approved by Your Majesty in person.

Consequently I have just drawn up a *supplément d'instruction* in accordance with what Your Majesty has already indicated. I entreat Your Majesty to read it, sign it with his approval and authorize me to give a copy to each Prince. I have these copies, to the number of seven, ready and waiting and I only need Your Majesty's order for them to be read out at the start of each committee. The point is of capital importance; otherwise, by an inconceivable stroke of mischance, the Assembly might suddenly adopt a course of action which would enrage the people and dishonour it in the eyes of all Europe. If Your Majesty will allow me to give him a more detailed verbal account I beg him to let me know.[13]

The *supplément d'instruction* was read out by each Prince to his committee on 28 February. It laid down certain principles concerning the Land Tax which the King did not regard as being 'open to discussion': that the tax should apply to all land without exception, was to vary with the yield of the crop and was not to be susceptible to any *abonnements*. Artois added that a tax payable in kind seemed the only way of meeting these conditions.

On the evening of 1 March Calonne had a meeting with his archiepiscopal opponents. In a letter to the King he tries to pass it off as going well — 'clouds of misunderstanding were dispersed' — and says that although there was strong opposition to a tax in kind, they no longer insisted on *abonnements* or their own *don gratuit*.[14] 'I was particularly pleased', he writes with unconscious irony, 'with the conduct of the Archbishop of Toulouse. I owe him the justice of saying as much.'

In the morning, Calonne met five deputies from each committee in a conference presided over by Monsieur, the Comte de Provence. It purpose was again to 'disperse some clouds' — over the Land Tax and the disparity between Necker's calculations and his own. Before the conference he wrote to the King: 'Your Majesty's letter leaves me in no difficulty, no doubt about what I should say. When a king takes such trouble to enter into the intricacies of his affairs and to guide his minister himself, he is sure to be well served.'[15] Nevertheless, despite a brilliant six-hour defence of his projects, Calonne left the conference with his authority shaken. Castries believed that he was beaten and that only 'the King's amour-propre still protects him'. Far from resigning to the inevitable, however, the King and his minister deliberately raised the stakes.

An appeal to the people, who he had said would be 'enraged' by the rejection of the measures, had always been implicit in what Calonne had said to the King. Now, as the Notables passed the month of March in captious debate, the appeal was prepared. The memoranda of the first two Divisions were published, preceded by a detachable *Avertisse-*

ment (which can either be translated as Preface or Warning) drafted by the barrister Gerbier on Calonne's instructions and probably corrected by the King.[16] In it the work of the Notables was ironically praised and there were provocative passages such as: 'People will doubtless pay more — but who? Only those who do not pay enough' and 'Privileges will be sacrificed . . . yes, as justice and necessity require. Would it be better to heap even more on to the non-privileged, the people? There will be loud squeals. . . . that was to be expected' and so on. On Palm Sunday, 1 April, the *Avertissement* was read out from the pulpit by all the curés in Paris and distributed in large numbers in the provinces.

Yet the *appel au peuple*, as many Notables including Lafayette and Miromesnil characterized it, fell strangely flat. Perhaps its ironical salon tone restricted its appeal. Many also shared Malouet's views of Calonne as 'the incarnation of every abuse he sought to eradicate'. Yet by this appeal, the King contracted an engagement to help the people were he ever in a position to do so.

On 2 April, Castries bearded the King over the *Avertissement*:

Castries: I do not know if Your Majesty realizes what is going on, the way in which M. de Calonne's scandalous pamphlet has been distributed throughout Paris and the indignation it has caused?

Louis: Yes, I know all that has been exaggerated.

Castries: How can one exaggerate the seditious distribution of it to all the curés of Paris and dissemination of it among the people? Would Your Majesty not be alarmed to see his subjects worked up against each other? I must warn Your Majesty that things are going to get more and more difficult for him because of the increasing outcry against his *Contrôleur-général*.

Louis: All that is the work of intrigue.

Castries: But is Your Majesty causing M. de Calonne to act so imprudently?

Louis: Hah! I have eight days.

The King's evasive 'I have eight days', in response to Castries's suggestion that Louis himself was the driving force behind Calonne's imprudence, refers to the recess of the Notables during Holy Week when it was rumoured that the King's opponents were to be imprisoned by *lettre de cachet*. Certainly, during this period, Calonne worked on the few Notables from the Third Estate, entertaining the provincial mayors furiously.

At this time the pressures on the King became intolerable. Calonne talks of 'the insinuation that his dismissal was the only way of terminating the affair and finally the false alarm instilled in the King by the incredible allegation [but one to which the King had always proved susceptible] that in eight days' time there would not be a sou left in the royal treasury'.[17]

Miromesnil tried to undermine the King's confidence in himself and in his minister by forwarding some treacherous letters from the former Finance Minister, Joly de Fleury, in which 'M. de Fleury asserts that he very much doubts that there was a deficit when you entrusted him with the administration of the finances, as he has recently indicated to M. de Calonne'. Joly, it will be remembered, had discovered the falsity of the *Compte rendu* soon after taking office and informed the King. Miromesnil went on to say that when he and Vergennes had gone through Calonne's figures they had lacked the necessary expertise — a fine time to make such a confession — and that some impartial Councillors and the two Keepers of the Treasury should be consulted, 'since M. de Calonne should not fear the light of truth from whatever source it comes'. He concluded this, his last letter to the King as a minister, with a section portraying Calonne in opposition to the whole establishment:

> I confess to you, Sire, that I feel — particularly after all that has happened in the last eight days and after my conversation of Monday evening with M. de Calonne of which I have already apprised you — that he wants to get you to dismiss the Assembly without concluding anything . . .
>
> I see that he is seeking to turn you against the bishops, against the nobles, against your ministers. He is making a kind of appeal to the people which may have dangerous consequences. Finally I see alarming consequences for your happiness and the rest of your reign.
>
> I throw myself at your feet and beg of you, Sire, not to blame these motions of my heart. It is totally devoted to you, to your *gloire*, to the prosperity of your state.[18]

Further pressure came from the Queen. Although her intimate circle — Artois and the Polignac group — was close to Calonne and supported him solidly throughout the Notables, she had never liked him and, as she moved into the centre of the political arena for the first time, she drew apart from her friends. Besenval accused her of 'protecting the mutiny of the Notables', to which she replied: 'No, I was absolutely neutral', earning Besenval's rebuke: 'C'était déjà trop!'[19] Pressed by Mercy-Argenteau, she was working to bring Brienne into the Ministry.

In his terrible isolation — the word used by Castries — Louis had no-one he could turn to. Vergennes was dead and Louis is said to have wept at his grave, lamenting 'he would have spared me all this'. He believed his policies to be right — and many historians would agree —

yet they had been universally rejected. He had appealed beyond the political élite to the people; there had been no response. He believed that the Intendants, who were to have a supervisory role over the Provincial Assemblies, were 'the best part of my system', and few historians would dissent from this view either, but no one had defended them in the Notables; indeed, some Intendants had even spoken against the institution themselves.[20] He could only turn to Calonne.

'Calonne, alone with the King at Versailles, conceived the audacious plan' — Castries is writing — 'of overthrowing the Ministry and filling it with ministers of his own choice.'[21] Malesherbes's cousin, Lamoignon, was to be Keeper of the Seals, Lenoir to replace Breteuil at the Maison, Puységur to replace Ségur at the War Ministry and d'Estaing, who had outspokenly defended the *Avertissement*, was to replace Castries. Castries and the Queen could see no further than Calonne's 'detestation' of Miromesnil and 'malignity' towards Breteuil. Marie-Antoinette's essentially trivial mind could not get beyond personalities and see that Calonne was advocating a new principle: that ministerial unity in order to get the King's business through a hostile assembly should replace the old notion of maintaining division among the ministers to preserve the King's independence of action. Calonne was running great risks and, as had happened in England, felt he had the right to ask for a ministry of his choice — to be in effect a Prime Minister in the English sense. The pressure of an assembly forced Louis at last to contemplate making such an appointment and on 5 April he agreed to dismiss Miromesnil and replace him with Lamoignon, who was informed by Calonne's private courier. Next, we learn from Lenoir who was to have succeeded him, Breteuil 'was dismissed momentarily and the order had been given to M. de Montmorin to go and ask him for his resignation as well as M. de Miromesnil's when the Queen caused the order concerning only M. de Breteuil to be revoked.

The Queen ranted and raved and 'would not leave the King until she had saved M. de Breteuil and overthrown the Contrôleur-général'.[22] Monsieur is then supposed to have entered and suggested dismissing both Miromesnil and Calonne. 'Sire,' he said, having a monopoly of bons mots in the Royal Family, 'whilst you are at it why not dismiss them both?' This Louis did, but the comedy masked a tragedy.

Besenval likened the fall of Calonne to that of Strafford at the start of the English Civil War, a comparison which Louis is likely to have made himself, given his almost obsessive interest in the life of Charles I. If it be accepted that Louis himself had been determinant in Turgot's fall, then the dismissal of Calonne was the first occasion since the Fronde when a king of France had been forced to dismiss a minister. Louis retained full confidence in Calonne and appointed as his successor

Bouvard de Fourqueux, whom he had ordered to take the job after La Millière had dared to refuse it, and who had been largely responsible for the memoranda of the third Division. Calonne did not immediately go into internal exile but stayed on for a fortnight, first at the Contrôle-générale, then at Bernis, his château near Paris, helping Bouvard with the memoranda of the fourth Division. Castries notes the 'secret attachment' of the King suggested by this.

Not only was Louis forced to dismiss Calonne, but forced by an assembly — the first of the Revolution — whose 'leader of the opposition', Brienne, became on 1 May *Chef du Conseil royal des finances*. Brienne himself said 'there is some glory in regarding the fall of the Minister as satisfaction due to the Assembly'.[22] Yet never, perhaps, since the days of Richelieu, had a king so publicly identified himself with his minister. As Mercy wrote to Joseph II on 19 May: 'The King's authority is all the more grievously compromised by the abandonment of the former *Contrôleur-général* in that the latter's plans had been so openly approved by the King that he had scarcely left himself any way of disowning him.'

This was an embarrassing situation for the ministers, for an 'absolute' monarch of sorts was still required. The fiction that the King's religion had been surprised by an evil adviser was not enough; the King had actually to believe it; his 'dear' Contrôleur was transformed into his 'expensive' Contrôleur. Calonne was accused of peculation on a heroic scale — the difference between Necker's *Compte rendu* and his own, four billion livres. A *comité des finances* was set up to investigate his administration and prevent the recurrence of such 'abuses'; Calonne wrote bitterly: 'In M. d'Ormesson, who has not been brought into this comité without design, they are sure of having a *rapporteur* who has thoroughly made up his mind against me in advance.'[23]

In this task of re-educating the King the clerical mind of the Archbishop of Toulouse was exercised to the full. On 17 June he wrote to Calonne:

> Far be it for me to disturb the repose you have planned for yourself. However, you cannot be ignorant of the fact that considerable sums of money have left the royal treasury without the King's authorization; you do not know what became of them and you should not be surprised by His Majesty's displeasure. It would have been wrong for me to conceal from him that of which the interest of his service requires that he be informed; and, as there is no doubt, I have not sought clarification from you.[24]

The money to which Brienne refers was spent supporting the Bourse at the critical juncture of the meeting of the Notables, a task made doubly difficult because Breteuil was supporting a syndicate of 'bear' speculators. Calonne admits to d'Angiviller that, under pressure of work, he had not always observed all the accounting formalities, though most of his predecessors had used such *acquits de comptant*.

If it had not been for Brienne's earlier assurances, he tells d'Angiviller, Calonne would have sent the King a memorandum defending his administration:

> I have every confidence in the King's justice. No one knows him better than I and when I can be heard no one will submit himself with greater abandon to his judgement and his virtues. He knows better than anyone what I have done for his service, why I have done it and to what I exposed myself in doing it, . . . but I hurl defiance at the prelate-minister who has rent my heart by wresting the King's esteem from me . . . and I scorn the hatred of his *corps* [the Clergy] to which he is not strongly attached but would happily sacrifice me.[25]

Calonne perceptively observed that his enemies needed to treat him as a criminal in order to justify 'surprising the King's religion'. The last use of the old formula was also its least conventional. The forcing of the King's mind was symbolized by Calonne's not only having to resign from the Order of the Saint-Esprit but to return the insignia to the King, including the star set in diamonds. Amelot, who had the unenviable task of asking Calonne for the insignia, broke through layers of protocol to say 'I cannot adequately express the pain I feel at being instructed to announce such devastating news to you'.[26] The only other occasion on which such an extreme step had been contemplated — and rejected as suggesting too much 'disorder' in the finances — had been when Terray had been dismissed in 1774, when also the mind of the King had been forced.

Calonne left France, which meant exile proper. 'How can I remain in this Kingdom', he wrote, 'where by this rigorous treatment [being stripped of the insignia] I seem to be treated as a criminal?' He retired, first to Holland, then, in August, to England, which he hated. In his absence, he was 'impeached' by the Parlement, though Louis quashed the proceedings. On learning that Calonne had left the country, he said sadly: 'He need not have worried, I would certainly not have allowed him to be harassed.'[27]

Brienne's appointment was preceded by an exchange of memoranda with the King which amounted to a negotiation. Louis's marginal comments on Brienne's first memorandum and his own memorandum would be sufficient in themselves to dispel the notion that the King was stupid and ill-informed.[28] His remarks are precise, clear, at times sardonic, and display a thorough mastery of the complex financial and administrative issues involved. Brienne says the King must be absolutely sure that an extra seventy millions of taxation are necessary and receives the sharp rejoinder: 'Naturally the King is far from desiring such a load of taxation if it is not necessary; on the contrary, he would be delighted to lower existing taxation but remember what is said at the beginning of the [Calonne's] memorandum about palliatives being worse than the disease.'

Furthermore, even granted that the new Land Tax were to bring in more money than is needed, the answer is not to reduce its yield but that of the less equitable and efficient taxes. Brienne naively suggests that money can be saved by lowering the rate of interest on government stock and is wearily reminded: 'Of course there is a substantial saving to me made by lowering the rate of interest but that can only be done when your credit is good and when you have enough money to dictate terms to the purchasers of stock' ('pour faire la loi aux capitalistes'). Weary also — and fulfilled — is his prophecy that Brienne's estimate of what economies can be effected is wildly optimistic: 'All in all, you'll be lucky to save twenty millions without retrenching on the Army and Navy.'

Louis's comments, however, were not entirely negative. What he was trying to do with this man who seemed to be able to manipulate the Assembly was to salvage as much as possible of the programme of reforms. He conceded that the presidency of the Provincial Assemblies would always go to the Clergy or Nobility, but the Third Estate was to have as many members as the other two combined and voting was to be by head rather than by Order — a fact little remarked upon at the time. Louis was able to insist that the powers of the Intendant remained substantially those envisaged by Calonne. The amount of the Land Tax would be raised from the fifty-four millions brought in by the existing two *vingtièmes* to about eighty millions; the amount paid by the clergy would be worked out in the Provincial Assemblies, but its collection would be left to clerical officials.

These negotiations were brought to a resolution by pressure from the Ministers, Lamoignon, Montmorin and Breteuil. According to Montmorin, they had at first pressed for Necker, and the King, worn down rather than persuaded, had finally said: 'Oh well, there is nothing for it then, we'll have to recall him.' He said it so sadly and so irritably, however, that Breteuil was able to get Brienne appointed instead. Louis is then said to have warned that Brienne was ambitious and restless and that they might live to regret the choice. Castries's version runs: 'All three went to the King together and talked to him about the political crisis; and all three, fearing Necker or rather to displease the King or at least not to please the Queen, demanded reinforcement from the King in the person of the Archbishop of Toulouse.' Brienne then asked the King for Necker as his auxiliary and was told 'that he had only been appointed to avoid Necker'.[29]

Necker had recently infuriated the King by publishing, in defiance of his orders, his reply to Calonne, which appeared on 10 April, the day after Calonne's fall; he should have waited. Enclosing a complimentary copy, Necker blandly assumed that the King would not take this 'defence of his honour and reputation' amiss. Castries was summoned to the royal presence and subjected to the following outbursts: 'He has had his book published without my orders; he has published a letter he wrote to me when it would have been good manners to notify even a private citizen. . . . He has cast doubts on my justice when I told you I would look into the whole matter. . . . Hah! he has let me down. . . . Hah! M. de Ségur's hanging around outside; tell him to come in.'

Necker was exiled to twenty leagues from Paris. On 4 June, without informing Castries, the King told Breteuil, as Minister for the Maison, that the exile could end. Castries confided to his diary that 'it would be too distasteful to serve such a master if one were serving him alone and not the State as well'. But what would Louis have thought if he had seen in Castries's diary à propos of the Notables' resistance: 'The Nation makes great strides towards liberty. . . . this safeguards the people from giving the sweat [of its labours] to an implacable master'?

The appointment of Brienne marks a crucial phase in Louis's development. There is something very sad in his having to employ a man whose meagre talents he had exposed in their exchange of memoranda. Nor, as a devout Christian, could he respect a man whom he had earlier denied preferment because 'An Archbishop of Paris must at least believe in God!' Louis also found Brienne physically repulsive: he was covered in eczema and the King was said to have had all documents emanating from him dusted before his perusal.

Furthermore, Brienne did not perform what he had promised. Louis had stressed that if he were to divulge the *arcana imperii* by giving the Notables a detailed statement of revenue and expenditure, 'success must be assured'. He had even authorized some lobbying of the Notables; and, above all, he had allowed the reforms to be diluted in accordance with the views of the Assembly. Nevertheless, the Notables had abstained from giving the revised measures any real endorsement — certainly nothing that would overawe the Parlement. Brienne got the backing for a loan of eighty millions but as regards the new taxes the

Notables, as Castries put it, 'enveloped their half-acceptance in so many words that those who refused and those who accepted are indistinguishable and one has to unravel their opinions in fifty pages of print'. The Assembly of Notables was dismissed on 25 May 1787.

The defeat and denigration of Louis's cherished plans, the way his mind was worked and the blows to his authority all wrought a profound change in the King. It is from this time that people note an insouciance about affairs in him, an apathy which is often engendered by depression. His hunting increased perceptibly: whereas in the early period of the Assembly it had been infrequent, in the fortnight after Calonne's fall he hunted on 11, 14, 16, 19, 21 and 24 April, even though the Notables were still in session. Mercy writes to Joseph II on 14 August: 'Against such ills the King's low morale offers few resources and his physical habits diminish these more and more; he becomes stouter and his returns from hunting are followed by such immoderate meals that there are occasional lapses of reason and a kind of brusque thoughtlessness which is very painful for those who have to endure it.'

On 19 May Mercy reports that Louis comes to the Queen's apartments every day and weeps at the critical state of the Kingdom. This is in marked contrast with Louis's extreme reluctance to discuss politics with Marie-Antoinette before 1787. Dependence is also frequently associated with depression. In short, most of the characteristics, good and bad, which are commonly attributed to Louis XVI — irresolution, dependence on Marie-Antoinette, sentimentality, kindness — emerge only after the Assembly of Notables, which marks the great watershed in his life and reign. The precise point at which the Ancien Régime ended and the Revolution began is a matter of debate, but in the history of Louis XVI the Ancien Régime ended with his decision to convoke the Notables and the Revolution began when he was forced to sacrifice Calonne.

Louis had received no support from his ministers, Miromesnil, Castries and Breteuil, who had sided with the 'mutiny' of the Notables. They had ceased to be the agents of the Crown in its secular struggle with the nobility and had become an undifferentiated part of the privileged orders. If Vergennes had lived, he would probably have sacrificed Calonne as he had earlier sacrificed d'Ormesson rather than have him remain in office until his retention or dismissal were alike damaging to the monarchy; which would have been a safer if more ignoble outcome. Henceforth we detect a Cassandra-like cynicism in Louis heralded by his warning that the ministers would live to regret the appointment of Brienne — as if there were prizes in politics for being right.

Louis had also been betrayed by the Queen, who was later to confess that her opposition to Calonne had been mistaken.[30] Even so, she lost her circle of friends. The Polignac group had remained loyal to the King throughout. They had not been strongly represented in the Notables but the Prince de Robecq, husband of one of their circle, had attempted to get his bureau to accept the Provincial Assemblies without more ado as early as 24 February.[31] In the course of his gallant defence of the King, Artois had come out with some uncharacteristic personal attacks on the nobility. When someone pointed out that it might arise that there were no nobles in a District, Artois interjected: 'If the presidency is reserved for them, nobles will crop up everywhere.' When it was suggested that military pensions should count as the equivalent of landed wealth in qualifying for a seat in the Provincial Assemblies, as these provincial noblemen had often exhausted their patrimony in the service of the King, Artois remarked, rather callously: 'The situation of these worthy soldiers is very unfortunate, but the fact that they have used up their own fortunes is hardly a qualification for administering those of others.'[32]

The Polignacs were punished for their loyalty to the King by a period of internal exile, returning to Versailles on 2 July.[33] On 17 July, the Princesse de Robecq wrote to Calonne that 'it is very lucky that in your misfortune Mme de Polignac should have returned' and adds that she 'tells the Queen every time she receives news of you: she wants to retain the right to speak to her about you'.[34] Relations with the favourite were patched up, but things were never the same and the split, represented at the ministerial level by the continuing rivalry between Breteuil and Calonne, was to weigh heavily on royalist reactions to the Revolution.

9

The Ministry of Loménie de Brienne, May 1787–August 1788

The appointment of Brienne marks the beginning of Marie-Antoinette's sustained involvement in politics. Hitherto, that involvement had been fitful, tangential, concerned with personalities rather than policy, but Brienne was her protégé and she had to support him in default of a disheartened, confused and resentful King. She started attending ministerial comités; nor did her increased influence pass unnoticed by the public. Her unpopularity, already evident at the time of the Diamond Necklace Affair, became pronounced in the summer of 1787, when she was first called Madame Déficit: these two strands fused in the popular belief that she had a room at Versailles paved with diamonds. During disturbances in August, Breteuil begged the King not to let her go to Paris.[1]

In his state of apathetic depression, Louis was induced to appoint Brienne, on 26 August 1787, *ministre principal*, a form of words designed to spare his susceptibilities, since he had declared that he would never have a *premier ministre*. Brienne was not given a formal *brevet* of appointment,[2] but on 27 August a circular letter informed each minister: 'The present situation demanding that there should be a common centre in the Ministry to which all parts relate, I have chosen the Archbishop of Toulouse as my *ministre principal*... consequently my intention is that you give him prior notification of important matters about which I need to be informed either by you and him together or in your *travail* with me.'[3] So that was it; the role of a first minister under Louis XVI at last received official definition, rather as, after many variations, the theme appears for the first time at the end of a piece of music, unadorned. What Maurepas and Vergennes had sought indirectly, through the title Chef du Conseil, had come to Brienne directly.

Castries and Ségur took the opportunity to resign. Personal relations between the King and Castries had continued bad and, on Brienne's advice, Louis had rejected Castries's plea for armed intervention in the Netherlands to repel the threatened Anglo-Prussian invasion:[4] 'Present the idea of *la gloire* to Frenchmen and you will effect the most useful . . . diversion from the present turmoil. Give the appearance of necessity to taxation, the mood will calm and perhaps you will see government recapture a part of what it is ready to lose.'[5] The mood of recrimination is caught by the snatch of conversation Castries records from a meeting of the Council on 19 July:

> Duc de Nivernais: '. . . we cannot hide from Your Majesty that the public mood is bad.' 'But why so?' said the King. No-one replied. [Castries] spoke up: 'Because the public views with some surprise, Sire, that whilst Your Majesty prepares to place new burdens of taxation on the people, he makes no personal sacrifice; that whereas he has made a bad choice [Calonne] which has led to the ruin of his finances, he seems disposed to make his subjects pay the price; that his building continues on all sides etc.

The 'building' to which Castries particularly refers was the stables for the newly acquired palaces of Rambouillet and Saint-Cloud, Castries being obsessed with the number of horses the King maintained. Louis must have found Castries's reproach about Calonne doubly unfair: when as king he had presided over a *comité des finances*, whose main purpose was to restrain Castries's extravagance, which Calonne considered the main cause of a deficit concerning which, as a Neckerite, Castries had in any case a *parti pris*. Nevertheless, instead of standing up to Castries as he had during the Notables, instead of saying that France could not afford to maintain a navy on a wartime footing, the demoralized King, as demoralized people often do, ceded the high ground and answered his minister on his own, trivial terms: 'But I don't have too many horses for the summer and it seems to me that although one could retrench during the winter one really can't be buying and selling horses every six months.' Fortunately Brienne stepped in to rescue the poor King by agreeing with him and closed a discussion of the crisis of the monarchy in terms of horse-trading. Nevertheless, the number of horses (which were used for all forms of transport) was reduced from 2,215 to 1,195.[6]

All in all, Castries's resignation should have come as a relief to both men, yet when Louis learned that Castries wanted to go, he sought to avoid him. When it finally came, Castries's resignation was accompanied by two observations to the Queen which show the gulf between him and Louis XVI. The first was 'that if there could be any question of an *homme de robe's* succeeding me, I should feel obliged to tell the King that his navy would be ruined'. Thus he rejected the class of royal administrators who had built the absolute monarchy and which the King most trusted. His second observation revealed divided loyalties which must have made being a minister a strain: 'As a Frenchman, I want the Estates-General, as a minister I feel bound to tell you that they could destroy your authority.'[7]

Brienne benefited from the resignations of Castries and Ségur (replaced by his own brother, the Comte de Brienne) and, with his enhanced status of *ministre principal*, was able to create the ministerial unity which had been lacking throughout Louis's reign. In particular, central control was established over departmental spending, whilst in March 1788 France's first budget in the modern sense was drawn up and published. Nevertheless, the general position of the Government was so weak, and the use to which Brienne put his new authority so inconsequent, that the changes were largely of symbolic importance, opening a chapter as the book was closing, though for Louis they mark a partial eclipse. Indeed he is obscured from sight for much of this period and one is left wondering at his relationship to the events of his reign. On one question, however, his ministers could always count on the smouldering King to flicker into life: that of combating the pretensions of the Parlement, and the central theme of this period is the mutual destruction of the Crown and the Parlement, the constituent parts of the polity of the Ancien Régime.

The Notables dispersed, taking despondency to the provinces and leaving behind them criticism of the King's proposals but no authority to implement even their own suggested modifications. The only chance now was to register the measures — representing the compromise thrashed out between the King and Brienne — in the Parlement en bloc. The early historian of the reign, Joseph Droz, writes: 'It was known that Louis XVI wanted Calonne's projects implemented, regarding this as essential alike for the maintenance of his authority and the prosperity of his people. All Paris believed that these projects, translated into Edicts, were about to be brought to the Parlement in a *séance royale* when they would be registered. The news from Versailles varied only as to the day fixed for this *séance*.'[8]

Brienne, however, chose to present the modified Edicts individually, starting with the least controversial. Those on the grain trade, Provincial Assemblies and the *corvée* were registered in June. Assuredly Calonne had not fallen on account of these. On 6 July the Edict extending the stamp-duty was rejected by the Parlement, which demanded a statement of royal revenue and expenditure and declared that only the Estates-General were competent to grant a permanent tax. Even the qualification permanent was removed when the modified Land Tax was presented in July, despite the efforts of a repentant d'Amécourt to secure a fair hearing for the new tax.[9]

Many have found this demand by the Parlement for the Estates inexplicable — political suicide, since the Parlement exercised a fiduciary political role only in the absence of the Estates. It has been suggested that the Parlement abdicated its political role because it felt powerless to resist royal 'despotism'.[10] A more likely explanation (for we are not about to observe a display of parlementaire weakness) is spite. Louis XVI, by convoking the Notables, had unilaterally shaken the structures of the Ancien Régime and had created in the minds of the parlementaires a condition of doubt as to the continuance of their political role: if the King could summon the Notables, the Parlement could go one better and demand the Estates.

Brienne had the Parlement exiled to Troyes (15 August–20 September) but negotiated. A leading part in the negotiations was played by d'Amécourt, who was now rewarded by being restored as *Rapporteur du roi*.[11] A compromise was hammered out whereby the King would abandon his new taxes in return for a massive loan of five hundred million livres staggered over a period of five years, at the end of which the Estates-General would meet. Louis's views on this transaction, which entailed the abandoment of his attempt to reform taxation, are not known. Marie-Antoinette told Joseph II on 23 November that the promise of the Estates 'caused her a lot of distress'. The compromise was to be solemnized in the Parlement on 19 November. Brienne thought he had secured enough support to allow a free vote (the best way to ensure the success of the loan) and indeed the Queen believed that during the debate 'the majority of opinions was for registration'.[12] There were, however, some intemperate speeches and the Keeper of the Seals, Lamoignon (Brienne had no seat in the Parlement), either losing his nerve or thinking it was time to reassert royal authority, whispered to the King, who, without counting the votes, pronounced: 'Having heard your opinions, I find it necessary to establish the loans provided for in my Edict. I have promised Estates-General before 1792; my word should satisfy you. I order my Edict to be registered.'

At this point the King's cousin, Philippe, Duc d'Orléans, First Prince of the Blood and the richest man in France, close to the throne yet for that very reason denied the naval career he sought or any other, condemned by the King to be a *frondeur*, stood up, hesitated a moment, then stammered out: 'Sire ... this registration strikes me as illegal ... it should be stated that this registration has been effected by the express command of Your Majesty' (the form used for a *lit de justice*). Louis, a little shaken, retorted: 'Think what you like, I don't care ... yes, it is legal because I want it.'[13] Shortly afterwards the King left and the Parlement declared the proceedings null and void. Orléans was exiled to his estates at Villiers-Cotterêts by a *lettre de cachet* delivered personally by Breteuil, whose obligations to the House of Orléans did not enable him to mitigate the rigours of a five-month exile with visitors not permitted. Here surely was an authentic victim of 'ministerial despotism'.

Louis, or Lamoignon, took the view that in the King's presence there was no need to count heads as the King represented the general will, as he explained to a parlementaire deputation: 'If a majority vote in my Courts constrained my decision, the monarchy would no longer be anything but an aristocracy of magistrates as detrimental to the rights and interests of the Nation as to those of the Sovereign.'[14] Here Louis enjoys the distinction of being the first to use the word 'aristocrat' in the specific, pejorative sense in which it was used during the Revolution.

Louis's conduct over the *séance royale* (as it was termed) of 19 November raises several questions. In the first place, the hybrid form, between a free registration and one by *lit de justice*, existed only in the antiquarian's mind of Lamoignon. Orléans was right in saying that this attempt by the King to 'have his cake and eat it' was illegal, i.e. without legal form, though whether he was right *to* say it is a different matter. Louis's petulant outburst, 'it is legal because I want it', was pure despotism, the arbitrary and formless will of a single man contradicting all he had written as a child in his *Réflexions*. If it had not been so *irréfléchi*, so obviously the product of temper, it would have been a grave matter. He must have felt thoroughly ashamed when he got back to his apartments. The exile of Orléans gave people pause: if this could happen to the highest in the land, who was safe? Two parlementaires considered to be in league with Orléans, Fréteau and Sabatier, were conveyed to state prisons.

Nor were these blows struck with ringing authority, Marie-Antoinette confessing to Joseph: 'It is irksome to have to take authoritarian measures; unfortunately they have become necessary and I hope they will inspire respect.' Joseph must have detected his sister's anxiety and also something of the paralysis of will that was beginning to affect the government — he certainly never found authoritarian measures irksome! The whole episode shows the royal government at its worst: indecisive, capricious, bad-tempered.

From the bungled *séance royale* to a final confrontation with the Parlement was only a matter of time. The first clear details of the plan — and this is the measure of her new involvement in government — comes in a letter of Marie-Antoinette to Joseph of 24 April 1788:

We are about to make great changes in the parlements. . . . The idea is to confine them to the function of judges and to create another assembly which will have the right to register taxes and general laws for the [whole] Kingdom. I think we have taken all the measures and precautions compatible with the necessary secrecy; but this very secrecy involves uncertainty about the attitude of large numbers of people who can make or break the operation . . .

The idea of removing the judiciary from politics and conferring their powers on a new body (a *Cour plénière*) was radical: Maupeou had merely changed the personnel of the Parlement. It also, as Marie-Antoinette says, would have enabled the King to make uniform laws for France rather than see the local parlements try to modify them in accordance with the local constitutions. But Brienne, routinely, planned to staff the new body with Notables, though in fact the Court only met once and Brienne did not even bother to appoint all its members. Lamoignon offered judicial reforms that were better worked out and his reform of criminal procedure represented the work of a lifetime. He sought to diminish the parlements' hold over the people by confining the cases they dealt with to the rare civil cases involving sums of over 20,000 livres, criminal charges against nobles and a few specialized cases. He abolished the *question préalable* by which a condemned man was tortured to reveal his accomplices and virtually abolished seigneurial justice by insisting that a manorial court be equipped with a strong prison and a graduate judge.[15]

The Government, however, did not proceed towards its coup with the confidence of a Maupeou and employed far more troops than he had considered necessary. A preliminary skirmish with the Parlement justified Marie-Antoinette's 'uncertainty' about the loyalty of 'large numbers' of key players. On 3 May, aware of the impending blow and unsure whether they would ever meet again as the Parlement, the parlementaires had finally enunciated the Fundamental Laws of the Kingdom, whose obscurity they had hitherto exploited. This list, very much a *pièce d'occasion*, included irremovable magistrates, the sanctity of the capitulations between the King and the various provinces at the time of their incorporation into France, and no taxation without the consent of the Estates. On 6 May, for their part in drafting the Fundamental Laws, Duval d'Éprémesnil and Goislard de Monsabert were arrested by armed force, but not before — according to two sources[16] — a Secretary of State, who can only be Breteuil, had tipped off d'Éprémesnil and given him time to seek refuge in the Parlement; upon which the nineteenth-century historian Chérest remarks: 'In default of the loyalty of its principal servants, the monarchy could not even count on their professional discretion.'[17] Having failed to prevent the arrest (but ensured it the éclat of taking place in full Parlement), Breteuil proceeded to throw responsibility for it directly on to the King by insisting that he send him a copy, entirely in his own handwriting, of the blank order signed 'Louis' which Breteuil had filled in and despatched in accordance with normal procedures.[18]

On the eve of the monarchy's last offensive the troops — the French Guards and the Swiss Guards — were loyal, but those responsible for giving them their orders, i.e. Breteuil, as Minister for Paris, and the Duc de Biron, Colonel-in-chief of the French Guards, wavered through fear of parlementaire reprisals should the King lose. On 5 May Biron told Breteuil that without direct orders from the King he could not put detachments of French Guards at the disposal of Breteuil's subordinate, the *Lieutenant-général de police*: 'If things turn out badly the Parlement could take me to task and I could only defend myself by exhibiting the King's orders.' Ministerial instructions were not enough, he had to 'know the King's personal intentions' ('avoir le secret du Roi') and despite the state of his health — he died in October — he wanted to go to Versailles to discover these.[19]

Calonne's impeachment by the Parlement in 1787 had made ministerial responsibility a reality. Furthermore, in a Council meeting to discuss that impeachment, two ministers at least, Castries, of course, and Malesherbes, the latter having been recalled that year as a minister-without-portfolio, had stated that such responsibility was desirable.[20] But the practical application now made by ministers was not that the King 'could do no wrong' but that he must take everything on his own head — a sign perhaps that the regime itself and not just the government of the day was being called into question.

On 6 May the members of the Parlement received *lettres de cachet* summoning them to Versailles for the 8th. There, after telling them that 'there was no transgression they had not committed over the past year', the King registered the Edicts and ordered the Parlement, without protesting, to go on vacation until the new order had come into being. They complied; Paris remained calm. Indeed, on 26 May Biron complained to Breteuil of the excessive deployment of troops, 'considering the calm which obtains . . . throughout Paris'.[21]

In the provinces, however, the May Edicts led to a period of serious disorder. (The contrast between Paris, quiet and garrisoned by loyal troops, and the rebellious provinces, where many of the noble officers were suspect, may help to explain why the King was to summon the Estates-General to Versailles, twelve miles from Paris, rather than to a provincial capital.) Some hardliners suggested that Louis put himself at the head of his troops and crush the disturbances in the worst affected province, Brittany, 'without fearing the consequences of civil war',[22] a course Louis was consistently to reject, though in the past he had been happy enough to use troops to suppress an *émeute* like the Flour War. In July the Breton nobility sent a deputation to Versailles to protest against the Edicts and Brienne had them imprisoned; Breteuil refused to sign the *lettres de cachet*, committing them to the Bastille, and resigned (25 July). He no longer believed in the system he had played such a large part in undermining and had, for some time, been advocating a written constitution.[23]

The provincial unrest took its toll of royal finances and by August the treasury was empty. The Declaration of 16 August suspended all payments for a fortnight when they would be resumed, half in paper, half in coin. Brienne's position soon became untenable and Marie-Antoinette was instrumental in recalling Necker, widely regarded as the only man who could restore credit. On 18 August she told Mercy:

> I greatly fear that the Archbishop will be forced to disappear from the scene completely and then whom can we choose to have overall direction? because we must have someone, especially with M. Necker. He needs to be restrained. The personage above me [the King] is in no fit state for this; as for me, whatever people say and whatever happens, I am only the second fiddle and despite the confidence of the first, he often makes me feel it.

And on the 25th: 'I tremble . . . that I am bringing him back. My fate is to bring misfortune.'

Louis's position on Necker was clear: quite apart from his conduct during the Notables, having resigned 'voluntarily' in 1781, he could not 'return to office'. Under Louis XVI ministers did not resign: they were dismissed or they died in harness. Apart from Louis's belief that a voluntary resignation necessarily showed ingratitude, there was the principle of royal government that the King should never re-employ a man in his old ministry:[24] Necker's was the first such re-appointment of the century.

The King told Brienne that he 'could not abide his [Necker's] manners or his principles but that he did not want Necker to know this', a task assisted by the Genevan's vanity. But as during the crisis over the Farms in 1783 and during the Notables, the fear of a collapse of credit — a blow both to his pride and his honour — again unnerved him. On 25 August he appointed Necker *Directeur-général des finances* and on the 27th vindicated his resignation in 1781 by granting him, as a *ministre d'état*, entrée to the Council, which was to enjoy a renaissance as a decision-making body during his second ministry. There was no one placed over him and indeed, during his second ministry, Necker seems to have possessed the essential attribute of a prime minister under Louis XVI, that the other ministers had to apprise him of important matters before raising them with the King.[25] But Louis did it all with a bad grace, and the new attitude of cynical compliance noted when he appointed Brienne is encapsulated in his remark: 'I was forced to recall Necker; I didn't want to but they'll soon regret it. I'll do everything he tells me and we'll see what happens.'

After the fall of Brienne, that of Lamoignon was probably inevitable. He negotiated with individual parlementaires through the Conseiller d'État, Foulon, in an attempt to save his judicial reforms at the price of abandoning the *Cour plénière*.[26] Necker, however, whether fearing a rival in Lamoignon or believing that nothing less than the unconditional restoration of the Parlement would restore credit, scotched the transaction. The King had promised Lamoignon a *lit de justice* maintaining the reforms, the parlementaires had been summoned to Versailles and the usual orders given to the troops. Then the whole thing was cancelled. Louis's diary gives the bare facts:

14. September: resignation of M. de Lamoignon.
15. September: There was to have been a *lit de justice*.
16. September: Visit to Meudon [where the ailing Dauphin had been sent for the air].
19. September: Swearing in of M. Barentin [as Keeper of the Seals; the reactionary protégé of Miromesnil, Barentin had been successively Avocat-Général in the Parlement and Premier Président in the Cour des Aides].

Lamoignon retired with a vast pension and the promise of a dukedom and an important embassy for his son. People thought such generous treatment unmerited; yet for the King's cause the head of the leading parlementaire family had irrevocably quarrelled with his corps; a future career in the Parlement was out of the question — hence the embassy. In May 1789, at the time of the opening of the Estates, Lamoignon was found dead in the grounds of his château at Bâville, a rifle by his side. He was the last true servant of the old monarchy.

10

Preparations for the Estates

Necker's appointment brought confidence that the Estates really would meet and the struggle for mastery of that body began in earnest. The genesis of that struggle, dating to the last weeks of the beleaguered Brienne Ministry, was the King's declaration of 5 July, lifting censorship and inviting advice from all sides about the composition of the Estates. The Declaration stated that the King was prepared to modify the old regulations concerning the Estates-General in accordance with the changes which had taken place in society since their last meeting in 1614, thus launching the debate which was to dominate political life for the next twelve months: the number of deputies the Third Estate was to send to the Estates and the voting arrangements of that body. The Third Estate, by 1788 the bulk of the population in wealth and numbers, claimed *doublement*, i.e. representation equal to that of the other two Orders, the Clergy and Nobility combined and, to make this effective, individual voting (*par tête*) rather than voting *par ordre*.

The King's Declaration was not intended to inaugurate a dispassionate enquiry after the truth: issued at the height of the *révolte nobiliaire*, it was an attempt by Brienne to prevent the nobility from dominating a body, the Estates-General, whose meeting they had forced the King to concede. Some viewed it as a policy of divide and rule, others, less cynically, as one of alliance with the Third Estate; both were traditional royal policies and, either way, the Declaration succeeded where the *Avertissement* had failed in bringing the Third Estate to life (*le réveil du tiers*). Brienne's wide-ranging and uncluttered radicalism is clear from the following extract from his memoirs:

> ... my preference was for a double representation for the Third Estate and voting by head — as I had established in the Provincial Assemblies and was doing in all the provincial Estates that were being set up. ... those for Dauphiné had been agreed and after my time were set up along the lines I indicated. ... Part of the Kingdom would have been divided

among Provincial Assemblies, with double representation and voting by head; they would have nominated their deputies to the Estates-General; elections by the *baillage* would not have taken place; . . .[1]

The implications of elections by the Provincial Assemblies rather than by the old electoral unit of the *baillage* are brought out in a long memorandum Malesherbes gave the King in July:[2] The Assemblies would elect a National Assembly — he uses the phrase — with deputies representing the whole nation, rather than an Estates-General with deputies representing the separate Orders. Brienne and Malesherbes thus cast doubt on the continuance of the separate existence of the Orders, at least at the political level. Lamoignon, consumed with prophetic ire, went further: 'The parlements, the Nobility and the Clergy have dared to resist the King; before two years are out there will no longer be any parlements, Nobility or Clergy.'[3]

At all events, the Brienne Ministry seemed to be establishing a framework in which competing interests were balanced and the King's independence of action secured by support from the Third Estate. This bold and experimental phase of royal policy-making was abruptly terminated by the appointment of Necker, who advanced the meeting of the Estates-General, but deferred the triumph of the Third Estate.

If Necker had been a statesman he would have issued — and to the sound of trumpets — a Royal Proclamation maintaining Lamoignon's reforms and at the same time granting the Third Estate *doublement*. Elections to the Estates would have been conducted through the Provincial assemblies and these, as Calonne had intended, would have been encouraged as vehicles for royal policy and propaganda. Instead, the Provincial Assemblies were put into hibernation and the Parlement was recalled unconditionally. Necker said that he would not himself have convoked the Estates, but for the King's solemn promise.[4] As it was, true to the guiding principle he enunciated in *de la Révolution française* — act only out of necessity but make your actions seem spontaneous — he now advanced the date appointed by Brienne (1 May 1789) to 1 January. However, in registering the Royal Declaration concerning the Estates, the Parlement took a step which seemed to throw Necker off course, by ruling that the Estates should be organized 'according to the forms employed in 1614', which implied not only a rejection of *doublement* but also the retention of the old electoral unit: it represented a riposte to the Declaration of 5 July and an attempt to foil the King's attempts to modernize the Estates.

The Parlement lost its popularity overnight, never to recover it, something which Necker was slow to register, perhaps because the Parlement was echoing his own doubts. His re-appointment after all embodied the triumph of the *révolte nobiliaire* just as his first ministry had advanced the ministerial aspirations of the aristocracy. He may have been 'born in the dust of the counting-house and married to a woman of the same estate',[5] but he had got to the top under the old order and married his daughter to the Swedish Ambassador, the Baron de Staël. People born to the purple sometimes rebel against the system, those who have worked their way to the top rarely, almost never. He was later to write: 'All my contacts, all my habits had been contracted among the order of society which rejected *doublement*.'[6]

If Necker had chosen to face down the Parlement, he would have found the King receptive. Louis had not given Brienne the degree of active support Calonne had enjoyed, but where the Parlement was concerned Brienne, like all his predecessors, had not found the King wanting. Louis had also been stung by the *révolte nobiliaire*, as Necker himself relates: 'I have not forgotten that on my return to the Ministry the King, personally affronted by the conduct of the nobility of Britanny, believed that he should buttress his authority with the loyalty of the Third Estate.'[7]

Thus the King did not influence Necker's response to the Parlement's pronouncement on the Estates, which was to defer their meeting to 1 May to allow time for consultations with the Assembly of Notables which met again between 6 November and 12 December. The Queen, still smarting from the *révolte nobiliaire* against her minister, was against reconvening them because, as Brienne says: 'A new Assembly of Notables, composed of the privileged whose mentality I well knew, could, in assembly, only be disposed against the Third Estate and therefore dangerous.'[8] Necker's action is more comprehensible if one does not assume he had decided on *doublement*. Castries, now an ordinary Notable and strongly against *doublement*, asked Necker what line he would like the Notables to take and was told 'that he had neither advice nor an opinion [to give] and that he would decide solely on the advice and opinions of the Notables'.[9] That advice, by six of its committees to one, was against *doublement*: the dissenting committee, presided over by Provence, was possibly for that reason more susceptible to royal pressure.

On 5 December, while the Notables were still in session, the Parlement 'interpreted' its original declaration, stating that 'no law or fixed usage stipulated the respective number of deputies'. There is evidence[10] that this declaration was got up by Necker in the belief that the prior consent of the privileged Orders to *doublement* was necessary or equitable. If, however, he thought that the authority of the Parlement still counted, he was singularly out of touch with the public opinion he so vaunted. Louis read the situation better and took the measure of the

Parlement. In September he had granted Lamoignon a *lit de justice* but, we may presume, had been caught out by Necker's manœuvre in the Parlement. Now he took his revenge, for this and all he had suffered at its hands. When a parlementaire deputation came to Versailles to present the declaration on the Estates, together with a request for certain constitutional guarantees, the King snubbed them and Necker with brutal relish: 'I have no reply to make to my Parlement; it is with the assembled Nation that I shall concert the appropriate measures to consolidate permanently public order and the prosperity of the State.'[11] The Parlement was seeking a post-1787 modus vivendi, asking the King to grant a constitutional charter which it would then register, but it received the reply that if it were not competent to register taxation, a fortiori it was not to modify the Constitution and he himself could only do this in conjunction with the representatives of the Nation.

Advice also came to the King from another quarter, the Polignac group, often referred to as the Queen's *société intime* but in reality the King's ally against her past political pretensions and increasingly a haven of intimacy and relaxation for the King himself. Recently they had given the King and their ally Calonne strong support in the first Assembly of Notables and had quarrelled with the Queen over this. By December 1788, though, they had realized that what had started the previous year as a necessary and desirable administrative and political revolution was fast becoming a social one. This is made clear in two publications associated with the group, Calonne's *Lettre au Roi* (published in London) and the *Mémoire des Princes*, signed by five of the Princes of the Blood (not Provence or Orléans), headed by the Comte d'Artois, whose Chancellor, Montyon, prepared the draft. Calonne and Artois defended the consistency of their position: throughout they had stood for the maintenance of royal authority and equal taxation; Calonne had never attacked a single legitimate right — for abuses such as tax-evasion were not rights; or, as Artois put it, 'all that was at issue was repairing not destroying'. Louis was not moved by such reasoning in December but, coming from a group which had provided both political support and friendship, it may have sown a seed of doubt, though the *révolte nobiliaire* had soured the soil in which it might have grown.

At last, with the benefit, such as it was, of the Notables' opinion, that of the Parlement and the *Mémoire des Princes*, the King came to decide the question of *doublement* and related issues in his Council, which emerged from fourteen years in the shadows to shine in meridian splendour *because Necker could not make up his mind*. Some have seen indecisiveness or detachment in the very nomenclature of the ruling which finally granted *doublement* on 27 December: *Résultat du Conseil touchant les états generaux* (*arrêt* — decision, decree — being more usual).

Malouet describes his friend Necker's havering: 'The *doublement* of the Third Estate was pronounced and I make no secret of the fact that I favoured it even against the opinion of M. Necker, who resisted it for a long time, foresaw the disadvantages and only yielded to the impression that the voice of public opinion always produced on him. No one outside his intimate circle knew how much he hesitated over the famous *Résultat du Conseil* or with what misgiving he promulgated it...'[12] The Archbishop of Bordeaux saw a printed first report by Necker refusing *doublement* and merely giving the major towns some extra deputies.[13]

The King did not share these doubts; both the protagonists in the Council — Necker tending towards *doublement* and Barentin decidedly against — attest, the latter resentfully, to the King's prejudice against the Nobility and Clergy, but he could not bring himself to pass up the opportunity for a thorough discussion. Indeed it has justly been observed that 'never perhaps was a royal decision subjected to a more thorough scrutiny'.[14] The method the King adopted was to preside over a series of conciliar committees consisting of the adversaries, Necker and Barentin, plus two further ministers. Since Barentin tells us that the latter two were different every time, we can calculate that the King wore out twenty pairs of ministers in sessions lasting from four to five hours each. The King took an almost academic delight in the minutiae of the organization of the Estates and 'never seemed to tire of the discussion'. 'His Majesty made frequent observations but it was impossible to divine his opinion.'

Finally, a double session of the Conseil des Dépêches was convened on 27 December. Exceptionally, the Queen was present. She had attended ministerial comités under Brienne in 1787/8 but never the Council. Barentin continues:

> It seemed that the King, having heard and digested everything, had only to pronounce. Nevertheless, he wanted to count the votes again. I adhered firmly to my original opinion as did M de Villedeuil; M. de Nivernais was less firm, playing the subtle courtier and not coming to a positive conclusion. M. de Puységur wavered. The King pronounced for *doublement*. The Queen maintained total silence; it was easy, however, to see that she did not disapprove double representation for the Third Estate.

Such is the account of Barentin, who was present; but Lenoir, the ex-*lieutenant de police*, was voicing a widely shared belief when he said that in adopting *doublement* the King had 'despotically' overridden the majority view of the Council by which he was supposed to abide.[15] The King may have brought indirect pressure to bear — notably the

141

presence of Marie-Antoinette — and two ministers had changed their minds during the final discussion; but even according to Barentin the basic disposition of the Council was 5:4 for *doublement*, whilst Necker says it was 8:1.

Apart from Barentin, Necker's main opponent had been Laurent de Villedeuil, Breteuil's replacement at the Maison du Roi. A former Intendant, he had followed a classical career within the royal administration. A rare bird now in the Ministry, he was an unrepentant defender of the tenets of the administrative monarchy. He thought the King could get out of convoking the Estates-General 'on grounds of the general unrest' and make do with an assembly nominated by the King.[16] So he was more royalist than the King, who had to pass beyond the authoritarian doctrines of the Council which, whatever their merits, enjoyed at that moment very little general support.

The *Résultat du Conseil* consists of five short paragraphs providing: (1) that there should be 'at least a thousand deputies' in the Estates; (2) that the electoral unit should be the *baillage*, the number of its deputies being determined by its population and taxation; (3) *doublement*.

This is followed by Necker's lengthy report (redrafted for popular consumption) which had formed the basis of the Council's discussions. The report emphasizes that by granting *doublement* there is no intention of prejudging the question of voting by head or by order (which the Minister seems to favour). In the last section Necker has the King thinking aloud with his ministers and promising to become a constitutional monarch. His pledges include regular meetings of the Estates, their consent to taxation and control over the budget (including the King's personal expenditure) and consultation with them on *lettres de cachet* and freedom of the press. The whole is punctuated with sentimental asides from the King, characteristic of the times: 'For several years I have known only moments of happiness' and 'What does spending money do for one's happiness?' In the words of the Duc de Luxembourg, the King granted 'more than the Estates-General on bended knees would have dared to hope for'. Calonne lamented the dismemberment of royal authority and wrote prophetically: 'A revolution followed by a counter-revolution (*une révolution contraire*) is the worst calamity that can befall a nation.'[17]

The *Résultat*, however, seems to have satisfied the tacticians of the Third Estate and there was public rejoicing throughout the Kingdom, reflected in this letter: 'The *Résultat du Conseil* has been rapturously received by the citizens of Paris. People embraced and congratulated each other and called down blessings on Louis XVI who had given them victory over the enemy. On parting they exclaimed: "Vive le roi et le tiers état!"'

The chief criticism of Brienne is that his policies were half-baked: he had had some good ideas — the *Cour plénière*, electoral alliance with the Third Estate and the modernization of the Estates — but he had failed to think them through. Necker is said to have lamented: 'Had I but had the fifteen months of the Archbishop of Toulouse!' by which he meant that royal authority had declined so far by the time of his recall that he had no scope for initiative. His lament therefore was also a confession. His only policy was to put the monarchy into the official receivership of the Estates and let them decide everything. There was early evidence of this approach when he advanced the date for their meeting to 1 January, a date before which it would have been difficult to have elaborated a royal programme. An ominous indication of his views on the management of assemblies had also come when he told Castries that he had 'neither advice nor an opinion' to give the Notables. This approach was all the more dangerous in that he was not confiding the destiny of the monarchy to a proven cog in the constitutional machine but to an antiquated body that had been racked with internal dissension.

Necker blindly accepted the Parlement's rejection of Brienne's plans to modernize the Estates: the *Résultat*, though it granted *doublement*, did not make structural changes — in particular retaining election by the *baillage* — and was to the political system what his first ministry had been to the financial. Indeed it may be that the *Résultat*, though hailed by the Third Estate as cementing the King's alliance with them, was in fact the unperceived turning-point when, in accepting the old format for the Estates, the King first allowed a body, the Nobility, which had lost its power, to dictate the agenda.

Unfortunately, Louis and Necker each reinforced the other's tendency to indecisiveness. In the context of the *Résultat*, Malouet said of Necker (in words that could equally be applied to the King): 'He had a rare talent for appreciating, both in the most minute detail and from the long view, the vices and disadvantages of every proposal, and it was these endless ramifications which so often made him indecisive.'[18] In the case of Louis, his indecisiveness was not only reinforced by Necker, but institutionalized by the mechanisms of the Conseil d'État. Having systematically neglected the Council as a policy-making body through-out his reign, Louis now saw fit to amplify its procedures: the *Résultat* is a textbook case of a judgement arrived at adversarially; but the intro-duction of pairs of ministers arguing, perhaps to make up the numbers, a brief in which they did not believe, whilst over a space of a hundred hours the King luxuriated in his indecisiveness, was a joyous embellishment of Louis's own devising, with the highly irregular appearance of Marie-Antoinette as the icing on the cake. These protracted discussions almost tempt one to say that if Louis abstained from taking formal advice for so long it was because, like an addict, he feared that once he started taking it he would never be able to stop.

A Bourbon king was only as good as the advice he received. Louis rarely took personal initiatives, but he had shown himself capable of responding to bold measures, in particular those of Turgot and Calonne. In 1788, his perception heightened by hostility, Louis was quicker than Necker to sense that the Parlement had shot its last bolt and he was readier for a more imaginative approach to the Estates. It was unfortunate that he did not possess a bolder minister. Malesherbes might have been such a man. In addition to his plans for a National Assembly, he also suggested that the King should take the initiative in presenting that body with a constitution. Nevertheless, Malesherbes was led by his own 'puerile'[19] distaste for office to refuse the King's request that he succeed his Lamoignon cousin as Keeper of the Seals (the Chancellor/Keeper had special responsibility for the holding of the Estates) and indeed to cease attending the Council altogether.

Both Malesherbes and the King took a very gloomy view of the future. In October 1788 they discussed Hume on Charles I, Malesherbes concluding that Louis would not share the fate of the English King because in France 'the political quarrel is luckily not aggravated by a religious one'. 'Very luckily,' the King said, squeezing Malesherbes's arm, 'so the atrocity will not be the same.'[20] The day before the *Résultat du Conseil* was announced Louis, on entering his private *cabinet*, found that the portrait of his grandfather had been replaced by one of Charles I. Indeed, there is at this time a fatalism about the royal entourage; Mercy, for example, noting the declining health of the Dauphin, concluded illogically that although his younger brother, the Duc de Normandie, was 'robust . . . , this kind of constitution is always dangerous for the cutting of teeth' and that he would probably go the same way.[21]

11

The Silent King and the Estates

We now come upon the central tragedy of the reign: the misunderstanding between the King and the Third Estate in the Estates-General which led to the collapse of royal authority and a damaging and widespread belief in the King's duplicity. Having virtually called the Third Estate into existence as a political force, the King was perceived to have betrayed their trust and thrown in his lot with the nobility; the truth was more complicated, but the perception was what mattered.

The Third Estate was an artificial social-political entity revived by Calonne and his king to preserve the monarchy's independence of action. It was a divisive move, as Miromesnil and Castries had bluntly told the King, and created the elements of a contest. At first the royal policy had fallen flat, the *Avertissement* elicited little response, but at some time between the summer of 1788 and that of 1789 the nobility ceased to be a threat to the monarchy, so there was no need to make it further concessions. The focus of political debate shifted from the question of royal 'despotism' to a struggle between the Orders: in other words, belatedly, the royal policy had succeeded. Louis and his principal adviser, Jacques Necker, never lucidly grasped when this turning-point occurred — as late as April 1789 Necker called the nobility 'still a great weight in the balance' — or what to do about it. The *Résultat du Conseil* had not suggested any great clarity of vision on the part of the Government.

Moreover, this confusion of aims was further clouded, for anyone trying to interpret it, by the King's inaccessibility and by a formidable development of his silences. Silence was now not just to questions but on questions. Louis made no attempt to influence the elections to the Estates-General, either by indicating suitable candidates or by drafting model *cahiers des doléances* to be adopted by the electoral bodies: in previous Estates-General these had formed a basis for royal legislation. His reticence went further: the nobility of the *baillage* of Clermont-en-Beauvaisis had imposed on their deputy, the Duc de Liancourt, a

145

mandate to limit the King's power. As Grand-Master of the Wardrobe he thought he should ask: 'If Your Majesty thinks I have contracted obligations which could displease him, would Your Majesty be good enough to inform me?' He would then have resigned; Louis gives him the illuminating reply: 'When I ordered the convocation of the Estates-General I permitted all my subjects to make any suggestions concerning the good of the State. When the Estates meet I will treat with them of all the great matters there presented. Until such time I must not reveal my attitude towards individual deliberations provided they have been conducted in accordance with the regulations.'[1]

A straw in the wind was provided by Louis's response to the Réveillon riots of 27–8 April. Réveillon was a wallpaper manufacturer who advocated a lowering of wages, though apparently without seeking to apply his theories to his own employees. When a mob burned down his house and his factory for his pains, Louis assumed that this riot, like the more limited ones of the previous year, had been instigated by the Parlement and deprived it of cognizance over the affair. This was the last occasion on which the King was seen to act in terms of the old politics.

In the same month there was an obscure attempt by Artois and the Polignacs to persuade the King to dismiss Necker and cancel the meeting of the Estates. A deputation from the Parlement apparently promised funds for the adventure but, as in the previous December, Louis gave them all a dusty response. Thus there was nothing in the King's external demeanour to diminish the high hopes of the deputies for the *tiers* as they gathered at Versailles throughout April for the opening of the Estates.

The Estates opened on 5 May. The Queen looked anxious; during the procession and solemn mass on the 4th, 'her brow was troubled, her lips tight-set and she made vain attempts to hide her agitation'. The King was radiant and delivered a short speech 'splendidly articulated'.[2] As was customary, it said very little and was in any case a compilation of drafts submitted by each minister. Where Louis makes changes it is generally to stress his feelings or to introduce greater precision, but there was one change of substance — Louis returned Necker's draft with the comment: 'At the beginning I have inserted "at the request of the Estates" because, as they cannot make laws by themselves, it is necessary to put that it is at their request, in accordance with their wishes, or something similar.'[3] This is important because it represented Louis's settled view of how legislation should be enacted in the post-Ancien Régime era: just as in December 1788 he had rejected the Parlement's request that he issue a constitution on his own authority, so he was consistently to maintain that the Estates themselves had no independent legislative power.

As with the opening of the Assembly of Notables, the main speech to the Estates was delivered by the Finance Minister. Necker spoke for three hours; his voice gave out and he had to employ a reader. Most of the speech was devoted to financial technicalities and tended to the conclusion that the King could have managed without calling the Estates. He gave no ruling on voting procedures, the subject uppermost in everyone's minds, and his advice tended if anything to favour voting by Order on most issues: he concluded this section by saying that a king could more easily dominate an assembly where voting was in common but that they must 'put the good of the State' first. His personal preference for a bicameral legislature such as England's emerges through an apparent slip of the tongue: stability would be greater if deliberations were by '*two* or three Orders'.

Left without guidance from the King or Necker, the *tiers* took a step which they hoped would lead naturally to voting by head: they insisted that the credentials of all the deputies be checked (*vérification des pouvoirs*) in the same chamber. For seven weeks the King allowed the Orders to wrangle over the issue. Meanwhile the deputies for the Third Estate of Brittany sought guidance from Bertrand de Molleville, who had been Intendant of Rennes at the time of the *révolte nobiliaire*, intending, as they put it, 'to do everything for the King, so to re-establish his authority that the nobility and the parlements could never damage it again'. They asked Bertrand 'to be their interpreter with M. Necker and transmit them his instructions which they would always follow strictly'. Bertrand found it impossible to see Necker, but his *premier commis*, Coster, gave him the message that 'the Minister declined all private communication with those deputies as repugnant to the purity of his principles, since it might be considered as ... a species of corruption'. These royalist deputies were radicals, their Breton Club becoming the nucleus of the Jacobin Club.[4]

If communication with Necker was difficult, with Louis it was well-nigh impossible. Although Necker was de facto prime minister, the minister with overall responsibility for the holding of the Estates-General was the Keeper of the Seals, Barentin, who took it upon himself to regulate the King's contacts with the deputies much in the manner of Maurepas. On 22 June he writes to Louis: 'I think I should point out to Your Majesty than when deputies are instructed to approach him he might think it best if they address themselves to me so that I can fix an appointment with Your Majesty. Otherwise he might be exposed to being interrupted by requests at any time. Moreover, some requests might occur which require that Your Majesty be given prior notification.' And on 12 June: 'I replied to the *doyen* [of the *tiers*, Bailly] that I would take Your Majesty's orders but that it was not proper to present him with anything he had not been apprised of in advance; that it was therefore necessary for him to give me the speech or address.' On 1 July Barentin considers that the King should admit a deputation, but only to tell them 'that he is going to assemble his Council immediately to enable him to decide what course of action he thinks he should adopt'. Spontaneity is thus excluded.[5]

Unfortunately Barentin, whose hostility to the Third Estate, already evident at the time of the *Résultat*, undergoes a crescendo in a series of seventy-six letters to the King between April and July, operated his system in a partial way: on 19 June, for example, he advises the King to see a deputation of the nobility because they had behaved well, but not one of the Third Estate. In fact Barentin could never find time for Bailly, who urgently needed to seek clarification from the King and explain his Order's hopes and fears, namely that the King was 'sold to the magnates' (as Mirabeau, a nobleman but now a deputy for the *tiers*, put it) or had all along planned this paralysis which had wrecked the Estates in 1614. Above all, Bailly would have been able to explain the steps by which the Third Estate was being driven to assume powers some of which properly belonged to the King.

On 3 June the Third Estate declared that it could not 'recognize any intermediary between the King and his people', on the strength of which Bailly asked Necker to get him an audience on the spot. He remained in the apartments adjacent to the Œuil-de-Bœuf whilst Necker went in to see the King but came back with the message that Bailly would still have to make an appointment with the Keeper of the Seals. It seems that Necker, as de facto prime minister, could prevent Barentin from seeing the King alone — hence all those letters — but Barentin could prevent Bailly from seeing the King alone. Louis, of course, instead of allowing himself to be trapped in a labyrinth of highly political protocol, should have knocked all their heads together, but he had always found it difficult to disentangle the status of conventions. So Bailly once more had to go to Barentin, who was out but finally transmitted the King's message: 'In my present situation it is impossible for me to see M. Bailly this evening or tomorrow morning or to fix a day to receive the deputation of the *tiers*.'[6]

Unfortunately Bailly had chosen a bad day: the Daupin had died at one in the morning; Louis was devastated — he never loved anyone as much as his eldest son. At a quarter to eight he heard mass in private — which he also did on the 5th and the 6th — and then he shut himself off. Only on the 7th does he note: 'La messe et le monde à l'ordinaire'.

The deputation of the Third Estate, exceptionally, managed to see the King on the 6th, but their importunity had drawn from him his celebrated remark: 'There are no fathers then among the Third Estate.' Thus tragedy is mixed with farce, reality with formalism. On 15 July Louis was to announce that in future access to him would be direct, without intermediary, but 'it had taken nothing less than the storming of the Bastille to bring down this barrier'.[7]

The difficulty in obtaining a private audience with the King was all the more disconcerting because of his total public silence, yet many believed that this was the correct constitutional stance. D'Éprémesnil, former leader of the *révolte parlementaire*, even 'observed that a letter entirely written in the King's hand could infringe the liberty of the Chamber [of the nobility] and the private and personal opinion of the King must necessarily restrict free debate and therefore should not be read out'.[8] Malouet strongly believed that the King should perform the *vérification des pouvoirs* himself and present the Estates with a programme: 'The subversive idea of a Constituent Assembly was born of the passive and uncertain state of the Monarch, who effaced himself before the new power he had called to consolidate but not annul his own.' But he had to admit that he was alone in his beliefs: 'All the deputies I was able to see before the opening of the Estates . . . [of every political complexion] all thought, to my great astonishment, as M. Necker, that the King should neither propose any plan nor adopt any regulatory procedure; that it was necessary to see the first deliberations of the Estates; that it was for them to pronounce on their organization.'[9]

On 3 June, a full month after the opening of the Estates, Véri asks:

What are the King's views and those of Necker, his solitary guide in this maze? I do not know. This is what I have learned. The Duc de Nivernais, deeply affected by the partisan struggles in the Estates, asked for an audience of the King with whom he unexpectedly found Necker. He strongly represented to him the necessity of taking a line in the debates between the *tiers* and the other two Orders and said that only his decision could bring about harmony in the other operations of the Estates. No reply from the King. The Duc insisted once more: still silence from the King. And finally Necker came in with: 'It's still too early.'[10]

Two weeks later Necker finally concluded that the time to intervene had arrived. His plans for a *séance royale* were given a first airing in the Conseil des Dépêches on 17 June but they had already had a favourable reception from the King some days before. A compromise was intended whereby matters of general interest, including the organization of future Estates-General, would be decided *par tête* but feudal and ecclesiastical

149

rights *par ordre*. Necker further intended that this separate discussion of matters specifically pertaining to the nobility would naturally lead to a bicameral legislature, like the English Lords and Commons.[11]

On the very day that Necker announced his plans for intervention to the Conseil, the Third Estate, unaware of what was afoot, declared themselves the National Assembly. This annoyed Necker, who seriously considered blowing up their chamber,[12] more than it did the King, who merely remarked, 'It's only a phrase'. When, however, the main hall of the Estates in which the Assembly met was closed in preparation for the *séance royale*, the Assembly, wrongly concluding that the King intended a dissolution, took a further step: repairing to an indoor tennis-court, they took the famous oath not to separate until they had given France a constitution (20 June). For Louis, this was the critical move: he had already showed his concern over legislative arrangements during the drafting of his opening speech; ultimately he would be driven to contemplate flight in order to secure a say in the framing of the Constitution.

It was unfortunate that the King and the Third Estate should each have been ignorant of the other's intentions, but the dramatic irony is lessened when one considers that even Necker's ministerial ally Saint-Priest told the King in a memorandum of 22 June: 'I fear that the Third Estate in its present state of exaltation will reject those absolutely just restrictions to be imposed on deliberating in common. I even fear that it will complain about the sovereign intervention of Your Majesty at this juncture.'[13] Louis liked his ministers to guarantee success, and this uncertainty, and lack of a clearly defined position, coupled with the Tennis Court Oath, emboldened Barentin, Artois and the Polignacs to attempt to capture the mechanism of a *séance royale* and fill it with the spirit of their own proposals. They had not at first found the King receptive; one of their group, the Comtesse d'Adhémar, writes:

> We never ceased repeating to the King that the *tiers* would wreck everything and we were right. We begged him to restrain them, to impose his sovereign authority on party intrigue. The King replied: 'But it is not clear that the *tiers* are wrong. Different forms have been followed each time the Estates have been held. So why reject verification in common? I am for it.' The King, it has to be admitted, was then numbered among the revolutionaries: a strange fatality which can only be explained by detecting the hand of Providence.[14]

The Polignacs had provided themselves with a congenial milieu in which to work on Louis by suggesting that he withdraw to Marly to mourn the Dauphin. It had always been easier for a small group to manipulate the King in one of the smaller palaces round Paris than at Versailles. Ministers did not have automatic access to the King. Thus on 20 June, Necker, sending Louis a note of the utmost urgency, has to add: 'I will explain myself more specifically to Your Majesty if he sees fit to give me his orders.' Necker later wrote that 'the visit to Marly had been arranged to make it easier to surround the King and to work his mind against the plans of the Ministry'; and Montjoie wrote: 'A vast silence reigned about the King; access to the throne was difficult.'[15]

One source says that Louis had not wanted to go to Marly and cut down the length of the stay (it lasted from 14 to 21 June).[16] A meeting of the Council at Marly had been planned for the 17th and the topic must have been important as the Duc de Nivernais was to travel there from Saint-Ouen 'if his health permitted'.[17] Instead, Louis managed to escape to Versailles on the 17th or 18th,[18] hold several comités and preside over the Conseil de Dépêches which lasted until 9.30 p.m. Here Necker raised his proposal for a *séance royale* and a further meeting of the Council to discuss it was arranged for the 19th, but at Marly.

Necker travelled to Marly in the same carriage as his ministerial allies Montmorin, La Luzerne and Saint-Priest. On the way he read out his memorandum in full but it was lost on Saint-Priest because of the 'jolts of the carriage on the pavings'.[19] When they arrived, the Queen summoned Necker and, together with Artois and Provence, tried to dissuade him from reading his memorandum to the Council. Marie-Antoinette, having supported the Third Estate, was now vacillating between the King and Artois. A gap in her correspondence with Joseph II makes it difficult to speak with certainty about her views in May and June, but in that month Necker's son-in-law, the Baron de Staël, writes of Artois's confidence 'now that he was won over the Queen'[20] and Mercy describes her as having been momentarily 'swept along by the infernal plot directed against the Finance Minister'.[21]

At all events, Necker refused her request and at the Council no substantive objections were raised. The King had remained silent but, according to Necker, was about to terminate the session by approving the proposals and fixing a date for the *séance royale*,

and the portfolios were already closing when suddenly we saw an official in attendance enter; he approached the King's fauteuil, whispered to him and immediately His Majesty rose, instructing his ministers to remain where they were and await his return. This message, coming as the Council was about to finish, naturally surprised us all. M. de Montmorin, who was sitting next to me, told me straight out: 'Everything is undone;

only the Queen could have allowed herself to interrupt the Conseil d'État; the Princes must have got round her and they want, by her intervention, to postpone the King's decision.'[22]

When the King returned, he adjourned the Council and indeed postponed the decision.

The next day, 20 June, Necker was detained in Paris by the extremity of his sister-in-law, Mme de Germany, but, realizing the pressures the King would be under, he sent him an urgent note: 'Several drawbacks to a *séance royale* which I had missed have been pointed out to me and it is thought that a simple letter of invitation [to the Orders] would serve better.'[23] But a *séance royale* suited Artois and his allies very well and it was on this day, that of the Tennis Court Oath, that the pressure on Louis reached its climax. The Chevalier de Coigny, one of the group, writes to the Bishop of Soissons:

This morning the Queen and his brother [presumably Artois] went to see the King and asked him what he was planning to do; he seemed as usual very uncertain and said that really the matter was not worth worrying about; that since previous Estates-General had not all acted uniformly in procedural matters one could let them arrange it as they liked.

'But look,' they replied, 'the *tiers* has just declared itself the National Assembly.' 'Its only a phrase.' 'It has passed a resolution declaring the present form of raising taxation illegal in future.' 'Heavens,' the King replied, 'he who pays the piper calls the tune and since they are the ones paying taxes it does not surprise me that they want to regularize the way it is raised.'

A deputation from the Parlement having failed to move the King, M. le Cardinal de la Rochefoucauld [*président* of the Clergy] accompanied by M. l'Archévêque de Paris appeared in their turn. Turning on the emotion, they threw themselves at His Majesty's feet and besought him in the name of Saint Louis and the piety of his august ancestors to defend Religion, cruelly attacked by the philosophes who counted among their sectaries nearly all the members of the *tiers*, etc.

This appears greatly to have shaken the King, who asked in an emotional voice where they had learned so much . . .

Then Mme de Polignac wheeled in the royal children and the Queen

pushed them into the arms of their father, beseeching him to hesitate no further and to confound the plans of the enemies of the family. The King, touched by her tears and by so many representations, gave way and intimated his desire to hold a Council on the spot; the Princes were

1. Louis as Dauphin in 1769, miniature.

2. Marie-Antoinette and the royal children, by Marie-Louise-Elisabeth Vigée-Lebrun. Madame Royale is on the left, the 'first' Dauphin on the right, and the 'second' Dauphin (Louis XVII) on the Queen's lap.

3. The Duchesse de Polignac, portrait by Marie-Louise-Elisabeth Vigée-Lebrun. Madame de Polignac was the Queen's favourite but the King's ally.

4. Louis XVI, portrait by J. S. Duplessis. The King wears the *Cordon Bleu* and star of the Order of the Saint-Esprit.

5. The Duc de Choiseul, portrait by L. M. van Loo. After granting Louis XV's disgraced minister an audience in 1775, Marie-Antoinette wrote: 'I bet old Maurepas can't sleep in his bed to-night'.

6. Marble bust of Miromesnil, Keeper of the Seals, 1774–87, by J. A. Houdon. Miromesnil was wont to say: 'Time is my first secretary'.

7. Turgot, *Contrôleur-général*, 1774–6, portrait by Joseph Ducreux. The young Louis XVI said: 'M. Turgot wants to be me and I don't want him to be me'.

8. Vergennes, Foreign Secretary, 1774–87, portrait by Gustaf Lundberg. Calonne called Vergennes 'the last minister truly devoted to [the King]'.

9. Necker, finance minister, 1776–81 and 1788–90, portrait by J. S. Duplessis. Louis personally made this unconventional appointment of 'a foreigner, a republican and a Protestant'.

10. Calonne, *Contrôleur-général*, 1783–7, portrait by Marie-Louise-Elisabeth Vigée-Lebrun. In December 1786 Calonne lamented: 'There is no one in France strong enough to carry out all that is necessary'.

11. D'Aligre, *Premier Président* of the Parlement 1768–88, anonymous print. Miromesnil warned him in 1786: 'Consider that when you seek to harm a minister of the King it is to the King that you render that minister harmful'.

12. *Buffet de la Cour*, anonymous satirical print. Calonne (monkey) asks the Notables (fowl) with what sauce they would like to be eaten. The Notables reply that they don't want to be eaten at all!

13. *The Recall of Necker*, 1788, anonymous print. Necker lamented: 'Had I but had the fifteen months of the Archbishop of Toulouse'.

14. *The Tennis Court Oath* of 20 June 1789, by J. L. David.

15. La Fayette, as commander of the National Guard in 1789, portrait by P. L. Debucourt. In 1792, La Fayette declared, 'we shall see which of us, the King or myself, has the majority in the Kingdom'.

16. Mirabeau, portrait by Briceau. Mirabeau told the Queen that the Revolution had 'facilitated the exercise of power'.

17. Sketch of Barnave at the Assemblée de Vizille in 1788. In 1791 he was to proclaim: 'Il est temps de terminer la Révolution'.

18. *The Return from Varennes*, anonymous print. Louis himself is treated to silence.

19. Drawing of Louis in prison in 1793, charcoal heightened by chalk by Joseph Ducreux. At this time he told Malesherbes, 'I would rather let people interpret my silence than my words.'

20. Louis reading his will to Malesherbes, anonymous print. Malesherbes had told the Convention: 'I have been summoned twice [in 1775 and 1787] to the Council of the man who was my master at a time when this function was coveted by everyone: I owe him the same service when it is a function which many consider dangerous'.

21. Execution of the King, 21 January 1791, engraving by Charles Monnet. The equestrian statue of Louis XV has been overthrown from the pedestal on the right.

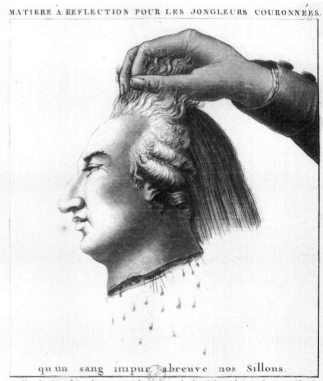

MATIERE A REFLECTION POUR LES JONGLEURS COURONNÉES.

qu'un sang impur abreuve nos Sillons.

Lundi 21 Janvier 1793 à 10 heures un quart du matin, sur la place de la revolution, ci devant appelé Louis XV Le Tiran est tombé sous le glaive des Loix. ce grand acte de justice a consterné l'Aristocratie, anéanti la super stition Royale, et créé la republique. Il imprime un grand caractère à la convention nationale et la rend digne de la confiance des français.......

ce fut en vain qu'une faction andacieuse et des orateurs insidieux epuiserent toutes les ressources de la calomnie; du charlatanisme et de la chicane; le courage des republicains triompha, la majorité de la convention demeura inébranlable dans ses principes, et le génie de l'intrigue ceda au génie de la Liberté et a l'Ascendant de la vertu.

Extrait de la 5.e Lettres de Maximilien Robespierre à ses commetans.

A Paris chez Villeneuve Graveur rue Zacharie St Severin Maison du passage N.72.

22. Louis's severed head is presented as a 'matter for reflection for the crowned jugglers', i.e. the Powers in coalition against France.

sent for and the Council met immediately without summoning the Contrôleur-général [*sic*], who knows nothing of this. Everything is settled: the King will issue a declaration which will satisfy the nation, will order the deputies to work in their respective Chambers and will severely punish the meddlers and intriguers. You may rest assured that he will not budge and a *séance royale* is announced; it is there that the plan that I tell you of will be unfolded . . .[24]

This second Council at Marly met on the 20th, with the King's two brothers present and Necker absent. Although there were to be two further meetings of the Council at Versailles, on Sunday the 21st and on the 22nd, the presence once again of the King's brothers on the 21st convinced Necker that the game was up, though the King's unease is shown by his asking Saint-Priest before the meeting on the 22nd for his memorandum, which he knew would be favourable to Necker's case.

The final draft for the *séance royale* differed only in emphasis from Necker's original and may indeed represent a compromise effected by the King between the position of Necker and that of Barentin, but the changes were more than an already doubtful enterprise could bear. Voting in common on matters of general interest was retained, but the King suggested that motions should only be carried by a two-thirds majority and insisted that the organization of future Estates should be decided by the Orders sitting separately. The King promised provincial Estates and approval by the Estates-General of taxation, loans and even the royal budget — all in all a recipe for an aristocratic, decentralized, constitutional monarchy. This compromise of royal authority would not have been necessary if Necker had not allowed the case for an active alliance with the Third Estate to go by default.

The deliberations had taken as long as those preceding the *Résultat du Conseil*, but as they had lacked form so they had led to a bad decision. For rule by counsel to be effective, it is essential that advice be taken in an orderly and formal way by people who are authorized to give it, i.e. the ministers. It was disastrous for the King to be taken out of his natural setting at Versailles, cut off from his official advisers and closeted with people like the Archbishop of Paris or even his brothers (Louis XV had not had a brother, whilst Louis XIV had always excluded his from affairs).

The *séance* itself, in which for the last time the King appeared in his full regalia, was a fiasco. Along the streets of Versailles, Louis was himself treated to complete silence — the 'lesson of kings', as the phrase went. The use of Lamoignon's unfortunate terminology — *séance royale* — suggested that the King was treating the Estates-General with no more respect than a disobedient *parlement*. In his *discours-programme*, similar in form to those he had recently pronounced in the Parlement, reference was made to the King's *volontés*, whilst the first clause began 'le roi veut'; even the nobility, the beneficiaries of the *séance*, jibbed at forms which would have been regarded as highly irregular at the height of the Ancien Régime. As for the Third Estate, they simply refused to obey the King's order to 'disperse immediately and proceed tomorrow morning each to the Chamber allocated to his Order'. To the Master of Ceremonies, Mirabeau addressed his famous apostrophe about only moving at the point of the bayonet. The versions of Louis's reactions to this are at total variance, ranging from 'No, not bayonets' and 'So they want to stay? Damn it let them' to 'Clear them out!' The very criers refused to proclaim the new laws, claiming that they had colds.

Necker had absented himself from the *séance*, which refurbished his fading popularity. As rumours of his resignation swept through the streets of Versailles, a vast populace poured into the Palace, reaching the doors of the royal apartments, where the Bodyguards were able to halt them. The King, at once furious with Necker and desirous of preventing his resignation, was heard through the door 'shouting at the top of his voice: "It is I, Monsieur, who am making all the sacrifices, making them with all my heart, whilst you take all the credit; you want to take all the thanks yourself." '[25]

Marie-Antoinette adopted a more conciliatory tone, as Vaudreuil, the lover of Mme de Polignac, recounts:

'Dare I ask the Queen', I said bowing respectfully, 'whether M. Necker accompanied the King to the Assembly?' 'No,' she replied with an air of surprise and annoyance, 'but why this question?' 'Just that if the principal minister is not put on trial today, tomorrow the monarchy will be destroyed.' Hardly had I pronounced these words when a severe gesture from the Sovereign ordered me to leave. I bowed even lower to show even greater respect: 'I am pained to see that I have incurred the Queen's displeasure but I will never hesitate between favour and duty.' After a third bow, even lower than the others, I retired, and was not recalled.[26]

According to Mercy, the union of the three Orders, effected by royal command on 27 June, was brought about by the 'moderation and wisdom of her counsels'.[27]

Louis's order to the nobility to sit with the Third Estate and the Clergy, who had already gone over to them, was obstructed by Barentin, who gave the Duc de Luxembourg, president of the nobles' chamber, to understand that it could be discounted.[28] The order had to be repeated and followed by a direct request from Artois, which must have cost him dear. Barentin continued to regard the articles enunciated in the *séance* as law even after the union of the Orders, and since Villedeuil, as Minister for the Maison, was effectively Minister for the Interior, they were able to promulgate them all over France. In an attempt to cover himself, however, Barentin did not seal the Declaration with the formal Yellow Seal nor countersign the version sent to the Imprimerie Royale. For his part, Louis, in persuading Necker to stay, told him that he did not insist on the articles which had angered the *tiers* and Necker was sure that 'his views were the same as mine'.[29]

Nevertheless, an important concomitant of the *séance* was not abandoned: the concentration of troops round Paris. On 22 June, the day Necker's version was finally jettisoned, Louis signed the first order, for the Swiss Reinach regiment to leave Soissons and arrive in Paris on the 26th. On the 26th, the day before he ordered the nobility to sit in the National Assembly, further orders were given, so that by 14 July there were some 30,000 troops assembled in the Paris region. On 4 July these troops were put under the general command of the Duc de Broglie, with the Baron de Besenval, lieutenant-colonel of the Swiss Guards, his field commander in Paris. On 11 July Necker was dismissed together with Montmorin, La Luzerne and Saint-Priest, and replaced by Breteuil, who returned to the ministry as *Chef du Conseil royal des finances*, La Vauguyon as Foreign Secretary, Broglie as War Secretary and the hated Foulon as Intendant of the army. It has always been assumed that the King's intention was to throw off the mask of conciliation, dissolve the National Assembly and subdue Paris by force of arms. There is not a shred of evidence for this assumption.

Obviously the troops were intended to provide a back-up for the disorders which might be occasioned by the *séance royale*, though they would not be in position in time for the *séance* itself; but an examination of the position of the King, of Broglie and of Breteuil reveals no offensive plans and, in the case of Breteuil, no plans whatsoever.

The King's instructions to Besenval give the general tenor of the military operations contemplated: Besenval must 'give the most precise and the most moderate orders to the officers commanding the detachments you may have to employ that they should only act as protectors and should take the very greatest care not to get into a quarrel with or to engage in any combat with the people, unless they are inclined to arson or to commit riot or pillage which threatens the safety of the citizen.'[30] Louis also gave signs of leaving avenues open and distancing himself from decisions. On 11 July he wrote Necker possibly the most gentle letter of dismissal he ever sent a minister:

When I engaged you, Monsieur, to remain in place you asked me to adopt a plan of conduct towards the Estates-General and you have shown me on several occasions that a plan of extreme complaisance was the one you preferred. Since you did not believe you would be of use in executing other plans, you asked for permission to resign if I adopted a different course of action. I accept your offer to leave the Kingdom during this moment of crisis and I count on your departure being as you promised prompt and in secret. It behoves your reputation for integrity not to give rise to any disturbances. I hope that when things have calmed down I will be able to give you proof of my sentiments towards you.[31]

There are several curious features about this dismissal. First, the last sentence of Louis's letter seems to give him a loop-hole for asking Necker back. Secondly, Necker notes: 'The King did not order me to leave the Kingdom because from this period he doubted whether he had the legal power to exercise such an act of authority towards anyone'[32] — the world of exile by *lettre de cachet* had at last come to an end. Finally Necker, not one to miss an opportunity for publicity, nevertheless executed an extremely prompt and secret departure. He was dining with his family when he received the King's letter but said nothing about it either to his brother or to his daughter, Mme de Staël. He took his wife with him and although they were going to Switzerland, they went via Brussels so as to cross the French border as quickly as possible and avoid being seen in Paris, Burgundy and Franche-Comté. They did not even change out of the clothes in which they had been dining.

On 14 July the National Assembly sent the King two deputations concerning the presence of troops in the Capital. Of Louis's second reply, Bailly writes: 'It produced a profound feeling of sadness; it should have been from the King himself. "It is not possible to believe", he says, "that the orders which have been given to the troops are the cause [of disturbances]." Which have been given! He does not say "Which I have given"; so it is not him. . . . we see that the Council and the King are not the same thing.'[33]

The Duc de Broglie was given wide powers: generalissimo as well as war minister, he commanded not only the troops-of-the-line but the royal Bodyguards, an exceptional infringement of the prerogative of the King who, unmartial though he was, must have been hurt as the kings had always retained personal command of their military Household. Even so, Broglie's use of these powers was extremely cautions. In a series of letters to Besenval he outlines his strategy.[34] There is no mention of offensive measures; even defensive ones are restricted. On 1 July he writes:

The King consents that you assemble all the forces on which you can rely to safeguard the Royal Treasury and the Discount Bank and that you confine yourself to defending these two positions . . . at a time when we are unfortunately not in a position to look to everything. I shall authorize the Marquis d'Autichamp to remain in his command at Sèvres and then, if it becomes necessary, to bring up the Salis Regiment as reinforcements to protect Versailles, falling back on the Palace if necessary.

On 5 July he tells Besenval to replace the garrison of the Bastille and 'as soon as the artillery regiment arrives you must send a small detachment of gunners to examine whether the cannon are in good order and to use them if it comes to it, which would be extremely unfortunate but happily is wildly improbable . . .'. Finally, on 11 July he writes: 'If there is a general insurrection we cannot defend the whole of Paris and you must confine yourself to the plan for the defence of the Bourse, the Royal Treasury, the Bastille and the Invalides.'

Of all the ministerial appointments made by Louis XVI that of Breteuil is perhaps the most surprising. He had been a dangerous *frondeur* in the ministry of 1783–6, and Marie-Antoinette had restrained Louis from dismissing him during the Assembly of Notables. After the coup d'état of 5 May 1788 Breteuil, as minister for Paris, had asked for holograph orders from the King to shift responsibility and had later resigned rather than take a more repressive line. Knowing the King's aversion to violent measures, one would not expect Breteuil to be more resolute, more prepared to take responsibility for subduing a city in arms than he had been in 1788 for containing relatively minor disturbances with the King's full co-operation. Nor was it an idle fear, for later in the year Barentin, Broglie and Besenval were put on trial for the new crime of *lèse-nation*. Small wonder then that Breteuil 'paid a great deal of attention to installing himself in his hotel and in forming his secretariat' — and did nothing.[35] Indeed, this could have been predicted: on 30 April, when the Polignacs already saw him as a replacement for Necker, Artois had asked him what was to be done. 'Nothing,' he replied, 'except to keep calm, always remain faithfully attached to the King and to the country and to look to the tutelary genius of France for that which one can no longer expect from the sensible measures which should have been taken.'[36]

There was more to it, however, than mere inactivity. The Princes in bringing back Breteuil had simply mistaken their man. In their political stance, Breteuil and Necker represented the right and left wings of a liberal-aristocratic coalition,[37] which shows the fine point on which the *séance royale* turned and how far Louis's options had narrowed. Breteuil was not a plain reactionary like Artois, who probably did want to subdue Paris by force of arms. One of Breteuil's intimates said that he 'had thwarted all the plans of the Marechal de Broglie'. Later, when he was Louis's plenipotentiary in 1790–2, one of his chief tasks was to be that of thwarting the Princes' plans for Counter-Revolution; All in all, it is extraordinary that the replacement of Necker by Breteuil should have been the signal for an armed rising in Paris.[38]

Besenval's response to that rising exceeded even the caution of his orders. A man said to be better fitted for the service of Venus than of Mars, he did not even try to prevent the crowd, led by deserters from the French Guards (Breteuil's response to the desertions was to look up precedents for granting an amnesty),[39] from seizing the arms from the Invalides with which on the 14th they stormed the Bastille (there is evidence that right up to this event Breteuil was negotiating with the Assembly).[40] Needless to say, its garrison had not been replaced nor its cannon refurbished. And yet the most recent study of the Royal Army suggests that it could and should have been used with good hopes of success and that the failure to do so destroyed its morale.[41]

At first no one dared to tell the King about the events in Paris, but on the night of 15/16 July an emergency meeting of the Council was held at which Breteuil advocated flight to Metz. Louis rejected this counsel, obsessed as he was by the fear of civil war or of his cousin Orléans seizing a vacant throne. Whatever the grounds for the latter fear, Barentin, no less, told the royal historiographer, Moreau, at two o'clock on the morning of the 16th: 'I believe we must have recourse to another dynasty.'[42] Louis came to regret his decision to stay, musing to Fersen in February 1792: 'I know I missed my opportunity; it was 14 July. We should have gone then and I wanted to; but what could I do when Monsieur himself begged me not to go and the Maréchal de Broglie, the commander-in-chief, replied to me: "We can certainly go to Metz but what do we do when we get there?" I was abandoned by everyone.'[43]

As for Breteuil, his advice rejected, he fled alone, disguised, it is said, as a monk. Alone of the new ministers he never resigned, perhaps because the Chef of a non-existent Conseil des finances was too nebulous for the National Assembly to comprehend, let alone include in its demand for dismissals. Possibly, in his haste, he simply forgot to resign and possibly it was at the King's insistence. For Louis's legalistic mind endowed the status of Breteuil with an embalming sanctity; it was his last 'free' appointment as the Declaration of 23 June was his last 'free' utterance; no matter if both had been made under pressure and no matter if two bad decisions were being engraved on tablets of stone.

Necker, Montmorin, Saint-Priest and La Luzerne returned, Louis profiting in his letter to Necker of the 16th from the escape-clause he had left himself in the previous one: 'I wrote that when things had calmed down I would give proof of my sentiments towards you.'[44] 'Nearly all the people', Droz writes, 'who had taken part in the projects which had been so speedily overthrown emigrated or retired to the provinces.'[45] Artois, his mistress Mme de Polastron, his friend Vaudreuil, Vaudreuil's mistress Mme de Polignac, the Bourbon-Condés, all packed up and left the country. The emigration had begun. Louis told them that he feared for their safety, but Lafayette, commander of the newly-formed National Guard, claimed that he forced the emigration of Artois and Condé, who 'shed tears of rage' at having to go.[46] There was certainly an element of exile: as the situation worsened, internal exile was being replaced by exile proper — first Calonne, then, briefly, Necker, now the Polignacs. Either way, all those who in a very real sense had 'surprised the religion of the King' in the period 19 June–14 July were removed.

On 17 July Louis went to Paris to show his acceptance of what had happened. Marie-Antoinette, fearing that he would be detained or murdered, begged him not to go, but he burst out: 'No, no! I will go to Paris; numbers must not be sacrificed to the safety of one. I give myself up, I trust myself to my people and they can do what they like with me.'[47] Provence was given the title of Lieutenant-General of the Kingdom during his absence. In fact Louis was deeply hurt by the Parisians' response to his gesture. In his 1791 Declaration he was to write: 'People stationed along the whole route took great pains to prevent those shouts of *vive le roi* which come so spontaneously to Frenchmen, and the speeches that were delivered to him, instead of testifying gratitude, were filled only with bitter irony (poor Bailly had referred tactlessly to Paris conquering its king).' When he returned to Versailles, Besenval writes,

the unfortunate king found himself almost alone. For three consecutive days he had no one with him except M. de Montmorin and me. The very valets served him as they pleased.... On the 19th I had entered the King's apartments, all the ministers being absent, to get him to sign an order giving post-horses to the colonel of the Évêchés Regiment. Just as I was presenting this order to him a footman interposed himself casually between the Prince and me to see what he was writing. The King turned round, noticed the insolent fellow and made to seize a pair of tongs. I checked his movement, prompted though it was by very natural anger; he squeezed my hand to thank me and I noticed that there were tears in his eyes.[48]

A few days later Saint-Priest, who had been given the portfolio of the Maison du Roi, ayant le département de Paris, went with Necker to 'put himself in possession of the municipal administration of the said town'. But there had been a municipal revolution in Paris. The royal *Prévôt des marchands* had been ousted by an elected mayor, Bailly. At the Hôtel de Ville, two seats had been prepared but Bailly offered one to Necker and sat down on the other himself. Saint-Priest, who had to find a seat among the aldermen, notes bitterly: 'For the sake of peace I had to suffer this insolence on the part of the Mayor, hitherto my subordinate, as replacing the *Prévôt des marchands* who took his orders from the Minister for Paris. But royal authority had already ceased to exist in Paris.'[49]

As he sat alone at Versailles, without ministers and badly served by the valets, Louis must have wondered what had happened since he lay awake for joy in 1786 thinking of his plans to reform France. Calonne had said he would not mind if he were the victim of the enterprise; now he was himself. He thought of the coalition of vested interests that had defeated him, the miserable and unsuccessful compromise with Brienne and Necker's total negativism. He was abandoned by everyone; even Malesherbes, who could perhaps have fused the old with the new, had said he feared office next to a mortal illness. He had been accused of raising the hopes of the *tiers* in 1787–8 and dashing them in the Estates-General, but things had become so embittered. Ought he not now to reconcile rather than divide? Had Calonne been right about revolution and counter-revolution? And the *tiers* wanted so much, not just fair taxation but, judging by the Tennis Court Oath, political power at his own expense and the destruction of the social privileges of the nobility — they were largely honorific, but honour mattered so much; it was all about vanity. His brother Artois, loyal ally in 1787, had been warning him of this for over six months; perhaps he was right, but he was surely wrong in wanting to subdue Paris by force. That was out of the question. He had used force to subdue the Flour War in 1775 — his own *liteutenant de police* had thought it excessive — and Maurepas had taught him that the police must act frequently, but you cannot hold down a city or a country, as Charles I had found; he had been executed for levying war against his peoples — Louis would never do that. Nor would he leave Versailles as Charles had left London — a fugitive king!

We do not know what went through Louis's mind because though he was to give an analysis of the later phases of the Revolution, he spoke very little of the period 1787–9. His conduct, however, provides the best clue to the striking feature of the events of the summer of 1789, their radicalism graphically captured in Malouet's description of the aftermath of the fall of the Bastille: 'If the Court had been at Paris instead of Versailles, it would have been the ministers, the Princes who would have been slaughtered instead of Foulon, Berthier [Intendant of Paris] and de Launay [governor of the Bastille]. It was as the agents of the Government that they were pursued. . . . here was a ferocious populace in search of victims and it would have taken them alike in the street or on the throne.'[50]

This mood had been created by a sense of betrayal by the King. The hope at the opening of the Estates had turned to malaise and, with the *séance royale*, to anger. The troop concentrations had added the ingredient of fear so that, combined with the well-known murderous proclivities of the Parisians, most of the elements of the Terror were already present, especially as a touch of the macabre was added when grass was rammed down the mouth of the aged Foulon in answer to his reputed quip, 'Let them eat grass'.

At the political level, the King's volte-face had effected, to his disadvantage, a synthesis between two strands of thought which might otherwise have remained separate: on the one hand, the parlementaire rejection of monarchical self-sufficiency and stress on the need for the consent of the governed; on the other hand, the traditional monarchical advocacy of equality and uniformity and of reason rather than precedent as the spirit of legislation.[51] This fusion led, among other things, to the idea that the 'Nation' could design a constitution from scratch which assigned to the King merely the role of 'first functionary'. Quickly, the National Assembly acquired the tone implicit in Sieyès's phrase 'the dictatorship of constituent power'.

It is harsh to be judged by action (or inaction) rather than by intentions, but with the King silent and inaccessible it was difficult to do otherwise. Also, by any normal standards he had displayed inconsistency. By his *appel au peuple* in 1787 Louis had contracted obligations which were remembered in 1789. He had sown dissension and, when it finally bore fruit, left it rotting in the fields. Had he gathered it, his constitutional concessions might not have been necessary; as it was, they were insufficient.

PART III

Captivity and Flight

Introduction

After the fall of the Bastille, the reign of Louis XVI is but one aspect of the French Revolution, a vast movement of which only the briefest outline will be given. The King became a *roi fainéant*, with far less theoretical and actual power than the King of England. For allied to the new personal distrust of Louis XVI there was the deep theoretical distrust among eighteenth-century political thinkers of what they termed The Executive Power. Political theory had played little or no part in the fall of the Ancien Régime, but these ideas rushed into the vacuum of power and experience caused by the collapse of royal authority in the summer and gave the Revolution a further impetus.

If Louis was feared or reckoned with it was because of the residual authority which some deemed that he derived from God and from his ancestors. The proponents of absoute monarchy, however, were virtually non-existent. Louis's brother Artois, in exile first with his in-laws at Turin, later at Coblenz, was an exception, but he had to dissemble to humour his émigré troops; for the 'aristocrats', whether sitting on the right wing of the National Assembly or forming the émigré armies at Coblenz, wanted to subject the King to the tutelage of parlements, provincial estates, and the whole panoply of an aristocratic constitution.

Not only was Louis's role reduced, but his voluminous official pronouncements and much of his ministerial correspondence present little interest: they rarely reflect his true political position and will be summarily treated. In particular, neither the Assembly nor (if only for their own protection) the ministers were privy to what became his central policy: to secure by flight from the Capital, where he was installed in the Tuileries on 6 October 1789 and regarded himself as a prisoner, an equal role with the Assembly in the formulation of the new Constitution.

It is also perhaps necessary to state that Marie-Antoinette's letters to her Austrian relatives during the Revolution, as before it, were not his letters: it is indeed difficult to know precisely what if any part Louis played in her secret diplomacy given that only a handful of his letters in this connection have survived and that the authenticity even of these has been questioned. In general it can be said that though her influence was greater than it had been before 1787, political divergence between the King and Queen continued right up to the fall of the monarchy.

Part III is concerned with Louis's own response to the Revolution and the deepening of his personal and political sympathies. The main sources for the latter are the manifesto (*Déclaration du Roi, adressée à tous les français, à sa sortie de Paris*) which he left behind when he escaped from Paris on the night of 20/1 June 1791 and his secret letter to his brothers of 15 September explaining his acceptance of the Constitution.* The Constitution, then, which in this letter Louis also uses as a synonym for the Revolution itself, is the King's central concern. Louis had never believed that the rights of kings were either indefeasible or indivisible — witness, at the beginning of his reign, his acceptance of the modification by treaty of the Young Pretender's rights and, at his own trial, his defence based on the legal situation obtaining at the various stages of his reign. He did believe, however, that a strong constitutional monarch was essential to govern 'a country as vast as France' and that the framing of the Constitution and the subsequent enactment of legislation should be carried out by himself and the Assembly as equal partners as demanded by the vast majority of the *cahiers*. This could only be achieved with the consent of that public opinion which had always been his guide and, after his contact with the outside world represented by his journey to Varennes, he accepted that he would have to wait until it swung his way. Even so, he never accepted that the pressure which the Jacobin Clubs put on the Assembly as well as himself represented that opinion.

---

* Unless otherwise stated, Louis's statements in this Part are taken from the *Déclaration*.

12

The October Days

During August and September, the National Assembly sought to institutionalize the political gains it had made in June and July and to fulfil the Tennis Court Oath through establishing the outlines for a new constitution and prefacing them with its Declaration of the Rights of Man. Already, however, the Revolution had been enlarged beyond the political dimension by a revolution in the countryside. The failure of the 1788 harvest led to tension as the *soudure* approached and this was heightened by hope that the seigneurial regime would be ameliorated and by fear — *la grande peur* — of aristocratic reprisals which the peasants imagined would be carried out by bands of marauding 'brigands'. The peasantry responded to these pressures by burning châteaux, destroying records of feudal dues and simply ceasing to pay them.

Many of the deputies for the Third Estate were substantial landowners who desired the restoration of order. Nevertheless, they dared not entrust the King to effect this with troops lest he turn them on the Assembly. Consequently they sought to defuse the crisis by a stratagem. The Breton Club got up some prominent liberal nobles to renounce their seigneurial privileges on the night of 4/5 August and this inspired a spirit of emulation on behalf of their more intransigent brethren who sat on the right wing of the Assembly. In its enthusiasm the Assembly declared that it 'entirely abolishes the feudal system'. What it meant was that serfdom or what was called *servitude personnelle*, i.e. anything which implied that the seigneur had some ownership over his peasants, was abolished outright. It was rare and, where it existed, very attenuated by 1789. Louis had abolished it on his Crown lands in 1779 together with *mainmorte*, which prevented the serf from transmitting his land to any but his children. Dues on peasant properties which were really the equivalent of rent were to be redeemed. There was a grey area between servitude and rent which was never defined; nor was the rate of conpensation for dues. Seigneurial justice was also abolished.

The August decrees also saw the entire implementation of the 1787 programme; indeed, in some respects it went further with the abolition of privilege in taxation, tithes, sale of office, and the different privileges of the towns and provinces of France. The entire 'corporate' organization of France disappeared overnight. Not surprisingly the King, in his message to the Assembly of 18 September, found little to criticize, only making four observations of substance.[1] He thought that where serfdom had in the past been replaced by a money payment, this should not be abolished without compensation; seigneurial justice should remain until, as Lamoignon had provided in 1788, something had been put in its place; if tithes were abolished, they should be replaced by a tax payable to the State. Otherwise the operation would merely result in the random redistribution of sixty to eighty million livres that the Treasury could well use; finally, Louis stressed the implications for Foreign Policy: the Treaty of Westphalia guaranteed the seigneurial rights of foreign princes with possessions in Alsace and Louis informed the Assembly that they had already lodged strong protests.

The Assembly's reception of Louis's observations symbolized the role the it was to assign him: only Lally-Tollendal thought it appropriate for the King to make any comment. The President was instructed to ask Louis simply to promulgate the decrees. Louis described this treatment in his 1791 manifesto: 'The Assembly . . . not content with degrading the monarchy by its decrees, even affected contempt for the King's person and received his observations on the decrees of the night of 4/5 August in a manner which can hardly be described as showing respect.' The King saved face by saying that since the decrees were statements of intent rather than finished legislation, he would *publish* rather than *promulgate* them.

Louis was not merely objecting to instant legislation, which he had been brought up to believe was arbitrary and formless. He was objecting to his exclusion from the legislative process. This exclusion operated at two levels. As regards ordinary legislation, the Assembly was prepared at least to accord Louis a veto, but over the articles of the Constitution itself, none. They would draw what they termed a 'religious veil' over this usurpation by according him the right of *acceptance* but not of *sanction* — in other words he could take it or leave it but not affect its validity. Louis, who in May had reminded Necker that '[the Estates] cannot make laws by themselves', was to complain bitterly of this treatment:

When the Estates-General, having styled themselves the National Assembly, began to occupy themselves with the Constitution of the Kingdom, remember the memoranda which the men of faction had sent in from several provinces and the agitation in Paris tending to make the deputies renege on one of the main clauses in all their *cahiers* providing that *legislation would be carried out in conjunction* with the King: in contempt of this stipulation, the Assembly has denied the King any say in the Constitution by refusing him the right to grant or withhold his assent to the articles which it deems constitutional, by reserving to itself the right to place such articles in this category as it sees fit.

The nature of the King's veto over ordinary legislation was the subject of lively debate in the Assembly. The group later dubbed the *monarchiens*, which dominated the Assembly's first constitutional committee, thought that the King should have an absolute veto to secure his participation in legislation, but they failed to carry the day: by 673 votes to 375 the King was accorded a suspensive or 'iterative' veto — to become law without the King's sanction a measure must be presented by three separate legislatures, which would take a minimum of six years. The *monarchiens* had led the Third Estate's struggle against the first two Orders but had become disturbed by the enlargement of the Revolution and feared lest its new social dimension would threaten the political gains of the early summer. They wanted to stop the Revolution at this point and felt that only the King could fill the vacuum created by the retreating nobility. Accordingly they sought to concentrate the powers of the executive by means of the absolute veto and divide the legislative by the creation of a second chamber largely nominated by the King. The debate on these two measures symbolized the conflict between the *monarchiens*, who wanted to use a strong Executive to suppress popular politics and preserve property rights, and those on the left, who were prepared to exploit popular disturbances and bring pressure on the King and on the Assembly.[2]

The *monarchiens* were not a homogeneous group; Mounier, for example, had led the revolt in Dauphiné the previous summer and was only driven to see the need for a strong Executive by the collapse of order. The dominant tendency of the group, however, may be termed Briennist: the three prelates, Boisgelin (Aix), Champion de Cicé (Bordeaux) and La Luzerne (Langres) had been Brienne's close collaborators and Malouet shared his views. Their theme was a strong monarchy in traditional alliance with the Third Estate. When the King, in his silence, had been thought to be favouring the nobility, Malouet, left without a doctrinal position, had remained silent himself for six weeks. In September he spoke again, rebuking the Assembly for droning on about the Rights of Man whilst France was lapsing into political and social disintegration. Their Briennist position largely accounts for their failure, for it alienated the right wing, the intransigent nobility on whom they counted but for whom the policies of Brienne had been anathema: they likened the second chamber to the *Cour plénière* and thought that its adoption would lead to *despotisme*. In any case they did not expect to be given seats in any second chamber and feared that one might help consolidate a Constitution they detested. For in pursuance of their *politique du pire*, they preferred total collapse which might lead to an aristocratic version of the Ancien Régime. Throughout the life of the National Constituent Assembly, the noble right, as the émigrés, had no care either for the restoration of an effective monarchy or for the personal fate of Louis XVI. After their defeat on the veto and the crushing defeat (by 849 votes to 89) on the second chamber, the *monarchiens* resigned from the constitutional committee.

The King did not give the *monarchiens* any formal support, even if he did sometimes discuss matters with Malouet. A second chamber was not of importance to him, though Necker had been a long-standing advocate. The question of the veto, however, symbolized his legislative role. An iterative suspensive veto — absolute against the Assembly, suspensive against the nation, as Duquesnoy put it — was actually less cumbersome than an absolute one, which in England was never used. Accordingly Necker favoured it. The King, for his part, was to characterize such a veto as 'purely illusory'. For the absolute veto symbolized the irreducible minimum share in legislation acceptable to him, given that he had reasonably assumed, in common with Malouet but practically no one else, that legislation would proceed as before: the King in his Council would draw up *lettres patentes* which would be debated by the Assembly (rather than the parlements) and, with appropriate modifications, become edicts. In his manifesto he was to complain that he had been 'denied the right formally to initiate legislation'. It mattered little that before the Revolution Louis had tended to exercise his influence on government by means of an informal veto rather than by personal initiatives: Miromesnil, for example, to demonstrate Louis's involvement in government, told Véri: 'But you do not see the *negatives* I witness.'[3] Louis was seeking for government its normal role in a parliamentary system.

On 4 October the King presented his observations on the constitutional articles, to the effect that the Constitution could not be judged piecemeal but only when it had been finished,[6] which remained his position during the two years it look to draft. The prefatory Declaration of the Rights of Man could not have appealed to one of Louis's down-to-earth views — in his manifesto he was to inveigh against 'a metaphysical and philosphical government which cannot work'. For the present, however, he contented himself with the observation that a declaration of principle should not precede its practical embodiment.

He made these observations against a background of mounting popular pressure on himself and on the Assembly itself, to some degree orchestrated by its left wing. Alarmed, the moderate deputies asked the King to withdraw to Compiègne and propose transferring the Assembly to nearby Soissons. Louis had himself proposed this to the Assembly on 12 July. Now he refused. The Bishop of Langres asked Necker why and received the 'impatient' reply: 'Monsieur, if you want to know the truth understand that our role is very arduous. The King is good but difficult to persuade. His Majesty was tired . . . he slept through the Council [an affectation he used to 'conceal his agitation'].[5] We were for translating the Assembly but the King woke up, said "No" and withdrew.' Malouet comments: 'The King, who had a passive courage, saw a kind of shame in withdrawing from Versailles; he was perfectly aware of the danger but he flattered himself he could avoid it by a display of force. If it came to using it, he could never decide to draw his sword against his subjects.'[6] The force to which Malouet alludes was the Flanders Regiment, which Saint-Priest, as Minister for the Maison, had summoned for the King's personal protection. On the night of the 4th this loyalist regiment drank imprudent toasts and sang the air 'O Richard O mon roi, l'univers t'abandonne' from Grétry's *Richard Coeur de Lion*. This incident served as the pretext for the long-expected march on Versailles.

At about ten o'clock next day Saint-Priest received intelligence that an armed force had left Paris and was making for Versailles.[7] It was a motley crowd containing many women and demanding bread and the King's sanction to the Assembly's decrees. Louis had just left to go shooting — not hunting as is usually stated. He had not hunted since 17 August, since it is harder to make contact with a hunt in full cry than a shoot. His diary notes: 'Monday, 5th, shot at the Porte de Châtillon [in the woods above Meudon]. Killed 81 head. Interrupted by events. Rode there and back.' He reached Versailles at about three o'clock, galloping with his retinue down the Grande Avenue to the Palace, and held the Council. It proved to be its last set-piece debate.

Saint-Priest proposed withdrawing to Rambouillet and was supported by Beauveau, La Luzerne (Marine) and La Tour de Pin. All four, as Saint-Priest observed, had been soldiers. The civilians — Necker, Montmorin (though a camp-marshal, he had not seen active service) and the Archbishops of Vienne and Bordeaux — opposed, Necker warning that if the King abandoned Paris there would be no money to pay the *rentes* or the troops.[8] In addition, they were under the mistaken impression that England would exploit such a situation to launch a naval attack. On 2 October La Luzerne had asked for 1,500,000 livres to lay in salt-beef so they could mobilize the fleet at a moment's notice: 'The King felt the weight of these arguments but, given the penury of the finances, he decided that only 300,000 would be spent on extra provisions.'[9]

With the Council, as so often, evenly divided, the King cast his vote for staying. In his manifesto he stated that he had 'sufficient warning to be able to withdraw where he pleased; but he feared that this step would be exploited to set alight civil war' — the likely consequence, Saint-Priest concedes. At six o'clock a message arrived from La Fayette, commander of the Paris National Guard, that he was marching to Versailles at the head of his troops. This force, a citizens' militia formed to preserve order during the July disturbances but also incorporating the former French Guards who had carried out the attack on the Bastille, posed more of a threat than the women. The debate in the Council veered towards flight. Orders were given for the carriages which had been waiting ready-harnessed in the Grande Écurie to be brought round, but the crowd cut the traces.

The Assembly took the opportunity to ask the King for his acceptance 'pure and simple' of the constitutional articles. At ten o'clock the King told their president, Mounier, that he would accept their articles. The irony of the situation was not lost on Mounier, who had no more liking for the articles than had the King. Dutifully he asked for the King's sanction in writing. Louis 'went to his desk, wrote it out in full and handed it to him, weeping'.[10] As Necker was to observe: 'We had to yield, but posterity will never forget the moment that was chosen to consecrate the theory of the rights of man and to insert the corner-stone of the temple of liberty.'[11]

In the early hours of 6 October, a portion of the crowd broke into the Palace, made for the Queen's apartments and outside the doors hacked down two of her Bodyguards whose resistance had nevertheless enabled her to reach the King along the secret passage constructed in 1775 to preserve her political influence; now it preserved her life: some accounts have the furious populace, disappointed of their prey, slashing the mattress of the Queen's bed to ribbons. That day Marie-Antoinette's blond hair went white at the temples.

With daylight the crowd gathered in the Cour de Marbre and clamoured for the King. He appeared on the balcony outside his bedroom, followed by the Queen and the two children. 'No children!' went up the cry, 'the Queen on the balcony alone!' She had to consent. Then, Saint-Priest relates, a new shout went up: ' "To Paris, to Paris!" was endlessly repeated and the King in a profound stupor kept going on the balcony, maintaining his silence, and returning to throw himself into an armchair in his room to rest. I took the liberty of telling him that by not consenting to leave he was exposing himself and the Royal Family to the utmost danger; that he must regard himself as a prisoner, subject to the laws imposed on him.'

The Royal Family were taken to Paris in a vast, grotesque procession, the heads of their Bodyguards held aloft on pikes. It took seven hours to cover the twelve miles from Versailles to Paris, where they were installed in the palace of the Tuileries, 'a long brown building in the west of the city', begun by Catherine de Medici and finished a hundred years later by Louis XIV.[12] It had last been occupied by the Court during the minority of Louis XV, from 1715 to 1722, and Louis was to complain that 'the disposition of the rooms [368 of them] was far from affording the comfort to which he was accustomed in the other royal residences and which any private individual with a competence may enjoy'.

Louis, however, had reason to complain of more than private discomfort. The October Days destroyed the last vestige of his independence of action. They also came widely to be regarded as the first great breach of legality in the Revolution — Mounier seceded from the Assembly as a protest — and even those who had profited from them affected regret. There were dark aspects to the October Days that will probably always be obscure, despite the committee of inquiry instituted at the Châtelet. La Fayette, Orléans, Mirabeau, any or all of them could have conspired to have the King and the Queen assassinated. Louis stood in the way of all three: of Mirabeau's desire for a modern absolutism, of Orléans's dynastic ambition; of La Fayette, who with cool contempt told Marie-Antoinette that he put the fate of the Revolution before that of the King and that he would have her divorced on grounds of adultery.[13] Louis certainly attributed many of his difficulties to Orléans and his fear of leaving him a vacant throne had been a further reason against flight. According to Necker: 'The King, inspired by personal notions which I never shared, feared the effects of this hothouse of plots [Orléans's residence, the Palais-Royal] more than the outcome of any other upheaval.'[14] La Fayette made Orléans the scapegoat by having him sent on an empty diplomatic mission to England, which amounted to exile.

In his diary, Louis tried to anaesthetize himself to the impact of the October Days by reducing them to the banality of some of his other entries. Thus that for 6 October runs: 'Left for Paris at 12.30. Visit to the Hôtel de Ville. Had supper and slept at the Tuileries.' The ordeal is treated as just another journey — 'soupé et couché à Rambouillet' is a frequent entry for the period 1784–9. In the recapitulation for the year 1789 we read:

    Excursions in 1789.
    Marly 14–21 June 7
    Paris 6 October–31 December 86
    Nights that I slept away from Versailles 93

It is a way of assimilating the terrifying to the mundane.

Slightly more ambiguous — keeping up appearances or nostalgia? — is Louis's maintaining his hunt intact and recording its activities, though in a different form to denote his absence: e.g. for 12 October 'le cerf chassoit à Port-Royal', the form used when he was present being 'chasse du cerf à . . .'. This was kept up for nearly a year until, in the entry for 14 September 1790, we read: 'le cerf chassoit pour la dernière fois'. As a silent protest against the October Days, Louis shut himself up in the Tuileries, which he scarcely bothered to furnish, and refused to hunt, though with his tendency to *embonpoint*, he needed the exercise. People asked: 'Why does the King not hunt?' It had become a political question.

For despite the form of face-saving in his diary, Louis did consider that the October Days had brought about a radical change in his position which is recorded in a letter he wrote to his Bourbon cousin, Charles IV of Spain, on 12 October:

> I owe it to myself, I owe it to my children, I owe it to my family and all my House to prevent the regal dignity which a long succession of centuries has confirmed in my dynasty from being degraded in my hands . . .
>
> I have chosen Your Majesty, as the head of the second Branch, to place in your hands this solemn protest against my enforced sanction of all that has been done contrary to the royal authority since 15 July of this year and at the same time [my intention] to implement the promises which I made by my Declarartion of the previous 23 June.[15]

It is significant that Louis did not send this letter on 15 July but on 12 October, so that what he seems to be repudiating is his sanction of the constitutional decrees under the direct threat of mob violence rather than the administrative and social decrees of August. Also, the promises he mentions in relation to the *séance royale* are to a constitutional monarch. At the same time, this letter inaugurates a dual attitude — that there are different orders of promises, those made under duress not being considered binding — and will soon lead to a dual policy.

13
Temporizing

As long as the King could hope to see the return of order and prosperity to the Kingdom result from the measures employed by the National Assembly and from his residence near that Assembly in the Capital of the Kingdom, he did not count the cost of any personal sacrifice. If this hope had been fulfilled he would not even have argued the nullity with which his total lack of liberty tainted all his undertakings since the month of October 1789.

Thus opens Louis's 1791 Declaration; and it had remained his policy until the end of 1790, when the ecclesiastical policy of the Assembly and the rapid deterioration of the political situation finally caused him to contemplate flight and resistance.

The 'personal sacrifice' refers to the King's prerogative power, not his personal convenience. For though he was to complain that the Tuileries was uncomfortable, the Assembly granted him plenty of money with which to rectify the situation and was almost aggrieved that he did not. In order to support the 'splendour of the throne', the King was granted the level of civil list he had requested, 25 million livres, in addition to the revenue from the estates around Versailles, Saint-Cloud, Fontainebleau, Compiègne, Saint-Germain and Rambouillet; Marly was to be sold. Although, as he complained in his Declaration, military and political pensions were later assigned to the Civil List 'even after its size had been determined', it was still a generous sum.

Paris became a court-capital again. The Court revived, expanded, adapted. Half the 1787 number of court officials moved into the Tuileries (only twelve of the twenty-eight in senior postions emigrated), whilst the ranks of courtiers were supplemented by recruits from a broader social spectrum. Bailly, the new Mayor of Paris, was given the *entrées de la chambre* as was the procureur of the new Department of Paris. La Fayette, who already had these *entrées*, received in addition those of the *cabinet*. The abolition of titles of nobility in June 1790 meant a fortiori that one no longer had to have proof of nobility stretching back to 1400 to be presented at Court. The expensive silk *habit-habillé* was no longer obligatory and a more simple tail coat or *frac* could be worn.

New groups paid their court — the *Corps des marchands* and the new electoral Districts of Paris, the focus of popular politics. Radicals and conservatives attended the King's *lever* and *coucher*. In a sense, the Court had always been politically neutral or rather the politics of the courtiers had not mattered to the kings as they did not play a political role. Most court officials had opposed Louis XV's attack on the parlements, but kept their jobs; most were loyal during the pre-Revolution, but two were dismissed; many were radicals at the beginning of the Revolution, such as the Duc de Liancourt, Grand-Master of the Wardrobe, and La Fayette's cousins the ramified Noailles family.[1] Liancourt, it will be remembered, had been told by Louis during the elections to the Estates that he had no need to resign over his politics provided he observed the electoral regulations. Paradoxically, the political complexion of the Court mattered more under a constitutional monarchy, witness the bedchamber crisis at the start of the reign of Queen Victoria, and plans were drawn up, one in the King's hand, to reimburse the *charges* of the existing officials and remodel the Court as a 'constitutional' Household. These, however, were shelved for lack of funds on the outbreak of war in 1792.

La vie endure, the Royal Family dined in public on Sundays and Thursdays and the twice-weekly receptions for ambassadors continued. Business as usual was the impression the leaders of the Assembly wanted to create. La Fayette, attempting to persuade Mounier to resume his seat in the Assembly, pointed out that the only external signs that the King was not free were his refusal to hunt and the absence of his personal Bodyguard. He did not add that the new guard, the Paris National Guard, was under his command, which made him a latter-day Mayor of the Palace and the King a *roi fainéant*, for whom the costly court merely represented, as Louis put it, 'the vain shadow of royalty'.

La Fayette exercised an occult power without responsibility. As Mirabeau put it: 'The multitude is totally ignorant of the dictatorship which La Fayette exercises so maladroitly ... and if it knew the sort of ministry without responsibility he wished to arrogate to himself, his public credit would be ruined.'[2] In a vain attempt to give the political situation some *consistance*, the King on two ocasions, in October 1789 and the following May, attempted to make La Fayette's pre-eminent position official. He offered him the Marshal's baton and the Constable's sword, even the position of Lieutenant-General of the Kingdom, but he declined. Bouillé, military commandant of the eastern provinces, considered that La Fayette should either have accepted this offer, or, if he feared for his popularity, have himself nominated commander-in-chief of all the provincial National Guards, disband and remodel the troops-of-the-line and found a consitutional monarchy: 'it was the wish of the King and of the nation'.[3] Instead, all he achieved was the permanent alienation of Marie-Antoinette by threatening her with divorce and some clumsy interventions in ministerial politics.

Ministerial office was a poor thing after the October Days, although one of the ministers, Bertrand de Molleville, remarked to the King that there were still more applicants than vacancies. In July, to humiliate the King, the Assembly had fêted the returning Necker Ministry but, as Louis observed, 'subsequently it treated them no better for that'. They were cut off both from the King and from the Assembly. Whereas the Cour des Ministres had been at the heart of Versailles, ministers, symbolically, did not have offices or appartements in the Tuileries. The Assembly's decree of 7 November prevented the King from choosing ministers from among the deputies. Some ministers had been so chosen in the summer, but the experiment had failed through suspicions that the ministers would be corrupted by the 'Court' — a vague but persistent code-word for the occult forces which were supposed to be operating on the King. The November decree reflected these suspicions but was particlarly directed against Mirabeau, whose ministerial ambitions were well known. This decree, apart from reducing the standing and calibre of ministers available to the King, made co-operation between the Executive and the Legislative very difficult and prevented the development of parliamentary government along English lines.

There was not much for ministers to do and they operated in a world of unreality. On the one hand, they were not acquainted with Louis's plans for flight, and on the other, the Assembly duplicated the work of their departments by the creation of its own committees. Lameth accused the Executive of 'playing dead', but in reality there was not much it could do, at least until the Assembly's completion of the Constitution ended the state of flux and its own dictatorshiop of constituent power. Louis, for example, was accused of letting the Revolution caricature itself by not resisting mad decrees, like the one of June 1790 abolishing titles of nobility and armorial bearings yet pompously protecting those on public monuments as belonging to sacred property rights. Even so, the reception accorded to his modest observations on the August decrees can hardly have encouraged him to give the Assembly the further benefit of his wisdom.

Under Necker's aegis, though, Louis did take several steps publicly to identify himself with the Revolution. On 4 February 1790, he went down to the Assembly and made a speech in which he 'placed himself at the head of the Revolution', swore to uphold the Constitution and, according to Elizabeth, the soul of the Counter-Revolution within the Tuileries, 'lost whatever crown was still left on his head'.[4] Of this proceeding, however, which amounted to a speech unaccompanied by a policy, Droz justly observes: 'If one merely utters sentimental phrases one obtains only fleeting applause. . . . Necker raised a peristyle which did not lead to any building.'[5] The King's request that the Assembly attend to the deficit was ignored. When Malouet, seeking to profit from the enthusiasm produced by the King's speech, asked the Assembly to confirm the King as head of the Army and the Administration, the Assembly did not even vote on his proposals.

Finally, having lost all control over the direction of the Revolution, Necker resigned in September 1790; upon which Elizabeth wrote: 'Have you heard the great news that does not cause a stir in Paris? M. Necker is gone. He took such a fright at the threat of being hanged that he was unable to resist the tender solicitations of his virtuous wife to take the waters. The Assembly, on reading this phrase, laughed and passed to the order of the day.'[6] La Fayette had contributed to Necker's fall, but he was unsuccessful in making Louis appoint the Foreign Secretary, Montmorin, as *Chef du Conseil royal des finances*, possibly because, in Breteuil, Louis considered that he already possessed one.

After the fall of Necker, the Assembly assumed responsibility for finance. It had already made substantial incursions into the King's use of the Executive by setting up its own committees to shadow government departments: as the King's manifesto was to say, the Assembly 'by means of its committees constantly oversteps its own self-appointed limits . . . and thus combines all the Powers'. Its control over finance, however, was the unkindest cut because Louis considered that he had acquired considerable expertise in this field: 'The King understands the problems of this Department, yet if that were possible he has been rendered more of a stranger to it than to the others.'

The reaction to Necker's departure symbolizes the rapid deterioration of the political situation of the monarchy. After the October Days, Malouet had founded the *Club des Impartiaux*, as a centrist counter-weight on the Assembly to the Jacobin Club, succesor to the Comité breton. His centre-right friends were joined by those from the centre-left, including La Fayette, La Rochefoucauld and Liancourt. Soon, however, they fell into disagreement over Malouet's insistence that the Assembly should define the constitutional powers of the Executive immediately, before the revolutionary torrent eroded it any further. La Rochefoucauld replied that the Executive was merely 'the keystone which could only be put in place when the other parts of the edifice had received their form and disposition'.[7] In other words, they differed over the question of whether the King or the Assembly should be invested by the Constitution with ultimate supremacy. Yet even when Malouet, La Fayette and Mirabeau acted in unison, as in the debate of 15–22 May 1790 over the royal prerogative of declaring peace and war, their proposals underwent such substantial modification that, as the King was to put it in his Declaration: 'With [peace] treaties having to undergo revision and confirmation by the Assembly, no foreign Power will be willing to contract engagements which could be broken by others than those with whom it was negotiating: in which case all the powers would be concentrated in the Assembly.'

Louis was to attribute this deterioration of the political situation largely to the influence of the Jacobin clubs:

> In nearly all the cities and even in several country towns and villages associations have been formed with the name Société des amis de la constitution [Jacobin Clubs]. In defiance of the laws, they do not permit the existence of any other clubs that are not affiliated to themselves, thus forming an immense corporation even more dangerous than any of those which previously existed.[8] Without authorization, nay in contempt of the laws, they deliberate on all aspects of government, correspond with each other on all subjects, make and receive denunciations, and post up their resolutions. They have assumed such a predominance that all the administrative and judicial bodies, not excepting the National Assembly itself, nearly always obey their orders.

The King sought a counter-weight in the formation of a public opinion which he still believed to be sovereign. This aim is at the heart of his relations with La Porte and Mirabeau.

Louis appointed Arnaud de La Porte, like Malouet a former naval Intendant, as Intendant of the Civil List when it was set up in 1790. The List was never part of the Maison du Roi and Louis had personal control of its considerable funds in a way he never had over the six departmental ministries. La Porte was the King's agent within the context of the Constitution, conducting negotiations over the formation of ministries, buying support, subsidizing pamphleteers, trying in general (and in vain) to direct public opinion. La Porte recommended Mirabeau to the King, describing him in March 1791 as 'the only man who, in the present circumstances, which are most critical, can really serve Your Majesty'.[9]

Mirabeau's political beliefs were almost identical to Malouet's, though there was no formal collaboration between them. His apostrophe to Dreux-Brézé on 23 June about only moving at the point of the bayonet and Malouet's silence were motivated by the same sense of betrayal by the King and despair that the nobility had captured the monarchy. In May 1790 Mercy-Argenteau approached him with a view to obtaining his services for the Queen, whom he met once on 3 July, and thus increasing her general influence. The extent of that influence on Louis is not clear-cut. Whereas the uxoriousness Louis first exhibited in 1787 continued, indeed became more pronounced, there is an important difference between Marie-Antoinette's political role in 1787–9 and that during the Revolution proper: she ceased to attend the Council or ministerial *comités*. As she was to tell Barnave on 16 December 1791: 'I do not go to see the King when he is holding the Council nor when he is with his ministers.'[10] Nor did she have any ministers of her own, as Brienne, Breteuil and even Castries had been. After the replacement of the Necker Ministry, Mercy was advised: 'The Ministry will have been replaced and the Queen will not have seized this opportunity to place a single one who is exclusively devoted to her.'[11] She even had difficulty discovering what had been decided in the Council, relying principally on the political weather-vane Montmorin, who survived the fall of the Necker Ministry. Of him, La Marck told Mercy (optimistically): '[He] is entirely and devotedly the Queen's ... he has better opportunities than anyone else to observe the King over a mass of cases where he eludes the Queen.'[12] The Comte de La Marck, the friend of Mirabeau, was a fellow-Belgian whom Mercy had placed about the Queen as a substitute for her lecteur the Abbé de Vermond, who had been forced to emigrate.

Mirabeau agreed to serve the Queen in return for 5,000 livres a month. Even so, as La Fayette, who was no friend, conceded, 'he would not for any sum have maintained an opinion which would have destroyed liberty and dishonoured his mind'.[13] Corruption consists not simply in receiving money but in changing conduct as a consequence. His ambition was to be the modern Richelieu and carry the monarchy forward to the next decisive stage of its development, its transformation into what would become the Napoleonic system. In a series of fifty Notes for the Court, he offered a stylish analysis of the Assembly's legislation which vindicated the consistency of his career as one who had collaborated with Calonne (with whom he may have been in contact in 1790 through d'Angiviller)[14] on the drafting of his projects, offered to defend Lamoignon if impeached by the Parlement, and advocated alliance with the Third Estate.

The National Assembly, he argued, had achieved what he had been seeking: the Revolution, properly understood, by destroying the *pouvoirs intermédiaires* 'facilitated the exercise of power' — notably, on 3 November 1789 the Assembly had 'buried alive' the Parlements by indefinitely prolonging their summer vacation, finally abolishing them on 7 September 1790. 'Richelieu', he adds, 'would have been pleased by the notion of forming just one class of citizens.' Mirabeau distinguished between the destruction of the corporate organization of the Ancien Régime, an irreversible achievement which could only strengthen monarchical authority, and the new Constitution which shackled it but could still be modified.[15] Louis may never have read these notes, indeed some of the expressions employed by Mirabeau suggest that he was not meant to, such as: 'The Queen . . . must have a clever agent about the King under her secret influence.'[16] In any case, he would no longer in 1790 have been swayed by these arguments. For whereas Mirabeau was feeling towards an egalitarian autocracy, the King, who could have used such advice from Necker in 1789, now inclined towards a constitutional monarchy which assigned its due place to the nobility — in short, the English system, which had always held a fascination for him, witness the analyses of proceedings in Parliament he inflicted on Vergennes.

Mirabeau's practical advice, if practical is the right word, consisted (1) in a plan, not adopted, for the King's open departure for Compiègne or Fontainebleau; and (2) to use Civil List money to mount an elaborate propaganda and secret service machine which, with its complex network of agents, ignorant of each other's activities, would have appealed to Louis's sense of secrecy for its own sake. Neither this nor La Porte's efforts, however, had any discernible effect on the general situation, which for Louis was aggravated by a measure of the Assembly's that affected not his royal prerogative but his Christian conscience, the Civil Constitution of the Clergy, which Talleyrand was to call 'perhaps the biggest political blunder of the Assembly'.[17] The Civil Constitution finally convinced Louis that there was no chance of ameliorating the Constitution whilst he was in Paris.

It would have been difficult for the French clergy to have been more conciliatory towards the Revolution. On 4 August they had renounced that separate corporate status they had defended so doggedly against Calonne. They accepted the loss of their lands, which were used to secure the national debt, bonds known as *assignats* which the Assembly soon made legal tender being issued against them. On 12 July, however, the Assembly issued its Civil Constitution of the Clergy, which introduced popular election of bishops and curés. It was not this doctrinaire measure, though, which led to difficulties but the new boundaries for the bishoprics which were to be the same as the new Départements that had replaced the old provinces. For this change required papal institution: as there were 135 old bishoprics and only eighty-three Départements, some bishops would have to resign and others be assigned new sees.

Pius VI was hostile both to the French Revolution in general and to the Civil Constitution in particular, and although formal condemnation did not come until his briefs of 10 March and 13 April 1791, he had already on 9 July 1790 sent Louis a warning letter: 'Do you think that a purely political body can change the doctrine and discipline of the Church, scorn the opinions of the Holy fathers . . . ?'[18] One can imagine Louis's unease when on 22 July he gave his sanction to the Civil Constitution.

Not satisfied with this, on 27 November the Assembly decreed that all priests must swear an oath of allegiance to the Constitution, including the Civil Constitution, or resign their livings. Louis postponed giving his sanction whilst he desperately and in vain urged the Pope to baptize the Civil Consitution and thus save France from schism.[19] Then on 26 December, with 'death in the soul', he finally sanctioned the decree. About half the curés took the oath but only seven bishops, including Cardinal Brienne, who received a stiff letter from the Pope and returned him his hat. Schism was thus a reality, with France divided into jurors and non-jurors.

In his last testament, Louis was to 'ask God to accept . . . my profound repentance for having put my name (albeit unwillingly) to decrees which may be in conflict with . . . the Catholic Church to which I have always remained sincerely attached'.[20] His aunt Adélaïde tortured him with a reproachful letter dated 18 January 1791 telling him 'you have deprived yourself of the only thing that could give you strength courageously to resist all the afflictions you have been made to suffer'. She asked for permission for herself and Victoire to retire to Spain or Rome 'until the persecutions end'.[21] The Aunts left for Rome on 19 February, creating the impression that this was the start of an exodus of the Royal Family.

The oath to the Civil Constitution also had practical implications for the exercise of Louis's personal devotions. Having sinned by sanctioning the decree, he wondered whether he had the right to make his Easter communion. In his perplexity, he wrote an anguished and confused letter to the Bishop of Clermont seeking guidance:

. . . May I receive communion and must I do it within the fortnight? You know the unfortunate predicament in which I find myself through my acceptance of the decrees on the Clergy; I have always regarded my acceptance of them as acting under duress, having never hesitated as regards my personal concerns to deal with Catholic pastors always, and being fully resolved, if I come to recover my power, fully to restore Catholic worship. A priest I saw thinks that these sentiments may suffice and that I can make my Easter communion. However, you are in a better position to see what the Church in general thinks . . . whether on the one hand this may not scandalize some and on the other, I see the factious — a reason admitedly which cannot weigh in the balance — already speaking almost threateningly. I beg you to consult such bishops as you see fit about this, ones on whose discrétion you can count. I desire also that you give me your reply tomorrow before noon and that you give me back my letter.[22]

The Bishop's reply was crushing. The King's sanction of the decrees 'has had the most disastrous consequences for religion'. The Bishop understood that the King had yielded to duress, but added: 'Your Majesty knows that it was only resistance to force which produced the martyrs.' He concluded that the King should postpone making his communion that Easter.[23]

Louis decided to go against this advice, but there was the further problem of where he should make his communion. The previous Easter he had gone to Saint-Germain l'Auxerrois, the parish church of the Tuileries, but its incumbent was now a 'constitutional' priest and Louis decided that the Royal Family would spend Easter at the Queen's palace of Saint-Cloud, where they could enjoy the services of non-juring priests. They had been allowed to spend the period 4 June–30 October 1790 at this palace 'at the gates of Paris', as Marie-Antoinette put it, but Louis returned to Paris twenty-two times to reassure the public. However, on this occasion, 18 April 1791, a crowd turned back the carriage in which the Royal Family was sitting in the very courtyard of the Tuileries. Louis and Marie-Antoinette were obliged to hear mass said by the 'constitutional' parish priest on Easter Sunday, though Elizabeth managed to get out of it. All the same, a letter to the King from La Porte suggests that the King may already have made his communion secretly in his private chapel. La Porte writes: 'This evening I am going to try to dispel [this] notion in the Cordelier Club.'[24]

The Saint-Cloud departure was a turning-point. As Marie-Antoinette wrote to Mercy on 20 April, it 'has confirmed us more than ever in our plans [for flight]'. It was also symptomatic of a galloping consumption in the body politic. The *Club des Impartiaux* had been founded in 1789 to strengthen the Executive; its successor, the *Club Monarchique*, founded by Clermont-Tonnerre and Malouet the following autumn, was instituted, according to its most recent historian, quite simply 'to save the monarchy'.[25] Popular pressure forced it to change address no less than four times before it finally closed after being stormed in a popular rising on 28 March 1791.

The King, as his manifesto makes clear, was well aware of this situation and how it was reflected in the ongoing drafting of the Constitution: '... the nearer the Assembly approached to the end of its labours, the more the wise men were seen to lose their influence and there was a corresponding daily increase of clauses which could only make government difficult, even impossible, and inspire contempt for it.' Among these clauses, the King specifically mentioned that passed on 8 June depriving him of the prerogative of mercy and several detailing the responsibility — criminal rather than political — of ministers.

Such troubles seemed to deepen the King's depression. Mme de Tourzel, who succeeded the exiled Mme de Polignac as governess to the royal children, notes that the King and Queen returned from Easter communion 'in a state of extreme depression. This state of mind was indeed habitual in the Royal Family.' In August 1790 Mirabeau had talked of 'the kind of torpor to which misfortune reduces people' and the following January, Montmorin 'said sadly... that when [the King] spoke to him about his affairs and his position it seemed as if he were talking to him about matters concerning the Emperor of China'. On 4 March, Louis became seriously ill with a high temperature and coughing of blood. Both Elizabeth and Marie-Antoinette believed that this illness, which lasted several weeks, was as much mental as physical in cause. Marie-Antoinette writes on 19 March: 'You already know how much I have been worried about the King's health; it was all the more disquieting because it is really the overflowing of his cup of sorrows which has made him ill.'[26]

Eighteen months of going along with the Revolution had led to a deeper captivity, a deeper depression, and France was now divided along religious as well as political lines: the crumb of comfort afforded him by Malesherbes in 1788 was gone. There must have seemed little for him to lose by flight.

14

The Flight to Varennes

Preparations for flight — October 1790–June 1791

It has generally been assumed that when Louis escaped from Paris on the night of 20/21 June 1791 his intention was to leave France, put himself at the head of foreign troops and French émigrés and bring about the forcible restoration of the Ancien Régime. An analysis of the escape plan and of the manifesto Louis left behind demonstrates the falsity of all these assumptions: Louis intended to set up his headquarters at Montmédy in Lorraine; the mobilization (apparently never effected) of eight thousand Austrian troops in Luxembourg was intended to give Louis's general, the Marquis de Bouillé, the pretext for assembling an army in Lorraine and, if all else failed, to afford the King and his family personal protection. One of the reasons for Louis's flight was precisely to forestall an émigré rising: the émigrés continually embarrassed him by speaking in his name yet would have put him in tutelage under an aristocratic form of government he had firmly rejected. Finally, in his manifesto there are no words suggesting a desire to return to the Ancien Régime.

Flight from Versailles had been proposed in the Council and rejected by the King on three occasions before the move to Paris. On each occasion, Louis had experienced a sense of shame at departing: 'A fugitive king! A fugitive king!' he had exclaimed on 5 October. The King's virtual captivity in the Tuileries removed that shame: escape was more honourable than flight. Captivity also put the King at an obvious disadvantage — his residual power could be used against him — which his escape would redress. For flight can be considered as a variant of the instrument of exile, whose essence had been absence from the King, rather than a disagreeable location, just as Hell is said to be absence from God. Escape from the Tuileries was, however, more dangerous than flight from Versailles, as the aborted journey to Saint-Cloud demonstrated. Nevertheless, by October 1790 Breteuil, the original proponent of flight on 15 July, decided that the time was propitious to return to the charge with the King.

After the fall of the Bastille, the Baron de Breteuil, keeping his distance from the Princes and other émigrés who blamed him for that event and who concentrated first at Turin then at Coblenz, settled at Soleure in Switzerland. From there he sent the King a memorandum via the Marquis d'Agoult, Bishop of Pamiers, who was returning to France from Switzerland. In this memorandum Breteuil, who regarded himself as Louis's last freely chosen minister, his *Chef du Conseil des finances* if not his prime minister, stressed the 'urgency of adopting any plan whatsoever' rather than drifting, which 'inspired general mistrust in all parties'. The best plan was for the King 'to leave Paris . . . in order to withdraw to a safe place within the Kingdom' and surround himself with the forces of General Bouillé.[1]

Of Bouillé, who was impatient of such labels as Revolutionary or Counter-Revolutionary and preferred to call himself a 'royalist', La Marck observes: 'Administrative reforms had always struck him as necessary and, as for improvements in the political structure, his opinions tended towards a form of constitution similar to England's. The King was not unaware of this viewpoint and that did not prevent his designating him the officer most worthy of his confidence, which proves once again that Louis XVI had sincerely opted for a constitutional system of government.'[2] Bouillé had drawn attention to himself in August 1790 by suppressing a mutiny of the garrison at Nancy, diplomatically employing both troops-of-the-line and National Guards, and Louis had sent him a nice letter with, rare for him, a gracious postscript such as Louis XIV might have written: 'I know that one of your favourite horses was killed under M. de Gouvernet; I am sending you one of mine which I have ridden and which I beg you to keep for love of me.' In the body of the letter he had told him: 'Look after your popularity; it may be very useful to me and the Kingdom; I regard it as the sheet-anchor which may one day be the means of restoring order.'[3] Lafayette tried desperately to win Bouillé over but, failing, made Louis write him a letter recalling him to Paris; but Louis sent Bouillé a secret letter countermanding this and he stayed put.[4]

So everyone thought of Bouillé, who was indeed devising a plan of his own (which envisaged the Assembly, suitably petitioned, asking the King to go and repel a preconcerted Austrian invasion from Luxembourg), when he received a visit from the Bishop of Pamiers, returning to Breteuil after seeing the King and bearing letters of credence dated Saint-Cloud 23 October.[5] Pamiers had found the King receptive; the October Days and above all the Civil Constitution had shaken his hope that the storm could be outridden whilst the final revision of the Constitution was about to begin without the benefit of his advice. Louis, however, did not finally commit himself to Breteuil until 26 November, the day before the Assembly passed the decree requiring the oath from priests, when he sent him plenipotential powers. (On sanctioning this decree Louis confided to Fersen, the Queen's handsome Swedish admirer who was to organize the Paris end of the escape: 'I would rather be King of Metz than remain King of France in this situation; but this will finish soon.')[6]

Breteuil's powers run as follows:

Monsieur le Baron de Breteuil, knowing the extent of your zeal and fidelity and desirous of giving you a new proof of my confidence, I have chosen you to be entrusted with the interests of my crown. As circumstances do not permit me to give you my instructions on such and such an object, to have a continuous correspondence with you, I am sending you these presents to serve as plenipotential powers and authorization vis-à-vis the different Powers with whom you may have to treat on my behalf. You know my intentions and I leave it to your discretion to make what use of them you consider necessary for the good of my service. I approve of all you do to attain the aim I have set, which is the restoration of my legitimate authority and the happiness of my peoples.[7]

Although the phrase 'restoration of my legitimate authority' is often taken to signify a return to the Ancien Régime, Louis uses it in a letter to Lafayette to summarize a programme submitted by the latter[8] and in his tenth note to the Court the same phrase is also used by Mirabeau, who is probably the common source.[9]

Bouillé did not like the plan outlined by the Bishop, considering in particular the escape from Paris too risky: he actually preferred Mirabeau's rival plan for an open departure: 'Un roi ne s'en va qu'en plein jour quand c'est pour être roi.'[10] Nevertheless, he put himself at the King's disposal and understated his objections lest he seem disloyal, for 'the King had learned by experience of the perfidy of men which had made him distrustful and suspicious'.[11]

Louis asked Bouillé to propose a fortified town to which he could withdraw in safety with his family, Bouillé offering him Valenciennes, Besançon and Montmédy, a small fortress-town in Lorraine which Louis selected. At the end of January Louis asked Bouillé for a route and Bouillé suggested the shortest one via Rheims and Stenay. Louis rejected Rheims because he had been crowned there and feared recognition. So Bouillé suggested entering Austrian Flanders via Chimay, then crossing the Ardennes to reach Montmédy the back way. But the King

> displayed even more reluctance for crossing the Emperor's territory to reach Montmédy than for going via Rheims, being set against leaving the Kingdom ... the King, who had read a lot of history and during the Revolution preferred to read that of England, had remarked that James II had lost his throne because he left his kingdom and that Charles I's death warrant had been grounded on the fact that he had levied war on his subjects. These reflections, which he often communicated to me, instilled in him an extreme repugnance for leaving France to put himself at the head of his troops or to cause them to move against his revolted peoples.[12]

So the Belgian route by which Monsieur was successfully to escape was ruled out and a very circuitous one was chosen instead, via Châlons, Sainte-Menéhoulde, Varennes (about which Bouillé was anxious as it was not a relay-station) and Stenay. Thus, so far from planning to leave the country, the King chose a poor route rather than leave France even momentarily.

One feature of Bouillé's own plan was retained, albeit in an attenuated form: that the Austrians should assemble a body of some eight thousand troops on the Luxembourg frontier to give him a pretext for his own troop concentrations. Marie-Antoinette undertook to arrange this, but communications between her and Vienna were slow and imperfect (as late as 22 May 1791 she could tell the Emperor: 'I am astonished you should know so little of our real intentions') and Imperial councils were divided between backing the plans of Louis and Breteuil, those of Artois, Calonne and the émigrés for an armed uprising in the Midi to restore the Ancien Régime, and doing nothing. In any case Mercy, now adviser to the Governor of the Austrian Netherlands, was resolved to turn a blind eye to any order from the Emperor to mobilize. The eight thousand troops never materialized.[13]

As for Louis's ultimate plans, Bouillé states:

> I never knew what course the King would have adopted at Montmédy and what would have been his conduct in relation to the Assembly in such difficult circumstances. Anyone who knew the King's religious character could not doubt that in taking his oath [to uphold the Constitution] his intention was to observe [it] scrupulously ... but this Constitution was then so imperfect; it was not finished; every day it became more vicious and impossible to uphold and to implement. ... I had therefore to suppose that once the King had recovered his liberty he

would have based his conduct on the disposition of the people and of the army and that he would only have employed force in the eventuality of his not having been able to come to a suitable arrangement with the Assembly which several leading members of that body — including Mirabeau, Duport and even the Lameth brothers — desired, realizing all the vices of their constitution, which tended towards a republic they did not want and anarchy which they dreaded.[14]

The idea was to get out of Paris before the Constitution had been finalized, which was expected in July, so that Louis would not be forced to accept it as it stood.[15] In the Declaration he left behind in the Tuileries, Louis tells the Parisians that he will 'return to their midst when he has freely accepted a constitution which will enforce respect for our holy religion, establish government on a stable footing. . . .' Bouillé lost his optimism about a settlement with the Assembly after Mirabeau's death on 2 April, but there were many deputies ready for an accommodation and Louis sought to strengthen their hand.

Louis's action in leaving his Declaration behind is generally considered foolish — he should have waited until he had reached safety. In fact he specifically instructed La Porte to deliver it immediately to the Assembly and he must have felt an imperious need to speak his mind at last. He told La Marck 'that he saw in the execution of this . . . project only a means of being free to address to the nation the language of reason and paternal benevolence'.[16] Any hostages to fortune were given with a sense of relief in what was in any case hardly a compromising document. For it offers not a wholesale repudiation of the Revolution but rather a detailed, at times rather boring critique of a constitution Louis wants to modify not reject. The Declaration, on which Louis worked for over six months, is unique in that the King could not have recourse to the advice of his ministers, since none was privy to his plans for flight. The Assembly suppressed it and few have bothered to read it through, but when a normally silent man speaks out he deserves an attentive hearing.

The Declaration, of curious form, begins and ends with a personal potted history of the Revolution. The middle section — beginning: 'Let us examine the various parts of government' — is a critique of the new institutions, in theory and in practice, tending to show that government needs to be strengthened. Apart from his claim for an equal share in the legislative process, he criticizes the excessive decentralization established by the Assembly and the fact that all the new bodies are 'elected by the people and do not depend on the Government'. Louis also criticizes specific policies of the Assembly, particularly in finance. The Assembly had not yet published an exact budget; it had abolished the old taxes without providing viable replacements — 'the ordinary taxes are greatly in arrears and the extraordinary resource of 1,200,000,000 of *assignats* are almost spent'. In other words, the Assembly had signally failed to solve the financial crisis for which it had been summoned. The general conclusion of the Declaration is that the Assembly by its incompetence has thrown away the patient fruits of his reign. The finances are in chaos, France's diplomatic hegemony destroyed and religious schism established.

Though Louis's criticisms are of a negative, sometimes peevish nature, one can derive from them a programme for a constitutional monarchy with a strong Executive. Marie-Antoinette's letter to Mercy of 3 February 1791 provides a positively stated if rudimentary programme of a different nature:

> The King is busy now collecting together all the materials for the manifesto which he must necessarily issue as soon as we are out of Paris. It will be necessary first to explain his flight, pardon those who have merely been led astray, flatter them with expressions of love; to except from the pardon the revolutionary leaders [*les chefs des factieux*], the City of Paris unless it returns to the old dispensation, and everyone who has not laid down his arms by a certain date; restore the parlements as ordinary law-courts without their ever being able to meddle with administration and finance. Finally, we have decided to take as a basis for the Constitution the Declaration of 23 June as necessarily modified by circumstances and events. Religion will be one of the great points to bring to the fore. We are now grappling together with the very difficult choice of the ministers we will want to appoint [personnes que nous voudrons appeler près de nous] when we are free. I thought it would be preferable to have one man at the head of affairs, as M. de Maurepas was formerly. In this way the King would avoid working with each minister separately and affairs would proceed with less fluctuation. Let me know what you think of this idea. The man is not easy to find and the harder I look the more disadvantages I find in them all.

This letter and the King's Declaration afford the rare chance of making a direct comparison between the political thinking of the Queen and that of the King at this time. Louis's Declaration is simply not based on the principles the Queen outlines here. The Queen's version is not just shorter but cruder, more immature and more vengeful. Louis does not mention pardons let alone punishments; the Declaration of 23 June is mentioned but is not central. Also Louis would never have exploited the religious schism as Marie-Antoinette here proposes. Louis simply intended, as he told the Bishop of Clermont, 'fully to restore Catholic worship if he came to recover his power'. Though neither of them desired it, Marie-Antoinette's approach would inevitably have led to civil war. In her reference to Maurepas, Marie-Antoinette shows that she does not think that Louis is up to his job, whilst Breteuil would not have been pleased to read the last sentence of his patron's letter. Not only did he want to be Prime Minister but 'to have [the Ministry] in his hand to avoid inconsistency'. He also planned to nominate all the other ministers: La Gallissonière for War, du Moutier for the Marine, La Porte for the Maison, Barentin to return to the Seals, and his close collaborators Bombelles and the Bishop of Pamiers to have Foreign Affairs and Finances respectively.[17]

The divergence between the positions of the King and the Queen have led the Girault de Coursacs to make a series of remarkable claims: that Marie-Antoinette kept everything from the King; that she originally planned to escape alone with the Dauphin, the King only resolving on flight after the Saint-Cloud Departure; that her correspondence with her brother the Emperor on the King's behalf was conducted without his knowledge; and finally that Breteuil's *pleins pouvoirs* were forged by herself and Fersen, who betrayed their ignorance by not dating them, an omission Breteuil rectified in the copies he sent to the Foreign Powers. As often, there is an element of truth in their assertions. During the Revolution as before, the King and Queen pursued different policies and concealed much from each other. During the Revolution as before, Mercy encouraged the Queen to have her own set of advisers: Mirabeau and later the 'triumvirs'. That the Queen wished to conceal matters from the King is clear from the following letter to Fersen: 'The Bishop [of Pamiers] should have told you already about the problems of writing to me. Only today, M. La Porte, who shows everything to the King, gave him your packet.'[18] This packet contained a long memorandum of Fersen's on the general situation and some skeleton letters for the Queen to write to foreign rulers. The King would not have resisted the temptation to open intercepted correspondence but would have found most of it in code. This seems to symbolize the situation.

It is hard to believe that Marie-Antoinette forged Breteuil's 'powers' and the handful of letters Louis sent abroad, though she may well have badgered him into writing the latter. At the same time when she purports to speak in his name or of his intentions, as in her version of the manifesto, she either gives a garbled version of his views or adds some of her own. In particular, her views on foreign policy and finance — the two fields in which Louis was most proficient — are wild and crude. For example, the notion that England and Holland must be given compensation to allow the Emperor to intervene in France; and that the King intended to restore its land to the Church and make the latter responsible for the redeeming the *assignats* at twenty percent below par — where would the Church find the money? Even wilder, the King was to choose this moment to break the habit of a reign and declare a 'partial bankruptcy', albeit with the proviso that holders of life-annuities were to be exempt. No wonder Breteuil insisted that all decisions, except those of the most pressing military nature, should be deferred until his own arrival at Montmédy.[19]

It is sad to relate but true that Marie-Antoinette spent no more time telling Mercy, in Brussels, about her political programme than she did in arranging with him how to send on ahead a travelling dressing-case fitted with silver boxes. In order to avert suspicion the Queen's sister, Christina, Governess of the Austrian Netherlands, asked to have a similar one made. Next, the Queen's cipher was removed from all the pieces and finally this *nécessaire de voyage* was sent to Brussels. These details are given by Marie-Antoinette's chambermaid, Mme Campan, and without the Queen's letters to Mercy would scarcely be credible. Nor would her statement that the Queen was 'determined to have a complete wardrobe with her' if we did not have Mercy's letter to Kaunitz in which, with horrified incredulity, he tells the Chancellor of whole crates of the Queen's belongings reaching him by public transport.[20]

The flight

So on the night of 20/21 June the King and Queen, Mme Elizabeth, the royal children and their governess, Mme de Tourzel, left the Tuileries — separately to avoid recognition. They were to reassemble at the Petit Carrousel where Fersen was waiting with a two-horse carriage to drive them out of Paris. The Queen left last; as she went from the Palace La Fayette's carriage, with blazing torches, passed so close that she could touch it with her cane. She pressed herself against a wall and then continued but got lost in the maze of small streets around the Tuileries. She even, some say, crossed the Seine by the Pont-Royal before finding her way back and arriving half-an-hour late. Louis had been more fortunate. A fortnight previously the Chevalier de Coigny, who resembled the King, had left the Palace at night wearing clothes similar to the ones the King was to wear. Accordingly, the King, after chatting with Lafayette and Bailly at his *coucher*, was able to leave the Palace by the grand staircase and the main entrance. 'So completely was he at ease', he told the rest of the party, 'that his shoe having become undone, he put it right without attracting attention.' When the Queen finally reached the waiting carriage and was safely inside, the King 'took her in his arms, kissed her, and said over the over again "How glad I am to see you here!" They all kissed each other; all the Royal Family did me [Mme de Tourzel] the same honour.'[21]

Fersen then drove the carriage out of Paris to the Barrière Saint-Martin, losing another half-hour by making a detour. Too much is made of these and other delays and mishaps and of the specially constructed carriage — the horrified italics are Bouillé's — which was waiting to take the Royal Family on the rest of their journey to Montmédy. 'What has not been said', Reinhard asks, 'about this *berline*?'[22] — 'the hearse of the Monarchy', as Fréron dubbed it. That it was big is undeniable, for it had to take six people and the provisions for an extended journey. People even quarrel about its colour, some insisting that it was grey, others inclining to the opinion that it was brown. Such are the accidents of failure, not its substance. Had the voyage succeeded, the carriage would have been of shining silver.

Fersen conducted the berline as far as Bondy, where a relay of six post-horses was put in. Here also they were joined by two waiting-women in a yellow carriage which was to precede the berline. An ordinary postillion took Fersen's place, with two disguised Bodyguards sitting on either side in case of trouble. 'Adieu, Mme de Korff!' shouted Fersen — Mme de Tourzel was posing as a Russian lady of that name, the King as her steward, and the rest as various servants and retainers.

As they left Paris behind them, their spirits rose: ' "Here I am," said this good Prince, "outside that town of Paris where I have experienced so much bitterness. You may be quite sure that once I am firmly seated in the saddle I shall be a very different person from the one you have seen hitherto." ' Keen cartographer that he was, Louis applied himself to his map as the towns and villages flashed by — La Ferté-sous-Jouarre, Montmirail, Vauchamps, Étoges. This was only the third journey of his life of any distance.

At Châlons the King was recognized by at least one person, accounts differ, but it was a loyal town and the carriage was not stopped. ' "When we have passed Châlons we shall have nothing further to fear," said the King. "At Pont de Sommevel we shall find the first detachment of troops and we shall be safe." ' The area of Bouillé's command began at Châlons and Louis had insisted, against his general's advice, on having detachments of cavalry placed in the towns between Pont de Sommevel and Montmédy. But when they reached Pont de Sommevel at six in the evening there were no troops to meet them. They were two hours late and the Duc de Choiseul, after waiting until a quarter to six, concluded that the escape had been postponed and withdrew his forty hussars.

Even so, it was not the time factor that was to be determinant. For when the berline reached Saint-Menéhoulde at eight o'clock, the troops were there all right — forty dragoons under Captain d'Andoins — but their presence had aroused so much suspicion in this ultra-revolutionary town that their captain had felt unable to use them: 'He rode up to the carriage for a moment and said to [Mme de Tourzel] in an undertone: "The arrangements have been badly made; I am going away in order not to arouse suspicion."' Furthermore, the King was again recognized and this time by an enemy — Drouet, the postmaster at Saint-Menéhoulde — but by the time Drouet had convinced the authorities and set off with a companion in pursuit of the Royal Family, they had a start of an hour and a half.

They thus safely reached Clermont at nine-thirty. Here again the relay of troops was present — a hundred dragoons under Colonel Damas — but again the town was seized by a panic-fear and would not let the troops leave with the carriage. Even more ominous, when Damas ordered his men to force their way out, the troops, who had been fraternizing with the inhabitants, refused to obey. Only Damas knew who was in the carriage, but one doubts whether this knowledge would have made the troops any more obedient.

Just outside Clermont, the King's party turned left off the main road, taking a minor road to Montmédy, via Varennes. They had been advised not to take the main road through the ultra-revolutionary Verdun. Unfortunately, Drouet had asked at the posting-house at Clermont (where the horses had been changed) which route the berline was taking — otherwise he would naturally have shot past the turning and on to Verdun. By cutting across country, Drouet was able to reach Varennes at about the same time as the King.

Since Varennes did not boast a relay-station, Bouillé had made private arrangements for a change of horses, but they could not be found. In what must have been a state of blind panic, the King and Queen went down the street knocking on doors. Varennes is in two halves, divided by the river Aire. The postillions could not be persuaded to continue their journey with tired horses, but they finally agreed to drive over the river and see if the relay were there. It was, and also another detachment of cavalry. But whilst Louis had been knocking on doors, Drouet had had time to assemble a small posse which stopped the berline under an arch in the town walls leading to the bridge. Passports were demanded and produced. Nevertheless, the procureur of the town, a small grocer aptly named M. Sauce, asked the occupants to step into his house above the shop. They agreed. The use of force by the two Bodyguards would quite possibly have enabled the carriage to cross the river.

At first Louis insisted that he was not the King. Finally, he declared in a loud voice: 'Yes, I am your king; here is the Queen and the Royal Family. Surrounded by daggers and bayonets in the Capital, I have come to the provinces to find, in the midst of my faithful subjects, the liberty and peace you all enjoy: I could not live in Paris without perishing, my family and myself. I have come to live among you my children and I will not forsake you.' He was very moved and embraced everyone present. They too were moved. He said he only wanted to go to Montmédy and was prepared to be escorted there by the local National Guard. He appealed to Sauce, but the procureur was scared.[23] He was a small man, standing in for the mayor who was away in Paris as a deputy to the National Assembly. The Queen appealed to Mme Sauce, who wept but replied: 'What would you have me do, Madame? Your situation is very unfortunate; but you see that would expose M. Sauce; they would cut off his head.'[24]

Then Choiseul and Goguelat arrived with the forty hussars who should have been at Pont de Sommevel. The crowd outside was not yet large, but growing. Choiseul and Goguelat were able to go in and see the King. 'Right!' said Louis, 'when do we start?' 'Sire, we await your orders.' Choiseul suggested that the King mount up with the Dauphin in his arms and the rest of the party mount up also. Then, surrounded by the hussars, they should try to break out. 'But do you answer for it,' said the King, 'that in this unequal struggle a bullet will not hit the Queen, or my sister or my children?' The plan was abandoned. At five in the morning another officer, Deslon, arrived with sixty dragoons, but there was now a crowd of ten thousand round the shop, summoned by the tocsin, and when Deslon asked the King for his orders, Louis bitterly replied: 'I am a prisoner and have none to give.'

One hope remained. Word had been sent to Bouillé, who was at Stenay, less than thirty miles away but over mountains, with the Royal Allemand regiment. Louis played for time. But at six o'clock there arrived not Bouillé but La Fayette's aide-de-camp Romeuf, with a decree from the Assembly ordering the King's return to Paris. At half-past-seven the berline headed on its mournful way back. Bouillé arrived at nine-thirty, but the horses were exhausted and the berline was in any case surrounded by six thousand National Guards and an immense crowd. Even if Bouillé could have caught up with the King, his intervention would have provoked a general massacre. So he withdrew to Stenay and immediately crossed the border. Later he received an emotional letter from the King:

You have done your duty, Monsieur; stop blaming yourself; you have dared all for me and my family and have not succeeded. God has permitted circumstances which paralysed your measures and your courage. Success depended on me; but civil war horrified me and I did not want to shed the blood of my subjects, whether deluded or faithful. My fate is bound up with that of the Nation and I do not want to rule by violence. You, Monsieur, have been courageous and loyal: I wanted to express my thanks; and perhaps one day it will be in my power to give you a mark of my personal satisfaction.[25]

The return to Paris was squalid. The berline was surrounded by a crowd so dense that it raised a thick cloud of dust like a fog. Though the sun was blistering, the occupants were not allowed to draw the blinds. Often the crowd compelled the berline to go at walking pace. Mme de Tourzel writes: 'It is impossible to give any idea of the sufferings of the Royal Family during this unfortunate journey — sufferings both moral and physical: they were spared nothing.' At Clermont and Sainte-Menéhoulde they were subjected to officious insults. Only at Châlons were they treated well: they were housed in the former Intendance where twenty-one years before the young Archduchess had been rapturously received on her way to wed the Dauphin. At the little town of La Ferté-sous-Jouarre the wife of the mayor served the Royal Family herself, dressed as a servant. She knew that otherwise the King would invite her to join them and did not want to invade their momentary privacy. This little gesture, with its delicate respect for fallen majesty, was one of the most affecting of the whole journey.

Just outside Épernay the Royal Family were joined by three commissioners from the National Assembly, Barnave, Pétion and Latour-Maubourg, who were to escort them back to Paris. Latour-Maubourg travelled with the waiting-women in the other carriage; Barnave and Pétion squeezed into the berline, bringing its complement up to eight. Pétion was consistently rude, talked of republics and regretted that France was 'not yet ripe for one'. He has left an account of the journey which is replete with naive presumption.[26] We are told that Mme Elizabeth was falling for his charms when he asked himself: 'What if this was a trick to buy me? Had Mme Elizabeth agreed to sacrifice her honour to make me sacrifice mine? Yes, at Court no price is too high, one is capable of anything; the Queen could have planned it.' Pétion's feelings were ones of forced contempt mixed with a good deal of superstitious awe for royalty. He was amazed that during the twelve hours it took them to reach Paris from Meaux none of the royal ladies had needed to relieve herself. Of Louis, he writes:

The King tried to strike up a conversation. . . . He asked me if I was married, I said that I was; he asked me if I had any children. I told him

I had one who was just older than his son. I said to him from time to time: 'Look at the countryside, is it not fine? ... What a fine country France is! There is no kingdom in the world that can compare with it.' I let out these ideas deliberately; I examined the impression they made on the royal physiognomy, but his expression is always cold, unanimated to a devastating degree and, truth to tell, this mass of flesh is insensible.

He wished to speak to me of the English, of their industry, of the commercial genius of that nation. He formulated one or two phrases, then became embarrassed, noticed it and blushed. This difficulty in expressing himself gives him a timidity I noticed several times. Those who do not know him would be tempted to take this timidity for stupidity; but they would be wrong: very rarely did he let out anything misplaced and I did not hear him utter anything stupid.

He applied himself greatly to following his maps and he would say: 'We are in such and such a *département* or district or spot.'

The Royal Family were clearly wasting their time with Pétion.

With Barnave, however, it was different. Whether he was converted on the road to Paris is doubtful. This mission, for which he had proposed himself in the Assembly, was, unlike Paul's, not one of persecution. Barnave was a gallant young man, only twenty-nine, and he was undoubtedly stirred by Marie-Antoinette's misfortunes to a personal devotion to the Queen. Nevertheless, the radical of 1789 had for some months been convinced that the Revolution must be 'stopped', as he put it, before it turned into an attack on property and that for this an entente with the Court was necessary.

It must have been difficult for Barnave to talk politics with Pétion sitting there, all suspicion, but he took time off to drink, throw chicken bones out of the window and tease the Dauphin. The party spent a night at Dormans — where Louis records in his diary that he 'slept for three hours in an arm-chair' — and another at Meaux before arriving back in Paris at eight in the evening of Saturday 25 June.

The Champs-Elysées was densely packed, but there was total silence. Everywhere placards proclaimed: 'Whoever applauds the King will be thrashed; whoever insults him will be hanged.' Everyone left their hats on. The King was taken back to the Tuileries and placed under the strictest house-arrest. A few minutes later, Pétion went into the King's bedroom: 'Already all the valets had preceded there in their usual costume. It seemed as though the King were returning from a hunting-party; they did his toilet. Seeing the King, contemplating him, you never could have guessed all that had just happened: he was just as phlegmatic, just as tranquil, as if nothing had happened. He immediately put himself on show.'

'He put himself on show', externally and internally; that is the clue. It was partly a matter of conditioning, the life on display he had known since a small child, partly a way of holding himself together. The flight to Varennes appears in his diary as an ordinary voyage. The detail is meticulous: there was no *coucher* at Dormans because there was no bed. Written across his diary for the month of July are the words: 'Rien de tout le mois: la messe dans la Galérie.' For August: 'Tout le mois a été comme celui de juillet.' He seems to be saying: 'What a boring month!' — in fact he had been suspended from his functions and was kept under such close surveillance that he was not allowed to go to the chapel to hear mass. His sanction was no longer required for bills to become law: the Minister of Justice applied the seal on the instructions of the Assembly.

The aftermath: suspension and the revision of the Constitution

During the three months of his suspension Louis lived in total seclusion, never so much as venturing into the Tuileries gardens until he resumed his functions on accepting the completed Constitution in September. The Duchesse de Tourzel tells us that 'Madame Elizabeth and the Queen made the King play billiards every day after the *dîner* so that he might get some exercise'. Indeed, as a substitute for the hunting diaries, he kept a record of his games against his wife and sister between July 1791 and July 1792.[27] It provides an interesting parallel chronicle to the political events for, though he usually won, in moments of crisis his game tended to fall away.

Yet from his seclusion Louis exercised an influence greater perhaps than at any time since the opening of the Estates and these months also offered the best chance since then of effecting a lasting settlement in France. For it is not exact to say that the King's flight weakened the monarchy: rather, it polarized opinion concerning it. On the one hand his flight gave birth to the first serious expressions of republicanism: among a handful of deputies, men such as Pétion and Buzot, who were later to be known as the Girondins; and more widely in the political demi-monde centred on the Cordelier Club and the electoral wards or Sections of Paris. The Cordelier Club got up a republican petition and on 17 July took it to the Champ de Mars to collect signatures. But on the other hand, the forces of order or of respectability rallied round the throne and the municipality replied to the petition by declaring martial law, in token of which Bailly, La Fayette and the National Guard arrived on the scene accompanied by a red flag. One shot was fired from the crowd and La Fayette ordered his men to open fire, killing some fifty of the petitioners. The popular leaders, men like Danton, Camille Desmoulins and Santerre, went into hiding and popular politics was dead for some months. All but a handful of the deputies in the Jacobin Club, Robespierre being the most celebrated, seceded and joined the more moderate Feuillant Club.

After the discovery of the King's flight, La Fayette did for a fleeting moment consider the declaration of a republic. A meeting of deputies was hastily assembled at the house of his friend the Duc de La Rochefoucauld, but its sense was decidedly against such a move and La Fayette did not insist. It was generally assumed that the declaration of a republic would be accompanied by a second revolution, one against property. Furthermore, Rousseau had said that republics only worked in small countries and in 1791 it was widely assumed both by advocates, such as Buzot, and opponents such as the Queen that a French republic would be a federal one.

These sentiments found expression in two moves by the Assembly to preserve the monarchy, the initial one highly formal, the other, by its Constitutional Committee, more creative. The immediate response of the Assembly was to stage-manage the measures taken in the wake of the King's flight in such a way as to preserve both the throne and its present occupant by employing a version, or rather the reductio ad absurdum, of the ancient convention of the 'King's religion being surprised'. Only because people were accustomed to the convention could such a blatant subterfuge have been contemplated. Even so, the relationship between convention and reality was strained to breaking point when the nation was immediately asked to believe that the King had not fled but had been abducted by General Bouillé, who soon obliged by sending the Assembly confirmation of this in a letter of 20 June. That this version also made the King appear an imbecile would not have troubled the Assembly.

After couriers had been despatched to the provinces with this official version, the gates of Paris were closed. When the King and Queen had been brought back, commissioners from the Assembly helped them to make prepared statements in which the King said that his journey had revealed to him the extent of support for the Constitution in the country; this part of the story was at least true, for Marie-Antoinette confessed to Mercy on 31 October that her journey had convinced her that 'there is not a single town, not a regiment on which we can rely'. Nevertheless, to make absolutely sure that the royal couple should have time to concert their 'story', it was arranged that the Queen should be in the bath when the commissioners arrived — she gave them her statement the following day.

Behind the formality and the farce, however, the conviction was growing among a good number of deputies that many of the criticisms levelled against the Constitution in the King's Declaration were justified and that it was in no one's interests to have a disgruntled monarch. At the very least, Varennes concentrated minds and gave the Assembly an enforced pause: on 24 June, elections to the successor assembly, the Legislative, were suspended, which would have pleased Louis, since in his Declaration he had complained of the unsuitable candidates the primary assemblies were throwing up. But his flight also, in spite of his recapture, did further his objective of assisting the movement to revise the Constitution. The starting-point for this had been Le Chapelier's proposal of 23 September 1790 that seven new members be added to the Assembly's Constitutional Committee to give a coherent final draft to a Constitution whose articles had been voted piecemeal over the past twelve months. Among the seven were Barnave, Alexandre de Lameth and Adrien Duport — the 'triumvirs' — who quickly established control over the Committee. These men had been leaders of the left in 1789 but now they wanted to consolidate the Revolution and in the spring of 1791 they had made contact with the Court. Though they did not actually meet the King and Queen, there had been exploratory talks through third parties. Montmorin, Mirabeau, Barnave and Alexandre de Lameth had certainly met together to discuss business, whilst the triumvirs' associates Beaumetz and d'André probably saw the King in person on 19 April.[28] Their complicity in the King's flight was widely assumed, though without hard evidence, and their reaction to his recapture is epitomised by Alexandre de Lameth's lament: 'What a disaster! In my terror at the speed with which public order is disintegrating, I hoped that a negotiation with the King, from a position of demonstrable and complete independence, could, through reciprocal concessions, give France the rest for which I seek in vain except through such a conjuncture.'[29]

According to some accounts, the Constitutional Committee had chosen commissioners to go and treat with the King at Montmédy and these were sitting in a coach ready to depart when news arrived of his recapture.[30] Indeed, of the Commissioners actually sent, one, Barnave, as we have seen, saw no reason to change his brief just because the King had been stopped. In snatched conversations on the return journey Barnave and Marie-Antoinette worked out an agreement of which the Queen later sent him a résumé: the Assembly would revise the Constitution in the light of the King's criticisms provided that the King would then frankly accept it, prevail on the Emperor to 'recognize it by any act' and conclude a new treaty with France, and finally induce 'the Princes and the émigrés or at least some of them' to return to France.[31] Nor was this merely a transaction: the points are naturally linked in a key passage in the Declaration: 'He [the King] placed his confidence in the wise men of the Assembly . . . when speaking about the intended revision of the decrees. . . . They recognized the need to give this government and the laws which ought to assure everyone's prosperity and place in society enough consideration to induce all those citizens to return to the Kingdom who had been compelled to expatriate themselves.' Since this agreement answered Louis's central complaint, that he had been denied any say in the framing of the Constitution and would have achieved the objective of his flight, there is no reason to doubt its sincerity as long as the revision stood a chance of success.

Louis told Malouet 'We have been very satisfied with Barnave', whilst he remained grateful to the triumvirs for scotching a move in the Assembly, immediately after his flight, to replace him with his brother Artois. The detailed negotiations were conducted by Marie-Antoinette and her sincerity at this stage is clear from the following letter of 12 August to Leopold:

My ideas are always the same: I do not think I am deceiving myself about the sincerity of some of those who were once our most dangerous enemies. One of them [Barnave] is endowed with the most animated and captivating eloquence and his talents exercise a very great influence on the Assembly. I have already witnessed to some degree the effect of his eloquence in winning back opinion and in making it resume confidence in the purity of our intentions. It has been for a long time the only resource we have. It is, I fear, too late to try others and they have become useless and dangerous.

The Constitutional Committee made the King's Declaration the basis of its operations.[32] Indeed, the original plan was to give Louis all the powers of the King of England (putting it this way may serve to bring home how little power the Constitution left him) — for example, the right of dissolution and the initiation of legislation; there was also to have been a bicameral parliament. These schemes foundered on the rock of intransigence represented by the right wing. Despite pressure from the Court — a rare occurrence in the constitutional context — its two hundred and fifty deputies preferred, in Ferrière's words, 'to risk the destruction of the monarchy and their own rather than surrender the hope of restoring the Ancien Régime'.

The Committee had to content itself with the support of fifty from the moderate right led by Malouet and Cazalès. This was insufficient for a frontal revision of the Constitution and the Committee had to employ the expedient of re-classifying certain constitutional decrees as ordinary unentrenched legislation subject to repeal. The Civil Constitution of the Clergy was put in this category, which meant that the King could in good conscience swear to uphold the Constitution but not the ecclesiastical settlement which everyone knew he detested; so also was the abolition of the King's prerogative of mercy on which Louis had also dwelt at length in his Declaration. But without the support of the right, the Committee was unable to have these decrees simply repealed, nor did it even manage to re-classify the decrees forbidding the King to command the Army in person or move more than twenty leagues from Paris.

In addition, the Committee proposed new measures in answer to the King's Declaration. Notably it was successful in obtaining for him a Bodyguard of his choice, 1,200 infantry and 600 cavalry, whose purpose, the debates made clear, was to protect him from insurrection as, during the October Days, had the one whose disbanding he had lamented at length in his Declaration. The Committee's attempts to enhance the prestige or diminish the perils of being a minister were largely unavailing, though it managed to introduce a clause allowing ministers to appear before, though not to be members of, the Assembly (a generous concession, Robespierre considered). In addition, through a procedural manœuvre which failed, Le Chapelier proposed legislation against the Clubs which virtually paraphrased Louis's Declaration, answering his criticisms point by point: affiliation and correspondence between Clubs was to be prohibited — the same analogy with the old parlements being drawn — as was the publication of their resolutions. On 26 August the Committee's proposal to restore the initiative in fiscal legislation to the ministers was rejected. Finally, the King was declared 'hereditary representative of the Nation' instead of merely its 'first functionary', which went some way to placing his theoretical authority on a par with that of the Assembly. But there was no disguising the fact that the revision had substantially failed. On 13 August Barnave told the Assembly that the previous evening the Committee had discussed whether it should resign in view of the Assembly's recent decrees.

Marie-Antoinette, cut off though she was in the Tuileries, conducting everything by correspondence, unable to use her charm, realized something of what was going on. On 16 August she writes to Mercy of 'the leaders who for the last eight days have realized that they are absolutely beaten'. It is at this point that the tone of her correspondence changes. For Barnave had failed to deliver his side of the agreement; the Constitution remains 'a tissue of absurdities'.[33] Barnave limply and disingenuously tries to convince the Queen that 'account has been taken of several things contained in [the King's] memorandum'.[34] The

Queen is amazed: 'These gentlemen say that "the Constitution is very monarchical"; I confess that I have need of enlightenment on this point . . .'[35]

Moreover, a last hope that the revision of the Constitution could be enlarged by observations from the King prior to his acceptance was dashed by Robespierre's withering speech of 3 September warning the triumvirs against attempting such a move and accusing them of personal ambition. The triumvirs failed to defend themselves, whilst the right laughed. Louis made himself ill with indecision about what to do, though there was no real alternative to acceptance. Finally he accepted the Constitution in a letter to the Assembly of 13 September, which, though largely drafted by Barnave and Montmorin, forms a pendant to his Declaration. It was a skilful letter highlighting the improvements to the Constitution made since his flight, to which, it was insinuated, they were attributable. 'You have shown a desire to restore order,' the deputies were told, 'you have considered the lack of discipline in the army; you have recognized the necessity for curbing the licence of the press.' He ended with a flash of candour: 'I should, however, be telling less than the truth if I said I perceived in the executive and administrative resources sufficient vigour to activate and preserve unity in all the parts of so vast an empire; but since opinions are at present divided on these matters, I consent that experience alone shall decide.'[36] Next day, as King of the French rather than King of France and Navarre, he took the oath to the Constitution before the Assembly, he standing, they, with the solitary exception of Malouet, seated.[37]

With the failure of the revision, Marie-Antoinette takes up an idea which had briefly crossed her mind in June 1790, that of an 'armed congress' of the Great Powers to put pressure on the Assembly or its successor — 'not war but the threat of war', as she put it. Her earlier letter to Leopold had characterized such measures as 'too late . . . useless and dangerous' whilst she had steadfastly rejected the advice of Mercy and Fersen that there should be no negotiations with the Assembly. The idea of a Congress was the hobby-horse of Marie-Antoinette and Breteuil alone: after Varennes, Mercy and Fersen advised her that the King should send Monsieur plenipotential powers, rescind those of Breteuil and subordinate him if need be to the Prince's adviser, Calonne.[38] Marie-Antoinette may have not forged Breteuil's *pleins pouvoirs* but he was nonetheless essentially 'her' minister as he had been ever since she had secured his appointment in 1783. In advocating a congress, Breteuil may well have been beguiled by his success at the Congress of Teschen in 1777. There is no clear evidence of Louis's views on a congress — he probably thought it was a waste of time but humoured his wife.

Breteuil and the Congress, however, were anathema to the King's émigré brothers Provence and especially Artois and their 'prime minister' Calonne. In part this was merely a continuation of the personal rivalries of 1785–7. Calonne took great delight in writing to Catherine II of Russia: 'After the catastrophe of Varennes, one might have expected that the Baron de Breteuil, desolated by the fatal consequences of his counsels, would have refrained from giving them, and would have ceased making use of the "powers" which he surprised from His Majesty['s religion]. These "powers" lapsed with the plan which occasioned them.'[39]

It was also, however, a matter of policy: Artois favoured direct military intervention in France by the Powers. On 27 August, whilst Louis was debating whether to accept the Constitution, Artois procured the Declaration of Pillnitz from the Emperor and the King of Prussia which stipulated that, provided the other Powers assisted, the co-signatories would intervene to restore the King of France to his rightful position. The Emperor knew perfectly well that English determination to remain neutral removed any obligation on his part to intervene in France. All Frenchmen, however, from the King down, were misled by the belief that England was itching to avenge the defeats of the last war. Accordingly Louis wrote a secret letter to his brothers complaining of the impossible position in which they had placed him:

> I was deeply hurt to see the Comte d'Artois go to that conference at Pillnitz without my consent. . . . do you really have to serve the fury of the men of faction by having me accused of carrying war into my kingdom? . . . For how can I persuade them that this Declaration is not based on your request? Will anyone ever believe that my own brothers are not carrying out my orders? Thus you portray me to the Nation as accepting [the Constitution] with one hand and soliciting [intervention] from the Foreign Powers with the other. What virtuous man could respect such conduct? And you think you are serving me by depriving me of the respect of decent folk.
>
> I hope you will come to your senses. Understand that victory is nothing if you cannot then proceed to govern and consider that one cannot govern a great nation against the current orthodoxy [*son esprit dominant*].

These lines were penned by Louis as a postscript to a longer letter explaining to his brothers why he had accepted the Constitution. As he was finishing it he received a printed copy of an open letter from his brothers, written by Calonne and assuming that his acceptance of the Constitution was forced and invalid. Louis considered that the procedure of publishing private advice was as disrespectful and insulting from his brothers as it had formerly been from the parlements. Lest his brothers continue to say that they were representing his real wishes — again like the old parlements — Louis had a second copy of this memorandum sent to the Emperor, who is thus able to give the lie to the King's brothers: 'Not only do I believe that my brother-in-law the King has genuinely [*sérieusement*] accepted the Constitution, and is against [*répugne*] any idea of counter-revolution, but I have positive proof. So do Your Royal Highnesses: he has communicated his real intentions to you in a secret memorandum which contains arguments for the decision he has taken which out-weigh those advanced against.'[40]

The King's memorandum is a moving document including a brilliant analysis of the mentality both of the revolutionaries and the émigrés; but above all it is a passionate and prophetic plea against war which, the King believes, his rejection of the Constitution would entail. Monarchical authority, he argues, can only be restored by force or by 'reunion' — by which he means allowing the people time to judge the defects of the Constitution for themselves. He first considers force:

This can only be employed by foreign armies — the émigrés by themselves are capable only of exercising a suicidal revenge — and this means recourse to war. The émigrés flatter themselves that the rebels will capitulate immediately before such immense forces, thus avoiding war [an implicit rejection by Louis of the utility of an Armed Congress]. But the leaders of the Revolution, those who control the levers of power both in Paris and in the provinces, are committed up to the hilt to the Revolution. They will use the National Guards and other armed citizens and they will begin by massacring those who are called aristocrats.

War will be inevitable because it is in the interests of all those in authority to fight; it will be terrible because it will be motivated by violence and despair. Can a king contemplate all these misfortunes with equanimity and call them down on his people? I know that kings have always prided themselves on regaining by force that which people have sought to snatch from them, that to fear in such circumstances the horrors of war is called weakness. But I confess that such reproaches affect me less than the sufferings of my people . . .

[So there would be no capitulation but a bitter war. Probably the foreign armies and the élite of the nobility would defeat] National Guards and regiments without officers. But these foreign troops could not settle in the Kingdom and, when they were no longer here, how could one govern if insubordination began anew? I know that my émigré subjects flatter themselves that there has been a great change in people's attitudes. I myself for a long time thought that this was happening but I am now undeceived. The Nation likes the Constitution because the word recalls to the lower portion of the people only the independence in which it has lived for the last two years and to the class above [the bourgeoisie] equality. The lower portion of the people see only that they are reckoned with; the bourgeoisie sees nothing above them. Amour-propre is satisfied. This new possession has made them forget everything else. . . . The completion of the Constitution was all that stood between them and perfect happiness; . . . time will teach them how mistaken they were, but their error is nonetheless profound. . . . One can never govern a people against its inclinations. This maxim is as true at Constantinople as in a republic; the present inclinations of this nation are for the Rights of Man, however senseless they are.

[And even discounting these considerations, how would one govern through the aristocracy?] Is the aristocracy which you say would be the support and refuge of the monarchy even united among itself? . . . there are as many parties on this side as on the other. One wants the old order; another the Estates-General and yet another an English-style government. What real strength could the Government derive from these different parties which would be even more divided among themselves if they won and several of which would rather treat with the Jacobins than with another faction of the aristocracy?

. . . I have therefore thought that [war] should be rejected and that I should try once more the sole means remaining to me, namely the junction of my will to the principles of the Constitution. I realize all the difficulties of governing a large nation in this way — indeed I will say that I realize that it is impossible. But the obstacles that I should have put in the way [by refusing to accept the Constitution] would have brought about the war I sought to avoid and prevented the people from properly assessing the Constitution because it would only have seen my constant opposition. By my adopting its principles and executing them in good faith, they will come to know the cause of their misfortunes. . . . Let the Princes conduct themselves in such a way as to spare me the decrees against them that the Assembly may present for my sanction; let the conduct of your entourage be such that I cannot be suspected of intentions contrary to the plan that I am going to follow. The courage of the nobility . . . would be better understood if it returned to France to augment the forces of the men of goodwill. . . . The true nobility would then have a splendid opportunity of regaining all its prestige and a portion of its rights. What I say of the nobility could equally be applied to the monarchy.[41]

The interception of this letter would have done the King's cause a lot of good — particularly the last sentence, in which the King limits his ambition to regaining, peacefully, 'all his prestige' but only 'a portion of his rights'.

The escape from Paris — the flight to Varennes — was Louis's first major personal initiative since the Convocation of the Notables in 1786; his Declaration, a manifesto in all but name, his first personal statement. In the interval he had drifted, following the impulsion of advisers in whom he did not believe. His initiative was the subject of hostile propaganda from the start — killed by condescension in the Assembly from those very members who sought to preserve the monarchy, stifled at birth and yet made the basis of the revision — and this has set the tone by which historians have continued to judge it.

Yet Louis did not write it in a vacuum but kept abreast of events; the lengthy section on the prerogative of mercy must have been written only days before the flight. And for the first time since the Revolution began, he seems to be swimming with the current, for in his manifesto he rightly detects a revisionist tide, which was to reach its high-water mark in Barnave's passionate speech of 15 July — 'il est temps de terminer la Révolution' — before retreating for three years, submerged by an ocean of blood. The Constitution was, as Marie-Antoinette observed, 'a tissue of absurdities' because many of its clauses were either too general to be applicable or too topical to endure.

If the intransigence of the right, as baleful an influence in 1791 as in 1789 and as little mindful of the monarchy, had not prevented the adoption of the King's modifications, France would have had not only a more workable constitution but one which would have worked better because it would have been freely accepted by the King.

All Louis's opponents who came into close political contact with him, from Brienne through the triumvirs to Dumouriez, ended up appreciating his predicament, and the moment this happened, authority melted from them. Brienne had said he would be a 'Notable in the Ministry'; he was nothing of the sort. For, as Mirabeau observed, a Jacobin in the Ministry was not the same thing as a Jacobin minister; but neither was he as influential.

15

The Last Year of The Monarchy, 13 September 1791–10 August 1792

Not only was the Constitution of 1791 defective, it was never given a chance, the conduct of everyone involved in its implementation, from the King downwards, being characterized by cynicism, irresponsibility and gross miscalculation. In his speech accepting the Constitution, Louis had made no bones about its imperfections but had 'consented that experience alone should decide'; to Bertrand de Moleville, Minister for the Marine, he confided the cynical variant to this approach which was to be his touchstone: 'My opinion is that the literal execution of the Constitution is the best way of making the Nation see the alterations to which it is susceptible.' He had outlined this approach in the secret letter to his brothers, but the generosity of spirit there displayed was cancelled by the word 'literal'. Marie-Antoinette's view was that nothing could be expected from the internal forces of the monarchy: the Revision had failed and 'there was not a single town, not a regiment on which they could rely', though if her attention had not been focused exclusively on the radical east, she might have detected in the Catholic west the first rumblings of what within eighteen months would be a general royalist insurrection. As it was, she pinned her hopes on her Armed Congress of the Powers to put pressure on France which the King, as mediator, would relieve at a price; it was a variant of Bouillé's original scheme to enable the King to profit from solving an artificial crisis.

Among the politicians a similar sense of unreality prevailed. The new assembly, the Legislative, which met on 1 October, was more radical than its predecessor and was to justify Marie-Antoinette's observation to Barnave of 31 August: 'Despite the decrees, the Constitution and the oaths, who can guarantee that [the next legislature] will not want to change everything and that the republican party will not regain the upper hand? If that happens, where is the force to prevent it?' The self-denying ordinance rendering ex-Constituents ineligible for the new Assembly worked against continuity. The aristocratic right wing entirely disappeared, many to join the Princes at Coblenz, and there were only about twenty nobles in the Legislative Assembly. The new right was made up of the constitutional monarchists, whether followers of La Fayette or of the triumvirs. They were in the most false and hopeless position of all, defending a constitution in which no one believed, in which they did not believe themselves, many of them hoping to modify it through a foreign adventure which would tend to strengthen the Executive, though La Fayette would have severely restricted the personal role of Louis XVI. Of the new deputies, 264 joined the Feuillant Club, to be joined by a further seventy by the end of the year.

The left wing was numerically inferior — 136 joined the Jacobin Club — but they tended to include the more eloquent speakers, notably a group of lawyers from the Département of the Gironde headed by Vergniaud; they were allied with Brissot and the ex-Constituents Pétion and Buzot. A smaller group were to acquire the name Montagnards because they sat on the extreme left of the Assembly where the seats banked steeply; they were suspicious of everyone else. From the outset the Girondins sought a confrontation with the King: by introducing savage legislation against the émigrés and the refractory priests and by seeking war with Louis's brother-in-law the Emperor, they aimed to manœuvre him either into identifying himself with their interpretation of the Revolution or appearing a traitor. Some were republicans, all wanted to capture the Ministry.

The King and the Constitution

Like his grandfather before him, Louis had always tended to evade responsibility for individual difficult decisions (this was reciprocated by his ministers). With the appointment of Brienne in 1787 the note of 'don't blame me' emerges and with his acceptance of the Constitution this becomes his settled view. The full text of his conversation with Molleville about the Constitution runs:

> Here then is what I think: I am far from regarding the Constitution as a masterpiece. I think that it has great defects and that if I had been permitted to make some observations some useful changes might have been made. But it is too late for that now: I have sworn to maintain it, warts and all, and I am determined, as indeed I should, to keep my oath rigorously. My opinion is that the literal execution of the Constitution is the best way of making the Nation see the alterations to which it is susceptible.

In this task Louis was aided by the fact that 'the Constitution was not very well-known by the public', whereas he had an 'amazing memory' and carried a pocket-sized edition around with him everywhere.[1]

Roederer, the *Procureur-Général* of the *feuillant* Département of Paris, describes the exasperation of the constitutional monarchists at this attitude: 'In accepting the good offices of La Rochefoucauld, of La Fayette, of the departmental administration, of the General Staff of the National Guard, he did not assist with any of his resources nor fortify them with any of his personal adherents nor with any conclusive act testifying to his sincerity; he did not encourage them by any mark of gratitude or of confidence.'[2]

The members of the departmental administration of Paris resigned in discouragement in July 1792, tormented, Roederer adds, by the 'secret anxiety or rather the intimate conviction of his political bad faith, a conviction repressed only by his need to hide it from themselves'.[3] In the same spirit Barnave asked that 'the King resume his wonted pleasures [hunting] and furnish his palace of the Tuileries'.[4] The general problem is put succinctly by Orléans's son Louis-Philippe in his memoirs. Louis XVI, he argued, possessed two kinds of authority, that derived from the Constitution and that derived from God and his ancestors, which no legislation could abolish overnight. His failing was in not putting the latter at the disposal of the former.[5]

The most striking example of Louis's detachment concerns ministerial appointments. On 31 October Montmorin tendered his resignation as Foreign Secretary and du Moutier was asked to succeed him but, Marie-Antoinette writes to Fersen, 'he has refused . . . and I even dissuaded him. He is a man to put by for better times.'[6] Writing to Mercy, La Marck elaborates on this: 'It appears that it is out of esteem for M. du Moutier that they [the King and Queen] have not wanted him in the Ministry. I also know that they have said that they regretted appointing M. Bertrand because they are satisfied with him.'[7] This attitude, however, can partly be explained by the perils which the Constitution attached to the office of minister, especially the provisions relating to ministerial responsibility which is conceived of as criminal rather than political: in November 1791 Isnard told the Assembly, 'by [ministerial] responsibility we mean death'. Article XXVII of the Constitution, which stipulated that there should be no Prime Minister, stemmed from the Constituent Assembly's obsession with pinning down individual ministerial responsibility. On the same grounds two of his colleagues objected when Montmorin, after his resignation, wished to continue attending the Council as a minister-without-portfolio.[8] Thus the Ancien Régime notion of a *ministre* as a life appointment and the late development of the office of Prime Minister ended for reasons quite extraneous to their origins. Also stemming from the desire for precise ministerial responsibility was the stipulation that there should be a 'Cabinet secretary' to keep minutes of Council meetings — a practice which to the regret of historians did not obtain under the Ancien Régime. Louis deferred making this appointment until June 1792, when he bowed to pressure from the Girondins in the Assembly.

If, however, the perils of the King and his ministers were now greater, their position had a solidity in relation to the Legislative Assembly it had not possessed in relation to the Constituent. For though the political situation continued to deteriorate to the point when many dared not accept ministerial office, the King's constitutional position was rescued from the shifting sands of the period when the legislature also possessed the 'dictatorship of constituent power'. Louis fought doggedly for his constitutional rights, in particular by his fearless use of the veto.

Moreover, if Louis sought to discredit the Constitution by the literal application of its provisions, the Girondins sought to destroy the compromise on which it was based by introducing divisive legislation. On 9 November they had a decree passed enjoining all émigrés to return to France within two months upon pain of being considered suspect of conspiracy, having their lands confiscated and being punished by death. On 29 November another decree declared that priests not taking an oath to the Constitution within eight days were to be 'considered suspect of revolt against the law and of evil intentions towards the Fatherland'. They were to be stripped of their pensions and held responsible for all religious disturbances in their neighbourhood.

These two decrees were the negation of the Rule of Law and prefigured the National Convention's Law of Suspects, for it does not follow that simply by being an émigré or a non-juring priest one is a traitor. Their main purpose was to embarrass the King, who used his suspensive veto on both decrees. The veto on the émigré law was accompanied by a second letter from Louis to his brothers which he wanted to be communicated to the Assembly, but, as he wrote on the projected speech: 'On n'a pas voulu l'écouter'[9] — the Assembly decided that the King was not allowed to give his reasons for applying his veto. On the decree concerning refractory priests, the *feuillant* Département of Paris smoothed his path by requesting him to use his veto. The Département's address was written by Duport and Barnave[10] and was Barnave's last service for the Court before retiring, disillusioned, to his native Dauphiné in January, no longer able to blind himself to Marie-Antoinette's political bad faith and realizing that all sides were moving towards a war with Austria which would destroy the fragile basis of the constitutional monarchy.

The outbreak of war

The key to an understanding of foreign affairs in 1791–2 — and one vouchsafed to none of the parties in France — is that Austria and Prussia, for fifty years mortal enemies, had come to a solid understanding which was ratified by a treaty of alliance on 7 February 1792.

The Emperor Leopold's initial response to the French Revolution had been one of cautious welcome. As Grand Duke of Tuscany, he had granted a constitution to his subjects and after he succeeded his brother Joseph as Emperor in 1790 his consistent advice to Louis had been to give the Constitution a chance. But in 1791 Frederick William II of Prussia gave him to understand that he would no longer oppose the Bavarian exchange provided that Leopold would allow him to pick up Danzig in a second partition of Poland. This meant that Leopold could no longer overlook the trouble being fomented by French revolutionary emissaries in Belgium, since the Elector of Bavaria could hardly be expected to take on a country in turmoil. Leopold believed that there could be no permanent pacification of the province until the revolutionary ferment in France itself had been bottled up. Accordingly, by January 1792 at the latest, he had decided on armed intervention in France — not merely a congress — delaying only to conclude his alliance with Prussia and for the campaigning season to begin.[11]

This knowledge makes a nonsense of the secret diplomacy of Marie-Antoinette who, for all the good it did, might have spared herself the 'prodigious fatigue' of this voluminous correspondence, carried on under the most arduous circumstances, employing a back-breaking code, often written in invisible ink, depending on the chance availability of a safe courier, sometimes sewn into a hat-lining, sometimes placed in a crate of tea. The attraction of an armed congress for her was not just the avoidance of war by the threat of it but also the hope that the Powers — especially Prussia — would restrain her brother Leopold's very real designs on the German-speaking provinces of France, particularly the patrimony of their father, Francis, Duke of Lorraine. Louis probably set little store by this secret diplomacy, but on 3 December 1791 he did write a letter to the King of Prussia, with whom Breteuil, still his secret plenipotentiary, enjoyed good relations. Louis referred to the idea of an armed congress 'at the moment when, despite my acceptance of the new Constitution, the men of faction openly display their aim of completely destroying the remains of the monarchy' — probably a reference to the decrees on the émigrés and the priests.[12] By the time this letter reached Frederick William, he had already decided on joint action with Austria.

Also unaware of the imminent Prusso-Austrian alliance was the

King's uncle, Louis, Comte de Narbonne, illegitimate son of Louis XV, lover of Necker's daughter, Mme de Staël, appointed in December Minister of War in the *feuillant* ministry and quickly becoming its driving force. Narbonne's plan was to secure the benevolent neutrality of Prussia, thereby isolating Austria and enabling France to conduct a military promenade through the territories of the Electors of Mainz and Trier, who were accused of harbouring concentrations of émigré troops. The victorious French army would then be used to close the Jacobin Club and restore monarchical authority. Narbonne received no support from the King who, through Breteuil, repudiated Narbonne's envoy to Frederick William, the Comte de Ségur. Louis, however, did announce on 14 December that he would summon the Elector of Trier, on pain of war, to disperse the émigré formations before 15 January 1792 and, to reinforce this ultimatum, Narbonne announced the formation of three armies under Luckner, Rochambeau and La Fayette, who relinquished his command of the National Guard. In fact the Elector felt in any case that the émigrés had outstayed their welcome: Louis's special envoy to Trier, Bigot de Sainte-Croix, reported to the Foreign Secretary de Lessart that 'the French émigrés are now the masters of the Electorate'.[13] Accordingly, though Breteuil — this time possibly acting on his own initiative — urged the Elector to resist the ultimatum, he immediately complied with it.

The Emperor's new attitude ensured that matters did not rest there, for whilst he accepted the dispersal of the émigrés, he saw fit provocatively to guarantee the Elector's territories from French attack. This enlarged the scope of the conflict and enabled the Girondins, who favoured an ideological War of Nations, to persuade Narbonne to raise his sights from the Elector to the Emperor himself. In the Assembly, Gensonné questioned whether the Emperor's declaration was compatible with the 1756 alliance and on 25 January the Assembly asked Leopold to clarify this point before 1 March, otherwise France would be obliged to go to war.

Narbonne's alliance of convenience with the Girondins led to conflict both with his *feuillant* colleagues in the Ministry, especially the Foreign Minister de Lessart, and with the King. Louis dreaded war — witness his letter to his brothers — despite the possible advantages which could accrue to him either from an unlikely French victory, which would tend to strengthen the Executive, or from defeat, which would give him a role as mediator. De Lessart, who enjoyed his confidence, explained the King's position in a private letter to Noailles, the French Ambassador to Vienna, dated 16 January: 'As you can well believe, the King is at the head of those who are against it [war]; his excellent mind, in conformity with his heart, seeks to reject the very idea. Even were it to be successful, he regards it as a calamity for the Kingdom and a scourge for humanity.'[14]

As much as war itself, however, Louis feared taking responsibility for its outbreak. De Lessart, who was desperately trying to dilute the acidity of the exchanges between France and Austria, posed the question of responsibility in a letter to the King of 19 February:

> Yesterday I went to the Diplomatic Committee [of the Assembly] to give them some idea of the state of relations with the Court of Vienna. I saw that everyone regarded war as inevitable and that the majority ardently desired it; but at the same time they were all for leaving to the King the whole burden of this great decision. They said that the King should make full use of his initiative and that the National Assembly should take no part and that it was better to risk everything [not going to war?] than explain itself on this particular.[15]

Meanwhile, Narbonne sought to put pressure on the King by threatening him with the joint resignations of La Fayette, Luckner and Rochambeau and by introducing them into the Council in a quasi-ministerial capacity. 'On Friday 2 March', Bertrand notes, '[Narbonne] brought them into the Council despite the King's repugnance for such an extraordinary proceeding.' They each remained standing to report on the state of their armies. The King then gave them a sign of dismissal and 'seemed pleased to have thus avoided their presence at the Council'. The generals, however, wanted to read a memorandum and 'since it seemed too long to be read standing, His Majesty sat down and invited the generals to do the same'. The memorandum was totally unimportant but the point was that, under the Ancien Régime at least, to be asked to sit down in the Conseil d'État was to be made a ministre. As if to underline the point, next day La Fayette turned up to a comité of ministers — meeting without the King, in a room adjoining that of the Council — in place of Narbonne to rebuke the ministers for their quarrelling. This is the occasion when La Fayette is credited with saying to the Keeper of the Seals, 'we shall see which of us, the King or myself, has the majority in the Kingdom'.[16] Finally, when Narbonne tried to break the King's favourite minister, Bertrand, Louis dismissed Narbonne on the grounds that he was trying to be a prime minister, a post that as Marie-Antoinette maliciously observed was now forbidden by the Constitution.

The Girondins threw their weight behind Narbonne and, though he was not reinstated, were able to bring down the *feuillant* Ministry by impeaching de Lessart and having him sent before the National High Court at Orléans to stand trial for *lèse-nation*. On this occasion

Vergniaud told the Assembly that 'presumption [of guilt] is sufficient to ground a decree of accusation'. Louis's response was to appoint a ministry not just of Girondin complexion but one which would indubitably be identified with the Girondins in the Assembly and throw responsibility for the consequent declaration of war squarely on to them. This is the gist of an extremely obscure letter to the King from his agent Radix de Sainte-Foy, who had been negotiating the Girondins' entry into the Ministry: 'They [the Girondins] prefer Lacoste to Kersaint for the Marine. As for us, we think that the latter [as more closely associated with the Girondins] would suit the circumstances better. This is not hard to comprehend since this is a kind of gamble which is being proposed to the King and the praise or blame for it [war?] must necessarily redound to its prime movers.'[17]

As expected, the new Girondin Ministry recommended a declaration of war against Austria, Louis insisting not just on the unanimous advice of the Ministry but on retaining the signed, holograph opinion of the individual ministers — a variant of the tactic he had employed when relations were sensitive with Austria in 1784–5. On this occasion, though, he had the opinions published by the Imprimerie Royale together with the précis he had made of the *rapport* of the new Foreign Secretary, Dumouriez.[18] Then, on 20 April, as prescribed by the Constitution, the King went to the Assembly to propose war on the King of Bohemia and Hungary, Francis II, son of the Emperor Leopold, who had died suddenly in March. The King's proposals were ecstatically accepted, with only seven dissenters. Louis was pale and stammered; there were tears in his eyes; he delivered his speech in a monotone as if to distance himself from his words, as in a modern Speech from the Throne.[19] On 3 August he was to tell the Assembly that 'my former ministers know what efforts I made to avoid war'.

The war, in Reihard's words, 'revolutionized the Revolution'. A King who thought that constitutional rectitude marked the limit of his duty to France was not acceptable at a time of national danger; nor was a queen suspected of betraying the French war plans to the enemy. Isnard accused her of this in the Assembly on 15 May but without the proof we possess. On 26 March, before the declaration of war, she had given Mercy a résumé of the campaign being planned in the Council, whilst on 5 June she wrote to Fersen: 'Luckner's army has been ordered to attack immediately; he is against this but the Ministry wants it. The troops are lacking in everything and in the greatest disorder.' On 23 June she writes again to Fersen: 'Dumouriez leaves tomorrow for Luckner's army; he has promised to rouse Brabant to rebellion.' It is arguable that her action was prompted less by treachery than by her fear that if Austria lost Belgium, and with it the Bavarian exchange, she would seek compensation at the expense of France's eastern provinces. Fear of Austrian expansion was becoming an obsession with her and stands in marked contrast with her views before the Revolution. It is echoed in Fersen's letter to her of 21 June:

> The Emperor plans a dismemberment [of France] ... but there is perhaps a way of preventing it, it is to give the King of Prussia a written undertaking for the payment [of his expenses]: he wants it but the King's signature is necessary. I still have one blank seal left which I have not mentioned to the B. [aron de Breteuil]. Do you want me to make use of it if it might be of use in assuring us of the King of Prussia's opposition to any dismemberment? ... it would be good to have three more [blank seals].

On 3 July the Queen sent the seals and, a surely unrelated event, Prussia duly entered the war. This reassured Marie-Antoinette. It was also a more serious threat to France: the French offensive against Austria in the Low Countries collapsed wherever it met with resistance, but the Austrians had not embarked on a major counter-offensive. Prussia, however, with a formidable army and with one eye on Poland, offered a swift and intense campaign.

The fall of the monarchy

The King did not make the Girondins behave responsibly by giving them power. They continued to devise decrees which would embarrass him. Between 27 May and 8 June he was asked to sanction a decree abolishing his constitutional Bodyguard, which had only been set up on 16 March, another establishing a camp of twenty thousand *fédérés* or provincial National Guards near Paris, and a third ordering the deportation of refractory priests. Louis wanted to veto the decree abolishing his constitutional guard, a useful force of eighteen hundred men for the most part loyal, but since none of his ministers was prepared to countersign his veto he was obliged to give his sanction.[20] Thus disarmed, however, he did not intend to deliver himself to the mercies of the *fédérés*; nor had he any intention of sanctioning the deportation of what he regarded as the only Catholic clergy in France. Exploiting a split which had developed within the Ministry, on 12 June he dismissed the most instransigent, Roland (Interior), Servan (War) and Clavière (Finance), retaining Dumouriez, Duranthon, the Keeper of the Seals, and Lacoste at the Marine. Dumouriez may have suggested this manœuvre, but he was nevertheless dismissed by the King on

16 June — Louis's diary specifically refers to a *renvoi* — and took up a command at the Front. It was hard to find replacement ministers. One who accepted, Mourges, resigned after twenty-four hours when he realized that countersigning vetoes was to be part of his job. On 18 June Louis finally persuaded Duranthon to countersign the vetoes, but he advised the King to conceal this fact until after the presentation to the Assembly of the two *feuillants* who had finally been prevailed upon to accept the Departements of War and Foreign Afairs. The strain plunged Duranthon into nervous depression; he told the King that 'public affairs are necessarily suffering from the state of stupor into which I have fallen'.[21] In early July, the King let him go.

Louis must have smiled inwardly, for he was in a similar condition himself. The impeachment of de Lessart — which was compared with that of Strafford — shook his composure, and the false position in which he was placed by the declaration of war must have been a great strain. His silences became more and more protracted. Mme Campan writes: 'About this time [May] the King fell into a state of despondence which amounted almost to physical helplessness. He passed ten successive days without uttering a single word, even in the bosom of his family; except, indeed, in playing backgammon with Madame Elizabeth, when he was obliged to pronounce the words belonging to that game. On one occasion he failed to recognize his son and asked who the child was.'[22] The activity involved in his use of the vetoes seems to have shaken him out of this fit of blank despair.

The dismissal of the Girondin ministers, amid a growing conviction that the King was planning to seize control of Paris before the arrival of émigré or allied troops, provoked a reaction similar to (and as unfounded as) that caused by the dismissal of Necker in 1789. A petition was due to be presented to the King asking him to withdraw his veto to the two decrees on 20 June, the double anniversary of the Tennis Court Oath and the flight to Varennes. Apprehensively, Louis wrote to his confessor, M. Hébert, on the 19th: 'Come and see me; I have never stood in so great a need of your consolations. I have finished with men; I look to Heaven. Great misfortunes are expected tomorrow; I shall have courage.'[23]

Fortified by the last sacrament, Louis, who expected to be assassinated and, according to Montmorin, 'for some months had been acting like a man preparing himself for death', had the courage to endure not the orderly presentation of a petition, but the occupation of the Tuileries for four hours by a mob drawn from the radical Sections. During this time Louis stood on a window-seat with nothing between him and the mob but a table and a handful of grenadiers. He humoured the crowd by wearing a cap of liberty and toasting the Nation, but would not give his sanction to the decrees. 'I am your king. I have never swerved from the Constitution,' Louis said. 'We'll come back every day until he sanctions the decrees', was heard from the crowd. 'Sire, do not be afraid,' said a grenadier. 'I am not afraid; put your hand on my heart, it is pure and calm' — and he thrust the soldier's hand on to his chest. The authorities — Pétion the Girondin Mayor of Paris, the Assembly, Santerre of the National Guard — let it go on for hours. Arriving on the scene, Pétion said: 'Sire, I have just this minute learned of the situation you are in.' 'That is very surprising, this has been going on for two hours.' The crowd finally left at eight in the evening. 'Pétion is my enemy', Louis had told Dumouriez, and when next day Pétion tried to justify his conduct, Louis told him to 'shut up' and turned his back on him. Marie-Antoinette feared that this would do the King damage.[24]

Louis's passive courage temporarily rekindled support for the monarchy. Baffled, the Girondins now had either to accept defeat or to overthrow the throne. In early July an orchestrated campaign began for Louis's dethronement (*déchéance*): the Assembly was flooded with petitions from Clubs, Sections, from town and country. On 31 July the Mauconseil Section declared that it withdrew its allegiance from the King. 'The *journée* of 20 June forebodes another,' said Marie-Antoinette,[25] whilst on 27 July Louis entered in his diary: 'alert the whole day'. Meanwhile, on 25 July, the Duke of Brunswick, general-issimo of the Prussian army, issued a manifesto which threatened Paris with total destruction if the Royal Family were harmed or the Tuileries invaded again. Marie-Antoinette had been pressing for such a declaration and Fersen had a hand in drafting it,[26] but its very vehemence was counter-productive and increased rather than diminished the perils of the Royal Family.

Faced with the imminence of a second rising, the King had two choices. One was to try to hold out in Paris until the Prussians arrived (Marie-Antoinette had their itinerary; by the end of August they reached Verdun, the last fortress between them and Paris). This plan would involve doing some kind of a deal with the Girondins (themselves engulfed in a wider movement they could no longer control), spending money lavishly on buying support in Paris and putting the Tuileries in some sort of defensive posture. The other choice was for the King to put his trust in La Fayette, 'the only man', as Elizabeth had put it, 'who by placing himself on a horse can give the King an army'.

Relations between the Queen and La Fayette continued desperate, but by the summer, Bertrand notes, the King's mistrust for La Fayette 'had largely been dispelled'. La Fayette in turn believed that the King's technical adherence to the Constitution was sufficient, since it allowed him only 'the exercise of a very limited and scarcely dangerous power'.[27] In this frame of mind, La Fayette made two attempts to save the constitutional monarchy on his own terms. First, on 28 June he left his army and appeared before the Assembly to denounce the *journée* of 20 June. Next day, according to Louis's diary, 'there was to have been a review of the 2nd Legion [of the National Guard] in the Champs Elysées'. La Fayette planned to review this loyal legion with the King, harangue it, and march with it to close down the Jacobins. La Fayette claims that the Queen told Pétion, as Mayor of Paris, to countermand orders for the review.[28] At all events, only a few Guards turned up and La Fayette returned to his army.

La Fayette's second attempt was a plan to get the King out of Paris. It had been arranged that La Fayette's Army of the Rhine and Luckner's Army of Flanders should exchange positions. This meant that at one point, at Compiègne, La Fayette's army would pass within twenty leagues of Paris. In terms of the Constitution the King could not step outside this limit and Louis, who wanted to play by the rules, insisted on strictly observing this.[29] La Fayette was to arrive in Paris and announce to the Assembly that the King was going to his palace of Compiègne, as was his entitlement under the Constitution. They would leave under the escort of the Swiss and loyal units of National Guards.

On 11 July Marie-Antoinette wrote to Fersen: 'The Const. [itutionalists] in conjunction with La Fayette and Luckner want to conduct the King to Compiègne the day after the Federation [15 July]. For this purpose the two generals are gong to arrive there. The King is disposed to lend himself to this project; the Queen is against it. The outcome of this great venture which I am far from approving is still in doubt.' This brief, coded note reveals a clash, in extremis, between the King and the Queen which is not just a tactical one of whether to leave Paris or stay put; not just a matter of personalities — Marie-Antoinette's 'it would be too appalling to owe our lives to that man twice', the first time being the October Days — but a symbolic clash over whether to rely on the Prussians or on the internal forces of the Constitutional Monarchy. For La Fayette intended that the King should issue a proclamation from Compiègne forbidding his brothers or the foreign troops to advance any further.[30] Mercy[31] and Fersen had both urged Marie-Antoinette to stay put in Paris, Fersen specifically warning: 'If you do [risk flight] you must never summon La Fayette, but the neighbouring Départements.'[32] In the end, it was Marie-Antoinette's opinion that prevailed rather than that of Louis, who informed La Fayette, politely, that his plan was not practicable.[33]

Apart from his wife's opinion, two further considerations must have weighed with the King. The first was that whereas the triumvirs the previous year had genuinely sought to increase his powers, La Fayette intended that Louis should play the *roi fainéant* to his Mayor of the Palace. As a foretaste of what he could expect from La Fayette, the *feuillant* Ministry offered its collective resignation on 10 July — a move concerted with La Fayette to throw the King on his mercy and make him accept the escape plan.[34] The second consideration was that if he abandoned Paris before the Prussians arrived, they might put his brothers forward. La Fayette has him saying: 'I do not want to fall foul of my brothers by going to Compiègne.' He stayed put as he had in 1789, when he feared that Orléans would seize a vacant throne. As La Fayette said: 'He feared the victor whoever it was.'[35]

Having rejected La Fayette's escape plan and also another for a withdrawal to Normandy.[36] Louis had to secure his position in Paris as best he could. Negotiations were opened with the Girondins Gensonné and Vergniaud through the Court painter Boze and the Keeper of the Seals, Dejoly. Vergniaud reminded the King that 'he had been sadly deceived if he had been led to believe that not to depart from the letter of the Constitution was to do all that he should'. He suggested that the King should enlarge his Council by including three popular ex-Constituents; also that he should take a personal initiative to bring about a cease-fire. The King, in a reply which Dejoly considered 'would not satisfy either a friend of liberty or a man of ambition. It is dry and negative', says nothing about enlarging the Council; the cease-fire can be effected only by 'les moyens généraux', i.e. official diplomacy. Louis acidly observes that 'we owe the declaration of war entirely to the self-styled patriot ministers'.[37]

Nevertheless, the Girondins, ever hopeful of storming the Ministry a second time, pursuing their tactic of 'threatening the Court and attracting it to them',[38] staved off the impending insurrection three times before it broke with the dawn on 10 August.[39] The Palace was in a far better state of defence than it had been on 20 June. There were a thousand Swiss Guards, absolutely loyal, another thousand mounted police and two thousand National Guards. There were also about three hundred armed nobles — two thousand had been summoned — who did more harm than good by antagonizing the National Guard. Montmorin was there and Malesherbes, who was not used to wearing a sword and was terrified of tripping over it and breaking his neck.[40] Both had contributed to the outbreak of the Revolution, as had the King, and they were staying in Paris to die with the monarchy. Otherwise, they feared their ministerial careers would be misunderstood.[41] It was the highest sense of ministerial responsibility, not political or criminal, but moral.

These forces, Reinhard considers, were 'enough to contain the insurrection, perhaps to crush it'. But all depended on the attitude of the National Guard, Parisian and provincial — the *fédérés* who were going via Paris to a camp at Soissons whose formation Louis had allowed. In prospect was an internecine struggle within the National Guard, one battalion turning out for the King, one against him, within a single battalion the grenadiers maybe for the King and the gunners against. But the balance was tipped during the night by the replacement of the Municipality, from which the National Guard took its orders, by a revolutionary Commune comprising delegates from the Sections. It was thus a dejected king who went down to review his troops at six o'clock. He was silent and depressed; his ingrained timidity stood him in bad stead; this was not physical fear — he scorned to wear the padded *gilet* Marie-Antoinette had provided — but, as she said, 'he fears above everything else speaking to assembled men'; he could find no rousing words. The most loyal troops had been placed nearest the Palace — they shouted 'Vive le Roi!' — but as he progressed, his reception became cooler. 'My God, they are booing the King!' shouted a minister; 'What the devil is he doing down there? Let's go and fetch him quickly.' He was brought back.

Roederer, of the Departement, advised that resistance was impossible and that the Royal Family should take refuge in the Assembly. The King looked at his ministers, his last Council, and said, 'Come, gentlemen, there is nothing more to be done here', and, raising his hand, 'let us go and make this last sacrifice to the Nation.' The Queen said nothing but turned green with chagrin. Louis said to the Maréchal de Mailly, whom he had put in charge of the Tuileries, 'We shall be back — once calm has been restored'.

Roederer led the little procession, the Royal Family, the Ministers, the Departmental officials, along a double line of soldiers to the Assembly. From the King's bedroom Mme de Tourzel's daughter saw this sad procession pass on its way: 'The idea of a funeral procession came to mind; it was indeed the cortège of the monarchy.' In the night there had been a fall of leaves and the gardeners had put them in piles along the route the procession took. The Dauphin kicked them carelessly. 'The leaves are falling early this year,' Louis said to Roederer.

On leaving the Palace, Louis had omitted to countermand the orders to defend it. This the Swiss Guards did, killing or seriously wounding about three hundred insurgents. When Louis, at about ten o'clock, finally gave orders to the Swiss to stop firing, they were butchered almost to a man.

The Assembly did as much for the King as it dared under mob pressure. Louis was suspended from his functions, not deposed: his fate was to be decided by a new assembly, a National Convention voted by manhood suffrage. Vergniaud even proposed that the Dauphin's governor, M. de Fleurieu, be replaced, from which Louis took some negative comfort.

The Royal family spent the day crowded together in the reporters' box. At two in the morning they were transferred to the neighbouring Convent of the Feuillants, where they remained for three days. Their final destination was to be the Temple, the grim medieval habitation of the former Knights Templar. Its massive central tower, with pointed roof, walls nine feet thick and mere slits of windows, looked like a prison. The precise point at which the King, who after all had sought refuge in the Assembly, became a prisoner is hard to discern. To Louis it seemed to come on 11 August, when his attendants were ordered to leave the Feuillants: 'I am then in prison, and less fortunate than Charles I, who was allowed to keep all his friends with him to the scaffold.' Knowing that the King was penniless, his courtiers emptied their pockets, but Louis said: 'Keep your purses, gentlemen, you will need them more than we shall, as you will have longer to live, I hope.'

On 13 August, at six o'clock in the evening, the Royal Family left the Feuillants and were driven, through immense hostile crowds, to the Temple. The carriage stopped at the Place Vendôme, where Louis contemplated the equestrian statue of Louis XIV which had been thrown down from its pedestal. 'That, Sire,' said the municipal officer, Manuel, with studied insolence, 'is how the people treats its kings.' 'It is fortunate', replied the King, who like many a fallen monarch was beginning to find the right words, 'that it confines its attention to inanimate objects.' Night was falling when the party reached the Temple, where they were met by the officials of the Commune — hats on head, addressing the King as Monsieur not Sire — which had assumed responsibility for their custody.[42]

16

The Prisoner of the Temple

In the Temple, no less than at Versailles, Louis's life was governed by a daily routine. He rose between six and seven o'clock, shaved and dressed himself. Then he retired into a little side-turret which served as oratory (he followed the Church year in the breviary used in the diocese of Paris) and study. Before he was moved to the Great Tower, he had access to the library of the Knights of Malta, which contained some 1,500 volumes, of which he read 250. One day, pointing at the works of Rousseau and Voltaire, he whispered to Hue, the Dauphin's valet-de-chambre, 'Those two men have ruined France'.

The main purpose of his reading was to prepare himself to educate the Dauphin and in particular he sought to brush up his Latin. He talked about the various Latin authors to one of the municipal officers, who adds perceptively: 'He struck me as very anxious to demonstrate that he is informed.'[1] On 22 November he applied to the Commune for a further thirty-three French and Latin authors. His request was granted, but only after one member of the Council objected: 'The prisoner was scarcely sure of a fortnight's existence and the books he was requesting would be enough to occupy him for a very long life.'

At nine o'clock the family came up to the King's room for breakfast, which would consist of coffee, chocolate, fruit, bread and milk foods. At about ten o'clock they all went up to the Queen's room on the third floor, where the ladies sewed whilst Louis instructed his son, mainly in Latin and geography; but, as the King's valet-de-chambre, Cléry, notes, 'it was the new geography of France that the King showed him'. The Dauphin's lessons in mathematics had to be abandoned because his jailers thought he was being taught to write in code.[2]

At noon the family walked outside to give the children some air and exercise, returning at two o'clock for the *dîner*, which was quite an elaborate affair with two main courses and dessert, red and white wine. The King usually drank half a bottle of champagne and a glass of liqueur with the dessert. This food cost 80,000 francs a month and was

223

provided by two chefs and eleven subordinates taken straight from the *bouche* or *cuisine* of the Tuileries.[3]

After the *dîner*, Louis and Marie-Antoinette would play piquet or backgammon until four, when the King had a nap. At six, Louis gave his son more lessons or played games with him. After supper, at nine o'clock, the King retired to his study and read until midnight.

This ordered life was punctuated by various privations and alarms. On the night of 19/20 August, the Royal Family were deprived of Mme de Tourzel and the Princesse de Lamballe, the Queen's companion and kinswoman. They were imprisoned in La Force. On 2 September, Hue was arrested. Soon the prisoners were left with only Cléry. The Queen and Mme Elizabeth mended the King's clothes whilst Marie-Antoinette asked Cléry to teach her daughter how to do her own hair, finding this preferable to being attended by the wives and relatives of municipal officers.[4]

Events from the outside world filtered through, sometimes slowly, sometimes with brutal immediacy. The Prussian advance continued, throwing into doubt the result of the insurrection of 10 August: the municipal officer, Mathieu, mindful of Brunswick's threat, asked one of Louis' servants: 'Beg him [the King] to write to ... [the King of Prussia] to halt his march and save himself and the town.'[5] The fortress of Longwy fell on 23 August and on 1 September news reached Paris that Verdun, the last fortress between the Prussians and Paris, was about to capitulate. At four o'clock on the 2nd the populace responded by breaking into the prisons and started to massacre the inmates. The slaughter continued uninterrupted until the 7th, by which time about half the prisoners had perished — roughly 1,200 people, only a third of whom were political prisoners.

Montmorin perished and another obvious target for the *septembriseurs*, the Princesse de Lamballe. The mob took her corpse and severed head to the Temple and sought admittance but were kept out by the expedient of stretching the tricolour sash of one of the municipal officers across the main entrance (Cléry had to find forty-five sous for the sash). Not to be thwarted, the mob lifted the Princesse's head aloft on the end of a pike so that it was visible from the windows of the Tower. A dispute arose between the municipal officers and the National Guard as to whether the Royal Family should show themselves at the windows. Louis asked a Guard what was going on, receiving the brutal reply: 'Very well, Monsieur, since you want to know, it's the head of Mme de Lamballe they want to show you. I advise you to show yourselves unless you want the people to come up.' The Queen fainted. The King replied: 'We were ready for everything, Monsieur; but you could have dispensed with telling the Queen this appalling news.'[6]

One of the first acts of the National Convention was the proclamation of the Republic on 21 September. Louis's municipal jailors now multiplied opportunities for calling him Monsieur and sat down in his presence. One of them, called Rocher, knowing that the *ci-devant* King had an aversion to pipe-smoke, took delight in blowing it in his face.[7] But despite having to endure such petty vexations, Louis found in his settled life, free from responsibility, bounded by welcome family duties and religious observances and lived from day to day, a serenity he had rarely experienced since 1787. Nor at first were the new masters of the country disposed to alter this state of affairs, though the King himself had long believed that his trial was inevitable. It was brought about by a change in the fortunes of the war and by the discovery, in the panelling of the Tuileries, of a document-safe, the famous *armoire de fer*.

On 22 September Dumouriez, after brilliant manœuvres, checked the Prussians at Valmy, very near Varennes, and allowed them to retreat. He then turned on the Austrians in Belgium, defeated them at Jemappes on 6 November, and a week later entered Brussels. These victories robbed Louis of his status as a valuable hostage and though Dumouriez personally favoured a restoration of the monarchy, this only served further to endanger the life of the King.

Then, on 20 November, Roland, the Minister of the Interior, made his dramatic announcement to the Convention concerning the discovery of the *armoire de fer*. Louis had constructed this himself after the insurrection of 20 June but he had had to employ the services of one Gamain to fit the lock. Louis's joinery had been so skilful that, but for Gamain's belated delation, the *armoire* might never have been discovered. The discovery was damaging to Louis because the papers found in the sack of the Tuileries had proved little more than that the King had continued paying his Bodyguards even after they had emigrated and joined the Princes at Coblenz. Nevertheless, the new discoveries did not provide any proof of dealings with the foreign Powers: since Louis and Marie-Antoinette systematically burned such papers, that proof came only when the papers of their correspondents became available. Soboul in *Le procès de Louis XVI* claims that 'the papers in the *armoire de fer* brought proof that Louis XVI was conducting a correspondence with Calonne'.[8] In fact they prove only that Calonne wrote letters to the King: on one of them Louis wrote 'point répondu' and Calonne received no letters from the King,[9] to his great grief. His rival Breteuil had fared better and the Convention had at its disposal letters found on the Prussians which hinted at Louis's relations with him, though the lead was not followed up.[10]

What the documents in the *armoire de fer* do reveal is Louis's dealings with Mirabeau, Talon, La Fayette and Dumouriez — the exercise of eighteenth-century patronage by a constitutional monarch but no less shocking to the deputies for that: they created the climate in which the trial of the King could proceed.

At eleven o'clock on the morning of 11 December Louis was instructing the Dauphin as usual when two municipal officers entered and took the boy away without explanation (as 'co-conspirators', his family were to be denied access to him). At one o'clock Chambon, who had succeeded Pétion as mayor, was announced and told the King that

> he had come to see him in order to conduct him to the Convention in virtue of a decree [providing] . . . that 'Louis Capet should be brought before the bar of the Convention'. 'I am not called Capet,' said the King, 'it is the name of one of my ancestors. I could have desired, Monsieur, that the commissioners had left me my son during the two hours I have spent waiting for you. In any case this treatment is in accordance with what I have experienced here for four months. I am going to follow you, not in obedience to the Convention but because my enemies are in possession of force majeure.'

Both Robespierre and Louis had thought it would be better for the country if a trial were avoided, Robespierre thinking that the King should simply be executed in accordance with the 'verdict' of 10 August, and Louis preferring and expecting to be assassinated: he had expected this to happen on 20 June and again he expected it on his way to the Convention for his second appearance on 26 December, making his will on Christmas Day. His reflections on the life of Charles I had convinced him that he must above all avoid a formal trial, because that would make the whole nation culpable, a thought which had been developed by Montmorin, in conversation with Bertrand in August: 'If the King is tried and formally condemned, you will not see a monarchy for a long time.'

Louis was brought to the bar and the President addressed him:[11] 'Louis, the French nation accuses you. The National Assembly decreed on 3 December that it would try you . . . you will be read the indictment containing the crimes of which you are accused. You may sit down.' The indictment consisted of thirty-five individual charges, some of them going back to 1789, leading to the general accusation of 'conspiring against liberty and an attempt against the safety of the State'. The general accusation was virtually meaningless, certainly not susceptible of legal proof. Furthermore, the Constitution of 1791, under which France continued to be governed until 1795, envisaged only three acts for which the King was responsible: retracting his oath to uphold the

Constitution, leading an army against the forces of the Nation and leaving the Kingdom. Louis had done none of these things and had, in any case, already incurred the only penalty provided — dethronement. Indeed, as Robespierre rightly observed, if the Constitution of 1791 were applied, the National Convention would be on trial and not the King. The trial was going to be a political one. The President put each charge separately to Louis and he was required to give an immediate reply. Some took him by surprise;[12] nor did he have any counsel — a Bourbon without counsel! — but he answered well, showing considerable presence of mind.

He did not follow the example of Charles I in challenging the competence of the Court, but offered a defence based on the laws in force at the various times when he was supposed to have committed the crimes. Thus to the charge 'You caused an army to march against the citizens of Paris' (in June–July 1789), he replied: 'At that time I could order troops to march where I pleased.' For the period between the fall of the Bastille and his acceptance of the Constitution, he relied on the amnesty for political offences issued at that time. For the period when the Constitution of 1791 was in force, he invoked ministerial responsibility where appropriate. The charges were badly framed and, as Marat observed, there were too many of them. Some were banal: e.g., 'You vetoed [the decree of 29 November against refractory priests]. What have you to answer?' This charge received the obvious reply: 'The Constitution allowed me the free exercise of a veto on decrees.' Some were illogical: e.g., 'After your arrest at Varennes your exercise of the Executive Power was suspended yet you continued to conspire. On 17 July the blood of the citizens was shed on the Champ-de-Mars.' Others were downright silly, as the accusation that he had pretended to be ill in the Spring of 1791 so that a sympathetic public would allow him to go to Saint-Cloud. To this Louis replied: 'This accusation is absurd.' Louis's replies were characteristic: solid but legalistic, negative, unimaginative. He did not offer his own interpretation of the events of the Revolution.

After the charges, Louis was presented with the evidence in the form of documents he had written or received. These he claimed not to recognize. This was pointless and lacking in dignity but he was being presented with the evidence without warning[12] and as he later observed, some of it could have been counterfeited.[13] When he came to Louis's letter to the Bishop to Clermont, even the impassive Barère had to ask: 'Don't you recognize your signature?' 'No,' 'The seal bears the arms of France.' 'Lots of people had it.' At first Louis tried to vary his answers: 'I don't recognize it'; 'Not in the slightest': 'No more than the last'. Then it was just 'No'. Finally he began to lose patience:

'No, no! no, sir, no!' So did the Convention. When Dufriche-Valazé said 'There are many other pieces; I think it would be superfluous to communicate them to the National Convention', the minutes note 'Expression of agreement on all the benches'. Louis finally said: 'I request counsel' and retired. After a violent debate, he was granted legal representation.

The King had missed his *dîner*. When he arrived back at the Temple he ate six cutlets, a chicken and some eggs and went straight to bed.[14]

Louis chose as his defence counsel Target and Tronchet, two of the most celebrated barristers of the 1780s. Target declined the honour, signing his letter to the Convention, 'le républicain Target'. Tronchet, who had been one of the commissioners who had examined the King after his return from Varennes, accepted but in the coolest, most grudging terms.[15] Others wrote to the Convention offering the King their services and among those who risked their life in this way it is good to be able to note Miromesnil.[16] Malesherbes also wrote: '. . . I have been summoned twice to the Council of the man who was my master at a time when this function was coveted by everyone: I owe him the same service when it is a function which many people find dangerous.'[17] Louis accepted the services of Malesherbes who, together with Tronchet, enlisted the services of de Sèze, who had successfully defended Besenval in 1789, to deliver the King's defence.

When Malesherbes was admitted to the Temple, Louis said to him: 'I am sure they will kill me. They have the power and the will. Never mind, let us work on my trial as if I were going to win. And win I shall, since the memory I shall leave behind will be without blemish.' Looking at de Sèze's emotional peroration, Louis said: 'We must delete it; I don't want to soften them.' A municipal officer notes: 'When the members of the [Convention's] Committee . . . brought him the 406 documents relating to his trial, he received them like a grand seigneur receiving the accounts of his steward.'[18]

On 26 December Louis made his second appearance before the Convention. He and his counsel were kept waiting outside the main hall of the Convention. Malesherbes addressed the King as 'Sire' and 'Your Majesty'. The deputy Treilhard rebuked him: 'What then makes you so bold in using here expressions proscribed by the Convention?' 'Contempt for you and for life!'[19]

De Sèze's defence developed the same arguments Louis had employed at the time of his first appearance. He spoke for three hours and Louis was so concerned for him that he wondered if he could have a substitute — like Necker at the opening of the Estates-General! There was something of an emotional peroration, including the words: 'The people wanted liberty, he gave it to them.' There were murmurs from the left and from the galleries and de Sèze crossed out the offending sentence. He ended by reminding them: 'History will judge your judgment and its verdict will be that of centuries to come.'

Louis then delivered a short speech:

You have just heard the arguments for my defence; I shall not repeat them. Speaking to you perhaps for the last time I declare to you that my conscience reproaches me with nothing and that my counsel have told you nothing but the truth. I have never feared a public examination of my conduct; but my heart is rent at finding in the indictment the imputation that I wished to shed the blood of the people and above all that the misfortunes of 10 August should be attributed to me.

I confess that the manifold proofs I have given at all times of my love for the people and the manner in which I have always conducted myself seemed to me sufficient proof that I took little heed of exposing myself to spare its blood and to remove such an imputation from me for ever.[20]

After some further questions about the keys to the *armoire de fer* Louis retired. On his way back to the Temple he heard some confused shouting. The guards raised the windows. 'I thought they were shouting Vive La Fayette!' Louis mused, 'that would be stupid.' When Malesherbes told him of such a plan to rescue him, Louis replied: 'Tell them that I will not pardon them if there is a single drop of blood shed for me. I did not desire it to be shed when it might perhaps have saved my throne and my life. I do not regret this.'[21]

The Convention did not proceed immediately to a vote. For a fortnight the parties manœuvred. Many of the Girondins, obscurely aware that the King's death would enlarge the conflict, at home and abroad, devised ways of saving his life — an appeal to the people organized in Primary Assemblies; a diversionary attack on the Duc d'Orléans, sitting in the Convention as Philippe-Égalité. Dumouriez came to Paris to put his laurels discreetly at the King's service, but his intervention was counterproductive. Danton is said to have guaranteed to save the King's life if Pitt would give him two million francs, and Pitt to have refused.[22] Louis himself believed that 'the majority of deputies could easily have been bought'. He had been lent money for the purpose but was scrupulous about using it for corruption. The Civil List, he told Malesherbes, had been a different matter, 'being only the just equivalent of the money from my domains.'[23]

Finally, between 14 and 20 January, the Convention voted on four motions. The first was phrased: 'Is Louis Capet, former King of the French, guilty of conspiring against liberty and an attempt against the safety of the State? Yes or no.' 691 voted 'yes', with twenty-seven abstentions. No one voted against the motion. The second motion, proposed on 15 January, concerned the appeal to the people. The voting was 287 for, 424 against, with twelve abstentions. The third motion was on Louis's punishment — death, banishment, imprisonment or whatever. The voting lasted thirty-six hours and could not have been closer: out of 721 voters, only 361 voted unconditionally for death — a majority of one. Given the closeness of this vote, a fourth motion was put, whether there should be a reprieve, but this was rejected by a majority of seventy. The Convention decreed that Louis should be notified 'within the day' and executed twenty-four hours after this notification. The Convention rose at three o'clock on the morning of 20 January 1793.

Malesherbes wanted to break the news to the King himself. All morning he hung around outside the Temple but was several times denied admission. He had, however, told him of the third vote, that of the death penalty, and saw him for the last time on the 19th. On taking leave of the King, Malesherbes says: 'I could not hold back my tears. "Tender-hearted old man," said the King squeezing my hand, "don't cry: we shall meet again in a happier life. I regret leaving behind such a friend as you. Adieu! As you leave the room, control yourself; you have to remember that they will be watching you . . . Adieu! Adieu!" '[24]

At two in the afternoon Garat, the Minister of Justice, informed Louis that he would be executed within twenty-four hours. Listening to the Convention's decree, Louis displayed no emotion except at the words 'conspiring against liberty', when a 'smile of contempt' played on his lips. Garat was astounded at the King's 'superhuman courage'. This stemmed from his religious faith. For much of his life he had been a pragmatist thrown among ideologues, but for its last act he had an ideology fitted to the occasion. After Garat had read out the decree, Louis produced a document from his portfolio. In it he requested 'a three-day stay of execution to prepare myself to appear before the presence of God'; the right to see a priest of his choice and to see his family 'without witnesses'.[25]

The Convention rejected the first but granted the other two requests. Garat then returned to the Temple at six o'clock, bringing with him the Abbé Edgeworth de Firmont, Mme Elizabeth's former confessor, who had been advised by Malesherbes of the King's choice of a man 'whose obscurity may save him from persecution'.[26] The King conferred with his confessor until half-past-eight, when the Abbé withdrew to one of the side-turrets so as not to alarm Louis's family, who were now admitted for the first time in six weeks.

His daughter, Mme Royale, has left this account of their meeting:

We found him greatly changed. He wept for our grief but not for his death. He told my mother about his trial, excusing the scoundrels who were bringing about his death. He repeated to my mother that people had wanted the Primary Assemblies but that he had not because that would have disturbed France. Then he gave sound religious teachings to my brother; above all he commanded him to pardon those who were about to cause his death. He gave his blessing to my brother and myself. My mother desperately wanted us to spend the night with my father. He refused, having need of tranquillity.[27]

As they parted from the King, their screams could be heard on the staircase, through the massive doors. His daughter was carried out fainting.

Louis turned to his confessor: ' "Ah! Monsieur," he said to me throwing himself into a chair, "what an encounter I have just had. Must I love and be loved so tenderly? But that is done, let us forget everything else in order to concentrate on the one matter, it alone in this moment must occupy all my love and thought." '[28]

At eleven o'clock Cléry proposed supper. Louis 'hesitated a moment; but on reflection accepted the offer'. Cléry has left this description of the King's last meal: 'The King ate, with a good appetite, two wings of a chicken and a few vegetables, drank two glasses of wine mixed with water and, for dessert, a little finger-biscuit and some Malaga wine.'

After supper Edgeworth suggested — what Louis had hardly dared hope for — the possibility of celebrating mass in the morning. The municipal officers not only acceded to this request, but scoured the neighbouring churches for the necessary accoutrements. Louis went to bed at about half-past-twelve: 'I [Cléry] undressed the King and as I was about to curl his hair, he said to me: "It's not worth it!" Then, lying down, as I was closing his curtains: "Cléry, you will wake me at five o'clock!" ' He slept soundly, no doubt with that 'continuous and most extraordinary snoring' for which he was noted.[29]

In the morning, just before nine, Louis left the Temple with the commander of the National Guard, Santerre, and Edgeworth, who was permitted to accompany him to the scaffold. He had wanted Cléry to cut his hair, to facilitate the task of the executioners, but they were refused scissors: 'These men see daggers and poison everywhere, they fear I will kill myself. Alas they know me very badly; to kill myself would be weakness. No, since die I must I will die well!' As he went out of his room he fought his last battle of etiquette: '[The National Guards'] faces were anything but assured. They all, however, had their hats on their heads. The King noticed it and asked for his own.'

He asked for his will to be given to the Queen — 'to my wife', he corrected.[30]

He was taken to the place of his execution — the former Place Louis XV — not in a tumbril but in a carriage, a security measure which helped him to die with dignity. Snow still lay from a heavy fall and the three-mile journey took an hour-and-a-half to complete. 130,000 men, practically the whole armed force of Paris, lined the streets. Louis looked 'pensive but not downcast'. On the way Edgeworth and the King recited alternate verses from the psalms for the dying.

When Louis descended from the carriage, three executioners rushed forward and tried to take his coat off. He pushed them aside, removed it himself and unfastened the collar of his shirt. He was further outraged when they sought to tie his hands behind his back. He looked to Edgeworth for guidance: ' "Sire, in this further outrage I see only a final resemblance between Your Majesty and the God who will be his recompense." "Assuredly . . . nothing less than His example would make me submit to such an affront." Then, turning to the executioners: "Do as you please, I will drain the chalice to the dregs." '[31]

Louis then mounted the scaffold hesitantly, supported on Edgeworth's arm: the steps were steep, his hands were tied behind his back and he was stout and out of exercise. At this point Edgeworth is credited with saying: 'Fils de Saint-Louis, ascendez au ciel.' Whatever he said must have given Louis courage, for he rushed forward to the front of the platform and tried to address the crowd. Santerre had ordered a drum-roll; Louis commanded silence. How many drums stopped beating we do not know; nor how many people heard Louis's words; nor indeed what exactly those words were. The most characteristic version, that of the *Semaines Parisiennes*, runs: 'I die perfectly innocent of the so-called crimes of which I was accused. I pardon those who are the cause of my misfortunes. Indeed, I hope that the shedding of my blood will contribute to the happiness of France and you, unfortunate people . . .' These words may have been broken off by Santerre, by the drum-roll or by the descent of the axe.[32]

Louis's neck was too fat to fit into the groove properly and the back of the neck and jaw-bone were 'mangled horribly'. It is doubtful if this caused Louis any pain, but it produced a lot of blood for which the spectators were literally thirsty. ' "It tastes quite good," some said; "No", others opined, "it's horribly salty." ' Others rubbed their hands in the blood to revenge 'what the wife of the tyrant had said after the Revolution about wanting to wash her hands in the blood of Frenchmen'. Since people wanted to dip handkerchiefs, pikes, envelopes in the blood which had collected in the trough under the guillotine, Sanson, the head executioner, suggested: 'Wait, I'll get you a bucket and then you can dip in more easily.' Not everyone behaved like this. An eighteen-year-old National Guard called Philippe Morrice nearly fainted and had to be revived with brandy. 'Luckily for me,' he relates, 'they were all decent chaps near me and, like me, they found no cause for merriment there.'[33]

Louis's body was taken to the local cemetery, that of the Madeleine, and placed in an anonymous grave. 'Let them take him where they like', wrote the deputy Choudieu, echoing perhaps the great hurt of 1789, 'What's it to us? We always wanted him; he never wanted us.'[34]

Conclusion

In some respects the picture of Louis XVI which has emerged is very different from the conventional stereotype of the stupid, lazy and impassive king. This correction restores to the story of the Revolution an element of tragedy that is absent if one shares with many Pétion's view of its central character: 'truly this mass of flesh is insensible'. The development of the stereotype, held by Louis's contemporaries as well as his historians, stems not from Marie-Antoinette's propagandists but from his own uncommunicative nature, which his education served to develop rather than correct. Louis was in fact fairly intelligent and fairly hard-working — even in prison he had sought to improve himself in order to instruct his son. Moreover, his particular aptitudes, for finance, law and foreign affairs, were suited to the areas with which he was expected to deal.

His reputation for indecisiveness, however, remains intact, though it should be recognized that its character was partly institutional, being determined by the tradition of ruling by counsel and counting votes in the Council. Over the three big decisions at the start of the Revolution (the *Résultat du Conseil*, the *séance royale* and the question of flight to Rambouillet) the Council was split down the middle; in the case of the *Résultat* one source, Lenoir, considered that Louis had acted *too* decisively, to the point of being despotic. However, although consulting the Council was the correct procedure, Louis was not above disregarding it, as over the convocation of the Notables in 1786, and on that occasion he wasted five crucial months making the decision. Over the recall of the parlements in 1774 the problem was rather different: the Council favoured one solution and his personal adviser, Maurepas, another.

This leads to the conclusion that, except during the heyday of Maurepas's *ministère harmonieux*, the Council was itself divided and on issues relating ultimately to the reform of the regime: these divisions were too fundamental to be explained in terms of Louis's failure to hold

234

a ministry together. Moreover, the King did not have untrammelled control over the composition of ministries: ministers often represented pressure groups which could not be disregarded, and ministries were in a sense coalitions. The *reculades* — the precipitate withdrawal of measures introduced with all solemnity — with which Louis was taxed were one natural consequence; the interests which had been ignored regrouped. The surprising thing about a measure such as d'Ormesson's abolition of tax-farming was perhaps not that it was shot down, but that it ever got off the ground.

The immediate cause of the fall of the Ancien Régime was the deficit. For all his understanding of finance, Louis contributed to its increase, by his repudiation of bankruptcy, his failure to impose departmental budgets and his decision to enter the War of American Independence. His repudiation of bankruptcy and the associated increase in the use of loans also implied a greater association of the governed, or at least of the subscribers, in the process of government. From an absolutist standpoint he should be criticized for this. The failure to impose a budget was an unqualified one, for the regime could possibly have absorbed the cost of the war if Castries had not been so profligate. Calonne certainly thought so. It seems with the benefit of hindsight that America would have achieved her independence even without French help. Even so, whether France would then have acquired the same diplomatic prestige is another matter.

In his memoirs Talleyrand referred scathingly to 'ce *fameux* déficit', by which he implied that the deficit was not the cause of the Revolution. Certainly it often disappeared from view during that event, and cynics suggested that the Assembly refused to tackle it so that it could keep the King in tutelage. Moreover, the deficit was endemic under the Ancien Régime and at certain times had been much greater, notably after Louis XIV's wars. The very fact, however, that it was endemic suggested that it represented something deeper than bad accountancy which the King should have corrected. It stemmed from the lack of consent to taxation, which Louis implicitly recognized by his turning to Provincial Assemblies, the Assembly of Notables and finally the Estates-General. Louis grasped this nettle rather than resorting to the 'cop-out' of abandoning a foreign policy (as Louis XV had done at the end of his reign) or doing a deal in extremis with the Parlements.

In attempting to tackle the deficit, Louis discovered, during the Notables, that the ideological basis for the absolute monarchy no longer existed. Calonne's measures were rejected out of hand precisely because they would have rejuvenated the system: the Land Tax was important not so much for the money it would have raised, not even as the collateral for a big loan, but as symbolizing that the regime had not lost the initiative. It is not easy to say why precisely support for the old monarchy had drained away. Perhaps it had been undermined alike by Maupeou's coup and by its reversal; perhaps by parlementaire remonstrances which may have had more immediate practical impact than the *philosophes*. What can be said with precision is that before 1787 the rot had reached the King's immediate agents of execution, the ministers, few of whom believed in the system. This could be simply explained by the failure of Intendants to reach ministerial rank, so that they were outnumbered by military aristocrats who favoured a devolution of power to the aristocracy as their price for paying taxes. It is noteworthy, however, that the Intendants, attacked in the Notables, did not have the will to defend themselves, even though Louis thought they were 'the best part of my system'.

To a large extent, then, an assessment of Louis depends on the intractable question of whether the collapse of the Ancien Régime was inevitable. The same consideration applies to the outbreak and course of the Revolution. We have suggested that the principal ingredient in its outbreak in 1789 was Louis's perceived volte-face in dealing with the Third Estate: this injected a poison into the body politic to which even the death of the King did not provide an antidote. It created the climate of distrust from which Louis never recovered. The image of 'Le Roi parjure, le Roi Janus' was established. What his precise motives were in 1789 we have not fully succeeded in establishing — he seems to have suffered from confusion of aims himself: certainly he did not analyse the situation in 1789 with the same clarity with which he analysed that in 1791.

The struggle in 1789 was not primarily about the extent of his prerogative power, for in the *Résultat* he had already conceded 'more than the Estates-General on bended knees would have dared to ask' and was to concede even more in the *séance royale* of 23 June. It was, however, about his right to make this renunciation voluntarily or at least in free discussion with the Estates. This was the principle on which his brother Provence, restored as Louis XVIII in 1814, issued his Charter. This free renunciation was also at the heart of his defence of the nobility — without which his sacrifice of power may not have been necessary. He seems to have believed that only free renunciation would be fair and only free renunciation would be lasting. Although Louis had pursued divisive policies in 1787–8, symbolized by the Avertissement, thereafter he sought to prevent divisions, between Orders and classes, émigrés and restants, jurors and non-jurors, and finally over his own fate — the *appel au peuple* — because it would have imposed a further division.

The failure of such an approach in a revolutionary situation was perhaps inevitable. It is symbolized by the title of a recent work on Malouet, *Le centre perdu*. Before the fall of the monarchy, there were three attempts to 'stop the Revolution': that by the *monarchiens* in August–September 1789, that by the 'Feuillants' in 1791, with which Louis's escape from Paris coincided, and finally by the Girondins before the *dix-août*. They all failed, and failed easily. Then, when least expected, Robespierre and the system of Terror, whose spirit at least had been present in 1789 and had sent de Lessart before the High Court in 1791, suddenly collapsed. Louis knew that one day it would, as he told his brothers; meanwhile one could not govern a country against its *esprit dominant*. He thought he could detect signs of a change in 1790, but in despair that the 'reasonable men' had lost control of the Assembly, escaped in 1791. On his return he knew he would have to wait, but the politically motivated outbreak of war denied him this chance.

Louis left a will but no political legacy. This was partly due to his uncharismatic personality, his difficulty in expressing himself and especially his feelings in public, in short his inability to win adherents; partly to his lack of a clearly defined position. Absolutism was to return, in brasher guise, under Napoleon, to remain part of the mainstream of French politics, but the Bourbons abandoned it in 1789. During the Revolution, Louis's centrist position earned him the distrust alike of the émigrés and the politicians at home. Truly, as La Fayette said, 'he feared the winner whoever it was'. The revolutionary authorities made sure no miracles were performed at his grave. They could have spared themselves the trouble. No real cult emerged of him either as martyr or king. In 1795 the Dauphin died from the studied neglect of his jailors after the execution of Marie-Antoinette and Madame Elizabeth. Louis XVIII, who had shed few tears at his brother's execution, raised a polite *chapelle expiatoire* on the site of his burial. That is all.

Notes

INTRODUCTION

1 K.M. Baker, *Inventing the French Revolution*, Cambridge, 1990, 115.

2 *Réflexions sur mes entretiens avec le Duc de La Vauguyon*, ed. E. Falloux, 1851, 254.

3 A.N. K164 no. 7.14, the King to Vergennes, 1 February 1785.

4 For a fuller discussion see J. Hardman, 'Ministerial Politics from the Accession of Louis XVI to the Assembly of Notables, 1774–87', unpublished D.Phil. thesis, Oxford University, 1972, 51–8.

5 See, e.g., the unpublished doctoral thesis of J.M.J. Rogister, 'Conflict and Harmony in Eighteenth-Century France', Oxford, 1971.

6 B. Stone, *The Parlement of Paris*, North Carolina, 1981, 180.

7 D. Van Kley, 'The Jansenist Constitutional Legacy in the French Pre-Revolution', in K. Baker, ed., *The Political Culture of the Ancien Régime*, Chicago, 1987, 169–201, 173.

8 B. Stone, *The French Parlements and the Crisis of the Ancien Régime*, North Carolina, 1986, 123.

9 Arsenal, MS 3978, 215–16.

10 Bibliothèque municipale d'Orléans, Lenoir papers, MS 1423, mélanges, 28.

11 Bouillé, Marquis de, *Mémoires*, 1821, 13–14.

12 Arch. Dept de la Drôme (Valence), Véri MS cahier 90.

13 Véri, Abbé de, *Journal*, ed. J. de Witte, 1928–9, 2 vols, I, 459–60.

14 W. Doyle, 'The Parlements of France', in *French Historical Studies*, VI (1970), 422.

15 E.g., D. Echeverria, *The Maupeou Revolution*, Baton Rouge, 1985, and W. Doyle, 'The Parlements of France'.

16 Lenoir MS 1423, mélanges, 45.

17 A. de Tocqueville, *The Ancien Régime and the French Revolution*, ed. H. Brogan, 1966, 207.

18 Letter of 24 June 1772 published by P. Grosclaude in *Malesherbes, nouveaux documents inédits*, 1964, 71.

19 J.M. Augeard, *Mémoires secrètes*, 1866, 39.

20 Quoted in W. Doyle, 'The Parlements of France', 163.

21 E.g., L. Laugier, *Un ministère réformateur sous Louis XV, le triumvirat (1770–4)*, 1975.

22 Lenoir MS 1423, mélanges, 28.

23 See, e.g., K.M. Baker, 'Politics and Public Opinion', in J.R. Censer and J.D. Popkin, eds, *Press and Politics in Pre-Revolutionary France*, Berkeley, 1987.

24 Talleyrand, *Mémoires*, 1891–2, 5 vols, I, 63.

25 P. Mansell, *The Court of France, 1789–1830*, Cambridge, 1988, 12.

26 A. d'Arneth and M.A. Geffroy, eds,

Correspondance secrète entre Marie-Thérèse et le Comte de Mercy-Argenteau, 1875, 3 vols, III, 30.

27 Mansell, *The Court of France, 1789–1830*, 11.

28 Louis XV, *Lettres à son petit-fils . . .*, ed. Amiguet, 1938, 172.

29 C.A. de Calonne [attrib.], *Lettre du Marquis de Caraccioli à M. d'Alembert*, 1781.

30 Letter of the Dauphin to the Bishop of Verdun, quoted in P. Girault de Coursac, *L'Éducation d'un roi, Louis XVI*, 1972, 71.

CHAPTER 1

1 For the subsequent influence of the idea of the King of France as an arbiter, see below, p. 99.

2 Quoted in P. Girault de Coursac, *L'éducation d'un roi, Louis XVI*, 1972, 98; this work is the basis for much of the information in this chapter.

3 Letter to the Bishop of Verdun, July 1762, quoted in Girault de Coursac, *L'éducation d'un roi*, 71.

4 See note 2 above.

5 Published by P. Chevallier, *Journal de l'Assemblée des Notables de 1787*, 1960, 79–92.

6 *Reconnaissance des environs de Versailles faite par Monseigneur le Dauphin en 1769*, B.N. Rés. Geo. C4349.

7 His credo for the conduct of Foreign Policy is contained in his instruction to Vergennes of 12 April 1775, 'honesty and restraint must be our watchwords', A.N. K164 no. 3, 1775 no. 14.

8 *Journal de l'abbé de Véri*, ed. J. de Witte, 1928–30, 2 vols, I, 221.

9 Louis XVI, agenda, A.N. AE1–4 dossier 1, a microfilm copy of the original in the Musée des Archives.

10 Girault de Coursac, *L'éducation d'un roi*, 88.

11 *Lettres de Louis XV à son petit-fils . . .*, ed. Amiguet, 1938, 156–7.

12 Duc de Cröy, *Journal*, 1718–84, ed.

Grouchy et Cottin, 1906–7, 4 vols, III, 135 and 144.

13 Girault de Coursac, *L'éducation d'un roi*, 285.

14 A.N. K163 no. 3, 1778 no. 5, 12.3.

15 Letter of 22 September 1784.

16 Barnave, *Introduction à la Révolution française*, ed. G. Rudé, 1960, 53.

17 Archives de la Marine, MS *Journal de Castries*, MS 182/7964, I, fo. 110.

CHAPTER 2

1 Duc de Croÿ, *Journal*, 1718–84, III, 115.

2 Louis-Philippe, *Memoirs*, ed. John Hardman, New York, 1977, xxx.

3 Necker, see below, p. 65.

4 J.N. Moreau, *Mes souvenirs*, 1898–1901, 2 vols, I, 224.

5 From Lefevre d'Amécourt's unpublished 'Ministres de Louis XVI', B.N. nouv. ac. fran. 22111 fo. 1.

6 D'Angiviller, *Mémoires*, Copenhagen, 1933, 64.

7 Abbé de Véri, *Journal*, ed. J. de Witte, 1928–30, I, 93.

8 Ibid., 93–8.

9 Lenoir Papers, MS 1421, Section 2, Religion.

10 Véri, I, 99.

11 J.M.J. Rogister, 'Conflict and Harmony in Eighteenth-Century France: a reappraisal of the pattern of relations between Crown and Parlement under Louis XV', unpublished D.Phil. thesis, Oxford University, 1972, 36. Rogister considers that the dismissal of Maurepas in 1749 was a major factor in the poor relations between Crown and Parlement in the 1750s.

12 Besenval, Baron de, *Mémoires*, ed. Berville et Barrière, 1821, 2 vols, I, 329–30.

13 Véri, I, 70–82; Malesherbes also believed that the King's superiority over the parlements rested on force,

Véri MS cahier 157.

14 Ibid., cahier 109.

15 Lenoir Papers (see note 9 above).

16 Véri, I, 99.

17 Munro Price, 'The Comte de Vergennes and the Baron de Breteuil', unpublished doctoral thesis, Cambridge University, 1988, 64–6.

18 Initially, Vergennes restrained Gustavus, who was urged on by d'Aiguillon, but once Gustavus had decided on the coup, Vergennes told him there could be no half-measures; J.F. Labourdette, *Vergennes*, 1990, 69.

19 J. de Maupeou, *Le Chancelier Maupeou*, 1942, 222 and 227.

20 P. Burley, 'Louis XVI and a new Monarchy', unpublished Ph.D. thesis, London University, 1981, 442.

21 Véri, I, 182.

22 Ibid., 160.

23 Ibid., 115.

24 In his Declaration of 20 June 1791.

25 The best example is Necker's letter to the King at Marly on 20 June 1789, A.N. K163 dossier 13 no. 1.

26 Croÿ, III, 144.

27 M. Antoine, 'Les comités des ministres sous Louis XV', in *Rev. Hist. de Droit*, 1951, 228.

28 Véri, I, 188.

29 Ibid., 130.

30 Ibid., 134.

31 Ibid., 151.

32 Ibid., 185.

33 Keith Michael Baker, 'Politics and Public Opinion', in *The Political Culture of the Ancien Régime*, 1987, 246.

34 *Journal Historique*, 8 November 1774, quoted in D. Echeverria, *The Maupeou Revolution*, Baton Rouge, 1985, 32.

35 A.N. O'354 no. 202, letter from the Minister for the Maison to the Keeper of the Seals, 17 October, returning Maupeou's letter.

36 Véri, I, 183.

37 Only Vergennes's copy has survived (published from the family archives by Coursac, Louis XVI, 127); the Vergennes-Tugny Archives also contain Louis's covering letter dated 20 December.

38 A.A.E., *Mémoires et Documents*, France, 1375 and 1628; there is also a plan in the Archives Nationales, K695 no. 24.

39 Véri, I, 202.

40 Ibid., 204–5.

41 Ibid., 162.

42 K.M. Baker, *Inventing the French Revolution*, Cambridge, 1990, 112.

CHAPTER 3

1 Louis-Philippe, *Memoirs*, ed. and trans. John Hardman, New York, 1977, 17.

2 P. Mansell, *The Court of France, 1789–1830*, Cambridge, 1988, 3–4.

3 Duc de Cröy, *Journal, 1718–84*, IV, 214.

4 Quoted in E. Lever, *Louis XVI*, 1985, 255.

5 Quoted in Luçay, Comte de, *Les secrétaires d'État en France depuis les origines jusqu'à 1774*, 1881, 265.

6 Véri, II, 395.

7 A. d'Arneth and J. Flammermont, eds, *Correspondance secrète du Comte de Mercy-Argenteau avec l'Empereur Joseph II et le Prince de Kaunitz*, 1891, 2 vols, II, 195.

8 A. d'Arneth and M.A. Geffroy, eds, *Marie-Antoinette: Correspondance secrète entre Marie-Thérèse et le Comte de Mercy-Argenteau*, 2nd ed., 1875, 3 vols, II, 356.

9 Besenval, Baron de, *Mémoires*, 1821, 2 vols, I, 324.

10 Arneth and Geffroy, II, 362, the Queen to Count Rosenberg.

11 Arneth and Flammermont, II, 454.

12 Véri, I, 388.

13 M. Price, 'The Comte de Vergennes and the Baron de Breteuil', unpublished Ph.D. thesis, Cam-

bridge University, 1988, *passim*.
14 Arneth and Geffroy, II, 356–7.
15 Besenval, *Mémoires*, I, 329–30.
16 Arch. Dépt de la Drome, Véri MS cahier 112.
17 Véri, I, 154–6.
18 Transcribed by Véri; his account of the Flour War is given in vol. I, 286–93.
19 His views are expounded in a letter of 5 May 1788, A.N. O'354 no. 54.
20 Véri, I, 292.
21 Lenoir MS 1423, mélanges, 45.
22 A.N. K164 no. 3, letter of 15 July 1775.
23 Véri, I, 314.
24 Ibid., 128.
25 Ibid., 318.
26 F. Hue, *Dernières Années du règne de Louis XVI*, 3rd ed., 1860, 442.
27 Letter of 2 June 1776, published in P. Grosclaude, *Malesherbes*, 1961, 134.
28 Price, 'The Comte de Vergennes and the Baron de Breteuil', 93; his section on the Affair, 92–113, is the most intelligible account.
29 12 April 1775, A.A.E. MDF 1897 fo. 37, quoted in Price (see note 28 above), 101.
30 A.N. K164 no. 3, Vergennes to the King, 23 February 1776 (draft).
31 Véri MS cahier 117.
32 Véri, I, 389–90.
33 A.A.E. MDF 1897 fo. 75, quoted in Price, 108.
34 A.N. K164 no. 3, Vergennes to the King, 23 February (draft).
35 E.g., Miromesnil's advice to the King in 1786 that d'Aligre could not be dismissed 'without being put on trial' and Necker's reappointment in 1788.
36 A.N. K164 no. 3, the King to Vergennes, 13 July 1776.
37 Miromesnil, *Correspondance politique*, ed. P. Le Verdier, 1899-, 4 vols, I, 171.
38 Véri, I, 175.
39 From a letter to the King of 5 August 1786, A.N. K163 no. 8.14.

40 Véri, I, 420.
41 Véri MS cahier 109.
42 Véri, I, 371–3; P. Burley, 'Louis XVI and a new Monarchy', unpublished Ph.D. thesis, London University, 1981, 456.
43 Véri, I, 459 and 451.
44 Véri MS cahier 109.
45 Véri, I, 395–7.
46 Ibid., 417–19.
47 P. Grosclaude, *Malesherbes*, 1961, 117–18.
48 Transcribed by Véri, I, 450–7.
49 Ibid., 447–8.
50 Véri, II, 147.
51 Letter of 30 April.
52 Arneth and Geffroy, II, 367.
53 D.L. Wick, 'The Court Nobility and the French Revolution: the Example of the Society of Thirty', in *Eighteenth-Century Studies*, XIII (1980), 272.
54 Mme de Polignac had a place as Dame d'honneur to the Comtesse d'Artois, her husband the Survivance as Premier écuyer to the Queen.
55 D'Ormesson, *Journal*, A.N. 144 AP 130. 84–6.
56 Arneth and Geffroy, II, 437.
57 Ibid., 466.
58 In 1780, when they backed Necker's candidates for the Marine, Castries, and War, Ségur; they probably hoped thereby to increase their influence on military promotions.

CHAPTER 4

1 Vergennes to Breteuil, 26 July 1776, Archives de Breteuil, L.A.B. lère serie, 1776, quoted in M. Price, 'The Comte de Vergennes and the Baron de Breteuil', unpublished Ph.D. thesis, Cambridge University, 1988, 111.
2 *Observations remises à Louis XVI et par ses ordres, le 3 Mai 1781*, published by J.L. Soulavie, *Mémoires historiques et politiques du règne de Louis XVI*,

1801, 6 vols, IV, 153. We follow Égret (*Necker*, 1975) in accepting the authenticity of this document. Vergennes's flattery and use of the word *prévoyance* are characteristic.

3 Soulavie, 153.

4 A.N. K159, Broglie to the King, 30 May 1774, published in M.E. Boutaric, ed., *Correspondance secrète inédite de Louis XV*, 1866, 2 vols, II, 395–6; Véri, *Journal*, II, 149.

5 A.N. K163 no. 13.8, unsigned and undated but Necker to Maurepas, August or September 1776.

6 Turgot, *Réflexions... mémoire remis par M. le Comte de Vergennes...*, published by Ségur, *Mémoires ou souvenirs et anecdotes*, 1827, 3 vols, III, 191.

7 Soulavie, 153.

8 Lefevre d'Amécourt, *Journal*, B.N. n.a.f. 22110 fo. 34.

9 A.N. K163 no 8.13.

10 The information contained in this paragraph is provided by B. Stone, *The Parlement of Paris, 1774–89*, North Carolina, 1981, 79–81.

11 J. Necker, *Sur l'administration de M. Necker par lui-même*, 1791, 235–6.

12 E.g., J. Bosher, *French Finances 1770–95*, Cambridge, 1970, and R.D. Harris, *Necker*, University of California, 1979.

13 D'Argenson, *Mémoires*, ed. Rathéry, IV, 42.

14 Published by Soulavie, IV, 121–31.

15 Véri, II, 380.

16 Letter of 8 October 1776, A.N. K163, 1776, 13.13.

17 Véri, II, 388–9.

18 De Witte MS cahier 100.

19 For a fuller discussion, see John Hardman, 'Ministerial Politics from the Accession of Louis XVI to the Assembly of Notables, 1774–87', unpublished D.Phil. thesis, Oxford University, 1972, 201–12.

20 Montbarey, *Mémoires du Prince de Montbarey*, 1826–7, 3 vols, III, 25; also II, 250, 327–8 and 197.

21 By R.D. Harris, *Necker*.

22 In 1787, Louis told Brienne that the Assembly of Notables could see the figures 'pour plusieurs années et pour une année ordinaire', *Journal de l'Assemblée des Notables*, 90.

23 See B. Stone, *The Parlement of Paris, 1774–89*, 115–16.

24 Quoted by J. Égret, *Necker*, 1975, 128–9.

25 According to a list for 1783 in d'Ormesson's papers, A.N. 141 A.P. 131, dossier 4.7

26 *Lettre... à d'Alembert*, 10, 19 and 21; H. Carré, *Quelques mots sur la presse clandestine*, 1893, 13.

27 See note 2 above.

28 MS Journal de Castries, I, fos 73 and 76; Castries Papers, A.N. 306 A.P. 18.7(1), letter to the Queen and draft letter of 22 April 1781; see also A. d'Arneth and J. Flammermont, eds, *Correspondance secrète du Comte de Mercy-Argenteau avec l'Empereur Joseph II et le Prince de Kaunitz*, 1891, 2 vols, I, 33 and 40, note 2.

29 D'Angiviller, *Mémoires*, Copenhagen, 1933, 114.

30 Castries had proposed Necker to the King on the fall of d'Ormesson, A.N. C223 (160) 26; the King's reply is given in Castries's diary, I, fo. 205.

31 See, e.g., K.M. Baker, 'Politics and Public Opinion', in J.R. Censer and J.D. Popkin, eds, *Press and Politics in Pre-Revolutionary France*, Berkeley, 1987, 304.

32 Soulavie, VI, 149–59.

33 See 'The Gazette de Leyde under Louis XVI', in Censer and Popkin, *Press and Politics*, 95–6.

34 J.F. Labourdette, *Vergennes*, 1990, 201.

35 B.N. fonds Joly de Fleury, n.a.f. 1438 fos 217–23.

36 Ibid., 1432 fo. 132, letter to de Lessart(?), 1787.

37 Castries, I, fos 91–3.

38 Lenoir Papers, MS 1423, mélanges, 27; de Witte MS cahier 102.

39 Lenoir Papers, MS 1423, mélanges, 39.

CHAPTER 5

1 Castries MS *Journal*, I, fo. 92.
2 Véri, II, 157.
3 A. d'Arneth and J. Flammermont, eds, *Correspondance secrète du Comte de Mercy-Argenteau avec l'Empereur Joseph II et le Prince de Kaunitz*, 1891, 2 vols, I, 227.
4 Vergennes to the King, 17 May 1782.
5 B.N. n.a.f. fonds Joly de Fleury, 1438 fo. 264; Miromesnil to Véri, *Revue de Paris*, 1953, 80.
6 A.N. K163 no. 8.14, Miromesnil to the King, 5 August 1786.
7 B. Stone, *The Parlement of Paris, 1774–89*, North Carolina, 1981, 23.
8 Miromesnil to Vergennes, 7 July 1782, quoted in M. Price, 'The Comte de Vergennes and the Baron de Breteuil', unpublished Ph.D. thesis, Cambridge University, 1988, 162; Miromesnil to Véri, *Revue de Paris*, 1953, 80–1.
9 Stone, *The Parlement of Paris, 1774–89*, 84–5.
10 Véri MS cahier 109.
11 B.N. 2487, fonds Joly de Fleury, no. 139; d'Ormesson, *Journal*, sections 55 and 59, A.N. 144 A.P. 130.
12 Besenval, Baron de, *Mémoires*, ed. Berville et Barrière, 1821, 2 vols, II, 125.
13 Castries, *Journal*, I, fos 147 and 192; Véri MS cahier 114; Arneth and Flammermont, I, 161, note 1; B.N. fonds Joly de Fleury 1441 fo. 142, quoted in Price, 'The Comte de Vergennes and the Baron de Breteuil', 183.
14 Véri MS cahier 114; Castries, Journal, I, fos 181–2; Besenval, II, 145; minutes for the seventh session of the Comité, A.N. 144 A.P. 131 dossier 5.
15 D'Ormesson to the King, 2 March 1783, A.N. 144 A.P. dossier 4.3; for Vergennes and de Crosne see Price, 'The Comte de Vergennes and the Baron de Breteuil', 199–200; d'Amécourt also believed that 'the choice of d'Ormesson was made by the King alone', *Ministres de Louis XVI*, fo. 96.
16 Miromesnil to the King, 27 May 1785, advising on filling a vacancy for a Conseiller d'État in the Conseil des Dépêches, A.N. K161 no. 28 bis.
17 D'Ormesson, *Journal*, A.N. 144 A.P. 130, section 58.
18 A.N. 144 A.P. 131 dossier 4.4.
19 D'Ormesson's account of the operation is contained in sections 60–3 and 68–73 of his *Journal*; we have followed this, which was also accepted by Véri — 'M. d'Ormesson is not a liar' (MS cahier 118) — as subtantially correct in preference to the more usual interpretation of the operation as rash, the view, e.g., of G.T. Mathews, *The Royal General Farms*, New York, 1958, 260–1.
20 Archives de Vergennes, *Lettres de Louis XVI*, quoted in Price, 'The Comte de Vergennes and the Baron de Breteuil', 242–3.
21 A.N. K164 no. 3, 1783 no. 4 (10 November) and 5 (12 December).
22 Archives de Vergennes, *Lettres de Louis XVI*.
23 D'Angiviller, *Mémoires*, Copenhagen, 1933, 113.
24 Montyon, *Particularités . . .*, 1812, 253.
25 For Calonne's ancestry, see A.N. 263 MI 1–2.
26 Lenoir papers, MS 1423, mélanges, 28; Joly de Fleury is also credited with having had a hand in writing the speech.
27 John Hardman, 'Ministerial Politics from the Accession of Louis XVI to the Assembly of Notables, 1774–87', unpulished D.Phil. thesis, Oxford University, 1972, 203.
28 Price, 'The Comte de Vergennes and the Baron de Breteuil', 284.
29 Véri MS cahiers 124–5.
30 *Journal de Castries*, entry for 1 April 1786.

31 Price, 'The Comte de Vergennes and the Baron de Breteuil', 284.
32 Rory Browne, 'The Diamond Necklace Affair Revisited', in *Renaissance and Modern Studies*, XXXIII (1989), 33.
33 Lenoir MS 1423, mélanges, 31–9.
34 Archives de Vergennes, *Lettres de Louis XVI*.
35 Vergennes to Noailles, 22 August 1785, A.A.E. C.P. Autriche 350, fos 119–20, quoted in J.F. Labourdette, *Vergennes*, 1990, 295.
36 Lenoir MS 1423, mélanges, 31–9; Véri MS cahier 140.
37 Lenoir MS 1423.
38 Augeard, 152, information supplied by Calonne and Augeard's mutual friend Président Lamoignon; Véri notes Calonne's desire to move as early as 1784 (MS cahier 121).
39 Arneth and Flammermont, II, 32–6.
40 Ibid.
41 Vergennes also tried to recover the diamonds but was told that only four were sufficiently distinctive to be recognizable (letter of Vérac from The Hague, 4 October 1785, A.A.E. M.D.F., 1399 fos 216–17).
42 Price, 'The Comte de Vergennes and the Baron de Breteuil', 321–9.
43 Adhémar to Vergennes, A.A.E. C.P. Angleterre 556 fos 282–3, quoted in Labourdette, *Vergennes*, 299.
44 Vergennes to Adhémar, 5 June, ibid., fo. 294, quoted in Labourdette, *Vergennes*, 299.
45 Arneth and Flammermont, II, 4 and 9.
46 Browne, 'The Diamond Necklace Affair', 33–4.
47 J.R. Censer and J.D. Popkin, 'The Gazette de Leyde under Louis XVI', in *Press and Politics in Pre-Revolutionary France*, Berkeley, 1987, 73–133, 100.
48 R. Darnton, *The Literary Underground of the Old Regime*, Harvard, 1982, 195 and 201–2.
49 B.N. n.a.f. 22111, Lefevre

d'Amécourt, *Journal du règne de Louis XVI*, fos 74 and 66.
50 Montbarey, *Mémoires*, 1826–7, 3 vols, III, 272–3.
51 P.R.O. P.C.1/125.68, Bertin to Calonne, December 1785.
52 E.g., Bertin told Vergennes 'vous connoissiez sa discrétion', letter of 16 July 1783, B.N. n.a.f. 6498.
53 D'Amécourt, *Journal du règne de Louis XVI*, fos 66–74.
54 A.N. K163 no. 8.21, 8 December 1786.
55 A.N. K163 no. 8.14, 5 August 1786.
56 Véri, MS cahier 109.

CHAPTER 6

1 E.g., on 6 February 1785 he writes: 'It is tiresome for a minister to have to bother Your Majesty with details which seem to relate to individuals rather than to his service', A.N. K164 no. 3, 1785 no. 5.
2 Louis's letters often begin: 'I am sending you the interceptions as usual'.
3 The two halves of the correspondence are contained in A.N. K164 no. 3 (for Vergennes) and Archives de Vergennes, *Lettres de Louis XVI*, kindly communicated to me by Dr M. Price.
4 M.E. Boutaric, ed., Louis XV, *Correspondance secrète inédite*, 1866, 2 vols, II, 424.
5 D'Ormesson, *Journal*, section 82, A.N. 144 A.P. 130; Bachaumont, *Mémoires secrètes pour servir à l'histoire de la République des Lettres*, London, 1777–89, XXXIV, 309.
6 Véri, I, 354.
7 A.N. K164 no. 3, 1776 no. 5, 23 February.
8 Ibid., 1785 no. 5, 6 February.
9 The best account of the relationship between Louis XIII and Richelieu is in O. Ranum, *Richelieu and the Councillors of Louis XIII*, Oxford, 1963.
10 Letter of 27 May, Archives de

Vergennes, *Lettres de Louis XVI*, quoted in M. Price, 'The Comte de Vergennes and the Baron de Breteuil', unpublished Ph.D. thesis, Cambridge University, 1988, 112.

11 Archives de Vergennes, the King to Vergennes, 4 March 1785.

12 Ibid.

13 Boutaric, II, 428.

14 Ibid., Broglie to the King, 14 June 1774.

15 Ibid., 404.

16 Ibid., 475, memorandum of 1 March 1775.

17 Archives de Vergennes, letter of 4 February 1778.

18 A.N. K164 no. 3; 1776 no. 5.

19 Ibid., 1775 no. 19.

20 Ibid., 11 April.

21 Ibid., no. 14, 12 April.

22 Archives de Vergennes, 6 December 1774.

23 A.N. K164 no. 3, 1775 no. 3.

24 Ibid., 1777 no. 3, 12 April.

25 Bertrand de Molleville, *Mémoires secrètes*, 1797, 3 vols, II, 32.

26 A.N. K164 no. 3, 1776 no. 9, 2 May.

27 Véri, II, 47; on 18 November 1775 Louis tells Vergennes that Beaumarchais's projects 'méritent grande réflexion' — Archives de Vergennes.

28 A.A.E., Espagne, vol. 588, no. 11; quoted in H. Doniol, *Histoire de la participation de la France à l'établissement des États-Unis d'Amérique*, 1886–, 5 vols, II, 736–7.

29 Ibid., 743; the King to Vergennes, Archives de Vergennes.

30 A.N. K164 no. 3, no. 7 fos 9–10.

31 Letters of 6 December 1774 and 11 April 1775, Archives de Vergennes.

32 A.N. K164 no. 3, 1778 no. 7, letter of 22 July.

33 6 March 1778, Archives de Vergennes.

34 A.N. K164 no. 3, 1778 no. 7, 22 July.

35 Véri, II, 95.

36 Ibid., 94 and 97.

37 Archives de Vergennes, the King to Vergennes, 13 February 1781.

38 Ibid., letter of 6 November 1784.

39 A.N. K164 no. 3, 1784 no. 4, 5 November, nos 3.4 and 3.6 (the opinions of the ministres); see also Castries, *Journal*, I, fo. 191 for his appreciation of the manœuvre.

40 A.N. K164 no. 3, memorandum of Breteuil, 11 November 1784.

41 Ibid., 1785 no. 1, 5 January.

42 Louis XVI to Joseph II, 6 January 1785, quoted in A. d'Arneth, *Marie-Antoinette, Joseph II und Leopold II*, 1866, 65–8.

43 A.N. 297 A.P. 3.122; Calonne describes the alliance as 'perhaps the most important that France could have contracted'.

44 Quoted in P. Girault de Coursac, *L'éducation d'un roi, Louis XVI*, 1972, 152, author's italics to indicate Louis's additions to Moreau's text.

45 Archives de Vergennes.

46 Ibid., January 1787.

47 A.N. K164 no. 3, 1786 no. 6.

48 *Journal de Castries*, II, fos 385–6; A.N. 306 A.P. 19.5, memorandum with corrections by Castries; 23.42, Castries's opinion delivered in the Council, 16 August 1787.

49 Castries's successor, La Luzerne, read the Council alarmist memoranda on 14 December 1788, and 12 August and 2 October 1789, B.N. n.a.f. 9434 fos 172, 213–4 and 209, published in John Hardman, *The French Revolution ... 1787–95*, London, 1981, 79–80.

CHAPTER 7

1 Véri MS cahier 122.

2 P.R.O. P.C.1/125.48.

3 A.N. K677.103, Calonne to the King, late August 1786.

4 See note 8 below; also *Correspondance secrète*, II, 127.

5 A.N. 144 A.P. 132 dossier 3.2, 24 February 1775; on Calonne's fall the memoranda were requested by Brienne (dossier 3.3). The main

difference between Turgot's plan and that of Calonne was that in Turgot's the total revenue raised would not be increased. D'Ormesson personally advocated replacing the *capitation* rather than the *vingtième* by the new tax but dutifully provided a draft Edict, leaving it to his Minister to write the preamble (which tends to disprove de Coursac's belief [Louis XVI, autoportrait, 10] that Louis wrote his own preambles).

6   A.N. K164.4, *Objections et réponses.*

7   Such I take to be the point of Miromesnil's warning to the King not to imitate the ecclesiatical policy of a Power (probably Joseph II's Austria) 'which is certainly very respectable but whose Estates in no way resemble your own'. A.N. K163 no. 8.22, letter of 28 December.

8   Drafts of Calonne's proposals are to be found among his papers at A.N. 297 A.P. 91 and 97.

9   Fragment of the *Journal de l'abbé de Véri*, ed. Duc de Castries, *Revue de Paris*, Nov. 1953, 84–5.

10 A.N. 297 A.P. 3.119 fo. 7.

11 MS *Journal* de Castries, II, fo. 335.

12 A.N. K163 no. 8.

13 Ibid., 8.22, letter of 28 December.

14 See M. Price, 'The Comte de Vergennes and the Baron de Breteuil', unpublished Ph.D. thesis, Cambridge University, 1988, 360–70.

15 Castries, *Journal*, II, fo. 335.

16 Letter of 28 December.

17 *Journal de l'Assemblée des Notables*, 46 and 50.

18 W. Doyle, 'The Parlements', in K.M. Baker, ed., *Political Culture*, Chicago, 1987, 165.

19 A.N. K677.102.

20 Undated, Archives de Vergennes.

21 *Correspondance, secrète*, II, 104, entry for 7 February.

22 A.N. 297 A.P. 3.119 fo. 7.

23 Castries, *Journal*, II, fos 343–4.

CHAPTER 8

1   MS *Journal de Castries*, II, fo. 342; other references to this diary are cited in the text by date.

2   The opening speeches are included in: *Procès-verbal de l'Assemblée des Notables . . . 1787*, Paris, 1788.

3   Castries, II, fo. 344.

4   A.N. 297 A.P. 3.119 fo. 5.

5   *Bibliothèque de l'Arsenal*, MS 3978, 212.

6   A.N. K163 no. 8.24 and 26, Miromesnil to the King.

7   Besenval, Baron de, *Mémoires*, ed. Berville et Barrière, 1821, 2 vols, II, 213–14.

8   Speech of Brienne, Arsenal MS 3978, 39; one is reminded of the mass exodus of nobles from the National Assembly.

9   See, e.g., a speech by Angran d'Allerai, Arsenal MS 3978, 215–16.

10 Arsenal MS 3976, 948.

11 Arsenal MS 3978, 196–7.

12 Calonne to Necker, 28 February, A.N. 297 A.P. 3.66.

13 Ibid., 65.

14 Ibid., 74.

15 Ibid.

16 *Journal de l'Assemblée des Notables*, 44.

17 A.N. 297 A.P. 3.119 fo. 5.

18 A.N. K163 no. 8.31.

19 Besenval, II, 261.

20 D'Ormesson Papers, A.N. 144 A.P. 133 dossier 6.4.

21 The following account is based on the version of Castries (MS *Journal*); Lenoir (Lenoir Papers, MS 1423, mélanges. 39); and Brienne, *Journal de l'Assemblée des Notables*, 60.

22 Brienne, *Journal de l'Assemblée des Notables*, 59.

23 Calonne to d'Angiviller, A.N. 297 A.P. 3.119.

24 Ibid., 113, Brienne to Calonne, 22 June.

25 Ibid., 119 and 121, from two letters to d'Angiviller, late July and 26 July.

26 Ibid., 113, Amelot to Calonne, 22
June.
27 Castries, II, fo. 381.
28 These memoranda have been
published in *Journal de l'Assemblée des
Notables*, 79–83.
29 Notes published by Marmontel,
Mémoires, ed. J. Renwick, 1972, II,
336–8; Brienne's memoirs, published in J.L. Soulavie, *Mémoires
historiques et politiques du règne de Louis
XVI*, 1801, 6 vols, VI, 248.
30 In letters to Fersen of 1791 and
1792, published by Klinckowström,
Le Comte de Fersen et la Cour de France,
1878, 2 vols.
31 Arsenal MS 3978. 98.
32 Ibid., 147 and 148.
33 Letter of Madame Elizabeth to
Mme de Bombelles, *Correspondance
de Mme Elizabeth*, ed. Feuillet de
Conches, 1868, 103–4.
34 A.N. 297 A.P. 3.114.

CHAPTER 9

1 J.F.X. Droz, *Histoire du règne de
Louis XVI*, Brussels, 1839, II, 14.
2 Castries, *Journal*, II, fo. 392.
3 Ibid.
4 See above, p. 100.
5 Castries, II, fo. 386.
6 Ibid., fo. 383; P. Mansell, *The Court
of France, 1789–1830*, Cambridge,
1988, 4.
7 Castries, II, fos 374 and 398.
8 Droz, *Histoire du règne de Louis XVI*,
II, 1.
9 B. Stone, *The Parlement of Paris,
1774–89*, North Carolina, 1981, 156.
10 W. Doyle, 'The Parlements', in
K.M. Baker, ed., *The Political Culture of the Ancien Régime*, Chicago,
1987, 165.
11 Stone, *The Parlement of Paris*, 156.
12 Letter to Joseph of 23 November.
13 Sallier, *Annales françaises . . . 1774–
89*, 1813, 128–9.
14 *Archives Parlementaires*, I, 284.
15 M. Marion, *Le garde des sceaux
Lamoignon*, 1905, *passim*.

16 Sallier, *Annales françaises*, 144 and
Weber, *Mémoires concernant Marie-
Antoinette*, ed. Berville et Barrière,
1822, 2 vols, 126.
17 A. Chérest, *La chute de l'Ancien
Régime, 1787–9*, 1884–6, 3 vols, I,
475.
18 A.N. 0'354 no. 5, 6 May, 7.45.
19 Ibid., no. 54.
20 Castries, II, fo. 387.
21 A.N. 0'354 no. 102.
22 Droz, *Histoire du règne de Louis XVI*,
II, 97.
23 M. Price, 'The Comte de
Vergennes and the Baron de
Breteuil', unpublished Ph.D. thesis,
Cambridge University, 1988,
360–70.
24 E.g., Lenoir MS 1423, mélanges,
329.
25 E.g., when Bertrand de Molleville
asked Montmorin to read out
in Council a memorandum on
dismissing the Estates, Montmorin
refused on the grounds that 'Necker
would stop me and desire to have it
communicated to himself before it
was read, on which the King would
order it to be delivered to him'.
A.F. Bertrand de Molleville, *Last
Year of the Reign of Louis XVI*,
Boston, 1909, 2 vols, I, 164.
26 Price, 'The Comte de Vergennes
and the Baron de Breteuil',
379–86.

CHAPTER 10

1 Published in J.L. Soulavie, *Mémoires
historiques et politiques du règne de Louis
XVI*, 1801, 6 vols, VI, 240–4.
2 This 200-page memorandum has
not survived; for recollections of
it, see J. Égret, *La pré-Révolution
française*, 1962, 322, notes 1 and 2.
3 Sallier, *Annales françaises . . . 1774–
89*, 1813, 186, note 1.
4 J. Necker, *De la Révolution française*,
1797, I, 51.
5 *Duc de Montmorency-Luxembourg*, ed.
Paul Filleul, 1939, 284.

6 Sur l'administration de M. Necker par lui-même, 1791, 47–8.
7 Ibid., 56–7.
8 Soulavie, *Mémoires historiques*, VI, 242–3.
9 Montmorency-Luxembourg, 288.
10 Sallier, *Annales françaises*, 288, note 1.
11 A.N. XIB, 8988.
12 Malouet, *Mémoires*, 1874, 2 vols, I, 220–1.
13 Article on Necker by Lally-Tollendal in the *Biographie-Michaud*.
14 Chérest, *La chute de l'Ancien Régime, 1787–9*, 1884–6, 3 vols, II, 221; the details of the discussion preceding the *Résultat* are to be found in Barentin, *Mémoire autographe . . . sur les derniers conseils du roi Louis XVI*, 1844, and Necker, *De la Révolution française*, 87ff.
15 Lenoir MS 1423, résidus, 122.
16 Barentin, *Mémoire autographe*, 67.
17 *Lettre au Roi*, London, 1789, 54.
18 Malouet, *Mémoires*, 1874, 2 vols, I, 249–50.
19 The word is Véri's.
20 Extract from Véri's diary published by Duc de Castries in *Revue de Paris*, Nov. 1953, 84–6.
21 Mercy to Joseph II, 23 February 1788.

CHAPTER 11

1 A.N. K679 no. 10.
2 Comte de Saint-Priest, *Mémoires*, ed. Barante, 1929, 2 vols, I, 221.
3 *Recueil des documents relatifs aux États Généraux de 1789*, ed. G. Lefebvre, 1953–, I (I), 253.
4 A.F. Bertrand de Molleville, *Mémoires secrètes pour servir à l'histoire de la dernière année du règne de Louis XVI, Roi de France*, London 1797, 3 vols, I, 157–9.
5 Barentin, *Lettres et bulletins à Louis XVI*, ed. A. Aulard, 1915, 10, 27 and 56.
6 Bailly, *Mémoires*, ed. Berville et Barrière, 1821, 3 vols, I, 94;

Barentin, *Lettres . . .* , 18–19.
7 *Recueil*, vol. I (2), 55.
8 Ibid., 171.
9 Malouet, *Mémoires*, 1874, 2 vols, I, 250 and 259.
10 *Recueil*, I (2), 48.
11 Necker, *De la Révolution française*, 1797, I, 252.
12 Malouet, *Mémoires*, I, 261.
13 Montmorin took a similar view, memoranda to the King, A.N. K679 nos 86 and 87–8.
14 Comtesse d'Adhémar, *Souvenirs sur Marie-Antoinette . . .* , 1836, 4 vols, III, 156–7.
15 A.N. K163 dossier 13 no. 1; Necker, *De la Révolution française*, I, 286; Montjoie, *Seconde partie . . .* , 44.
16 Adrien Duquesnoy, *Journal*, 1894, 2 vols, I, 90.
17 Barentin, *Lettres . . .* , 34.
18 Accounts differ; there is no mention of this journey in Louis's diary.
19 Saint-Priest, *Mémoires*, I, 223.
20 *Receuil*, I (2), 94.
21 Mercy to Joseph II, 4 July 1789.
22 Necker, *De la Révolution française*, 253; Barentin's account in his *Mémoire autographe sur les derniers Conseils du Roi Louis XVI*, ed. M. Champion, 1844, agrees with Necker's that no objections had been raised in the Council.
23 A.N. K163 dossier 13 no. 1.
24 Letter transcribed in Adhémar, *Souvenirs sur Marie-Antoinette*, 171–5.
25 D'Angiviller, *Mémoires*, Copenhagen, 1933, 158.
26 Vaudreuil-Artois, *Correspondance intime*, ed. L. Pingaud, 1889, 2 vols, I, xxvii–xxviii.
27 Mercy to Joseph II, 4 July 1789.
28 That, at least, is our reading of the second and third paragraphs of Barentin's letter of 27 June.
29 J.F.X. Droz, *Histoire du règne de Louis XVI . . .* , Brussels, 1839, II, 247; Necker, *De la Révolution française*, I, 313.
30 *Moniteur*, 1790, no. 4 (III-33), cited by P. and P. Girault de Coursac, eds, *Louis XVI à la parole*, 1989, 195.

31 A.N. C185 (123) 9.

32 Necker, *De la Révolution française*, II, 5.

33 Bailly, *Mémoires*, I, 367–8.

34 These are published by P. Caron in 'La tentative de contre-révolution de Juin-Juillet 1789', in *Revue d'Histoire moderne*, VIII (1906), 25–30; Caron draws a perverse conclusion from his own evidence.

35 Droz, *Histoire du règne de Louis XVI...*, II, 299.

36 Quoted in M. Price, 'The "Ministry of the Hundred Hours": A Reappraisal', in *French History*, vol. 14, no. 3 (1990) 317–39, 331.

37 M. Price, 'The Comte de Vergennes and the Baron de Breteuil', unpublished Ph.D. thesis, Cambridge University, 1988, 334, note 100.

38 Price, 'The "Ministry of the Hundred Hours"...', 339; Raigecourt-Bombelles, *Correspondance du Marquis et de la Marquise de Raigecourt avec le Marquis et la Marquise de Bombelles pendant l'émigration, 1790–1800*, ed. M. de la Rocheterie, 1892, I, 168.

39 Price, 'The "Ministry of the Hundred Hours"...', 335.

40 Ibid., 336–7.

41 S.F. Scott, *The Response of the Royal Army to the French Revolution... 1787–93*, Oxford, 1973, 59 and 80.

42 J.N. Moreau, *Mes souvenirs*, 1898–1901, 2 vols, II, 439–41.

43 Journal de Fersen, in Klinckowström, *Le Comte de Fersen et la Cour de France*, 1878, 2 vols, II, 6.

44 A.N. C185 (123) 1.

45 Droz, *Histoire du règne de Louis XVI...*, II, 345.

46 Marquis de La Fayette, *Mémoires*, 1837, 6 vols, II, 362; Comte d'Allonville, *Mémoires secrètes*, 1838–41, 10 vols, II, 68.

47 Montjoie, *Éloge de Louis XVI*, 141.

48 Baron de Besenval, *Mémoires*, ed. Berville et Barrière, 1821, 2 vols, II, 367.

49 Saint-Priest, *Mémoires*, I, 240–1.

50 Malouet, *Mémoires*, I, 290.

51 D. Echeverria (*The Maupeou Revolution*, Baton Rouge, 1985, especially 217–95) demonstrates that a few thinkers had effected this fusion during the Maupeou period; D. Van Kley ('The Jansenist Constitutional Legacy in the French Pre-Revolution', in K.M. Baker (ed.), *Political Culture*, 169–201, 195) argues that it was effected by the political clubs in 1788–9. However, the King's volte-face in the summer of 1789 leading to the abandonment of the old royalist position is the most satisfactory explanation of the *prevalence* of the new standpoint.

CHAPTER 12

1 A.P. IX, 28–31.

2 The best and most recent treatment of the *monarchiens* is R. Griffiths, *Le Centre Perdu, Malouet et les 'monarchiens'*, Grenoble, 1988, especially 55–80. See also P.R. Campbell, 'Louis XVI King of the French', in C. Lucas, ed., *The Political Culture of the French Revolution*, Oxford, 1988, 178–80.

3 Véri MS cahier 113.

4 A.N. C31 (263).6.

5 See, e.g., Saint-Priest, *Mémoires*, ed. Barante, 1929, 2 vols, I, 229.

6 Malouet, *Mémoires*, 1874, 2 vols, I, 304–5.

7 We have based our account of the October Days on Saint-Priest, *Mémoires*, I, 8–23.

8 Necker, *De la Révolution française*, 1797, II, 77–9.

9 B.N. n.a.f. 9434 fo. 209.

10 Mallet du Pan, *Mémoires et correspondance pour servir à l'histoire de la Révolution française*, ed. A. Sayous, 1851, 2 vols, I, 181, note.

11 Necker, *Sur l'Administration de M. Necker par lui-même*, 1791, 328.

12 P. Mansell, *The Court of France, 1789–1830*, Cambridge, 1988, 19.

13 A. de Bacourt, ed., *Correspondance*

entre le Comte de Mirabeau et le Comte de La Marck, 1851, 2 vols, I, 57, La Marck to Mercy; Marquis de La Fayette, *Mémoires*, 1837, 6 vols, III, 148–55.

14 Necker, *De la Révolution française*, 77–9.

15 Published in A. Mousset, *Un témoin ignoré de la Révolution, le Comte de Fernan Nunez*, 1924, 228.

CHAPTER 13

1 P. Mansell, *The Court of France, 1789–1830*, Cambridge, 1988, 21–3 and 29–30.

2 A. de Bacourt, ed., *Correspondance entre le Comte de Mirabeau et le Comte de La Marck*, 1851, 2 vols, I, 329, first Note for the Court.

3 La Fayette, *Mémoires*, 1837, 6 vols, II, 414; III, 136; Bouillé, *Mémoires*, ed. Berville et Barrière, 1821, 170 and 174.

4 *Correspondance de Madame Elizabeth*, ed. Feuillet de Conches, 1868, I, 145.

5 J.F.X. Droz, *Histoire du règne de Louis XVI...*, Brussels, 1839, III, 121.

6 *Correspondance de Mme Elizabeth*, I, 290.

7 R. Griffiths, *Le Centre Perdu, Malouet et les 'monarchiens'*, Grenoble, 1988, 89.

8 A reference to the Parlements' *théorie des classes*.

9 A.N. C187, La Porte to the King, 2 March 1791, quoted in Mansell, *The Court of France*, 33–4.

10 A. Söderjhelm, ed., *Marie-Antoinette et Barnave, Correspondance secrète*, 1934.

11 La Marck to Mercy, 21 November 1790, Bacourt, II, 385.

12 Vienna, 88 FA, dossier 3 fos 143–6, cited in P. and P. Girault de Coursac, *Enquête sur le procès du Roi Louis XVI*, 1982, 262.

13 La Fayette, *Mémoires*, 1837, 6 vols, II, 367.

14 Mercy at least thought that 'M. de Calonne could be implicated in the negotiation' of d'Angiviller to bring Mirabeau into contact with the Court: Mercy's notes, Vienna, 71 FA Sam. dossier A–B fos 2–3, cited in Girault de Coursac, *Enquête*, 192.

15 See especially the eighth and twenty-eighth Notes for the Court, I, 355 and 424.

16 Extract from the ninth Note; for a discussion of the extent of Louis's involvement with Mirabeau, see Girault de Coursac, *Enquête*, 186–206.

17 Talleyrand, *Mémoires*, ed. Duc de Broglie, 1891–2, 5 vols, II, 123.

18 A.P. LIV, 580.

19 There were some draft letters to the Pope, largely inspired by Boisgelin, Archbishop of Aix, found in the *armoire de fer*. These have been published in A.P. LIV, 475–8.

20 Published in F. Hue, *Dernières années du règne de Louis XVI*, 3rd ed., 1860, 480.

21 Sale in the Hotel Druot, 6 May 1958; the date 18 January 1791 is written in the King's hand.

22 Undated but 14 April 1791, A.P. LIV, 474.

23 Ibid., 474–5.

24 Ibid., 467, La Porte to the King, 20 April 1791.

25 Griffiths, *Le Centre Perdu*, 95.

26 Duchesse de Tourzel, *Mémoires*, ed. Duc de Cars, 1904, 2 vols, I, 302; A. de Bacourt, *Correspondance entre le Comte de Mirabeau et le Comte de La Marck*, I, 390; II, 211; Marie-Antoinette, *Lettres*, ed. La Rocheterie et Beaucourt, 1895–6, 2 vols, II, 23.

CHAPTER 14

1 Bouillé (son of the General), *Souvenirs*, 1906, 180.

2 A. de Bacourt, ed., *Correspondance entre le Comte de Mirabeau et le Comte de La Marck*, 1851, 2 vols, I, 167.

3 The King to Bouillé, 1 September 1790, published in A.P. LIV, 513–14.

4 Bouillé, *Mémoires*, ed. Berville et Barrière, 1821, 165–9 and 174.

5 Ibid., 213.

6 Bouillé, *Souvenirs*, 185.

7 J.M. Roberts, *French Revolution Documents*, Oxford, 1966, I, 291.

8 La Fayette, *Mémoires*, 1837, 6 vols, II, 449.

9 Bacourt, I, 367.

10 Ibid., 331.

11 Bouillé, *Mémoires*, 245.

12 Ibid., 223, note 1.

13 Comte de Pimodan, *Le Comte de Mercy-Argenteau*, 1911, 274–5, 284 and 289; Mercy to Marie-Antoinette, 27 April and 11 May 1791; Bouillé, *Mémoires*, 266.

14 Bouillé, *Mémoires*, 223–4.

15 E.g., Marie-Antoinette to Mercy, 14 April 1791.

16 Bacourt, I, 166.

17 Fersen (on behalf of Breteuil) to Marie-Antoinette, 26 July 1791, Klinckowström, *Le Comte de Fersen et la Cour de France*, 1878, 2 vols, II, 236.

18 Ibid., cited in P. and P. Girault de Coursac, *Enquête sur le procès du Roi Louis XVI*, 1982, 302.

19 Breteuil to Fersen, 30 April and 29 May 1791, published in Klinckowström, II, 110 and 131.

20 Marie-Antoinette to Mercy, 4 June 1791; Mercy to Kaunitz, 22 June 1791, published in Pimodan, 289; Campan, *Mémoires sur la vie de Marie-Antoinette par Mme Campan*, 1849, 237–9.

21 Duchesse de Tourzel, *Mémoires*, ed. Duc de Cars, 1904, 2 vols, I, 324–5; her eye-witness account forms the basis of this section.

22 M. Reinhard, *La chute de la royauté*, 1977, 27.

23 From the minutes drawn up by the Municipality of Varennes and published as an appendix to E. Bimbenet, *La fuite de Louis XVI à Varennes*, 1868.

24 Campan, 250.

25 Louis to Bouillé, 3 July 1791, published by Feuillet de Conches, ed., *Louis XVI, Marie-Antoinette et Mme Elizabeth, lettres et documents inédits*, 1864–9, 6 vols, 469 and taken from the Bouillé archives.

26 Published in L. Mortimer-Ternaux, *Histoire de la Terreur*, 1862–81, 8 vols, I, 353–71.

27 A.N. KK375. *Registre de perte et gain des parties de billard faites par le Roi contre la Reine et Mme Elizabeth à commencer du trente juillet 1791.*

28 *Marie-Antoinette et Barnave*, ed. O.-G. Heidenstam, 1913, 39 and 79.

29 Théodore de Lameth, *Notes et souvenirs*, ed. Welvert, 224–5 and 388.

30 Duc de Choiseul, *Relation du départ de Louis XVI le 20 Juin 1791*, 33–5; F. Hue, *Dernières années du règne de Louis XVI*, 3rd ed., 1860, 220–1.

31 *Marie-Antoinette et Barnave*, 42.

32 The view of G. Michon, *Adrien Duport et le parti feuillant*, 1924, the best account of the Revision despite its hostility to the King and the triumvirs.

33 Marie-Antoinette to Mercy, 26 August 1791.

34 *Marie-Antoinette et Barnave*, 86.

35 Ibid., 78.

36 *Marie-Antoinette et Barnave*, 95–107; J.M. Roberts, *French Revolution Documents*, for the text.

37 For a discussion of the implications of the new title, see P.R. Campbell, 'Louis XVI, King of the French, in C. Lucas (ed.), *The Political Culture of the French Revolution*, Oxford, 1988; R. Griffiths, *Le Centre Perdu, Malouet et les 'monarchiens'*, Grenoble, 1988, 104.

38 J. Arnaud-Bouteloup, *Le rôle politique de Marie-Antoinette*, 1924, 260; Klinckowström, I, 141–2, Feuillet, II, 168–9 (an identical letter, one copy coming from Fersen, the other from Mercy); Pimodan, 296–7.

39 Calonne to Catherine II, 28 September 1791, P.R.O. P.C.

I/127.388.

40 Archives of Austria, Frankreich Hoffcorrespondenz, 7, cited in P. and P. Girault de Coursac, eds, *Louis XVI à la parole*, 1989, 270.

41 Archives of Austria, Familien Acten 88.3 fos 108–125, published by Feuillet de Conches, II, 365–75 and Girault de Coursac, *Louis XVI à la parole*, 263–8.

CHAPTER 15

1 Bertrand de Molleville, *Mémoires secrètes*, 1797, 3 vols, I, 210 and II, 139; Dumouriez, *Mémoires*, 1822–3, 4 vols, II, 139.

2 Roederer, *Chronique de cinquante jours*, 1832, 281.

3 Ibid., 282.

4 *Marie-Antoinette et Barnave, correspondance secrète*, ed. Alma Söderhjelm, 87.

5 Louis-Philippe, *Memoirs*, ed. and trans. John Hardman, New York, 1977, 119–23.

6 Klinckowström, *Le Comte de Fersen et la Cour de France*, 1878, 2 vols, I, 199.

7 A. de Bacourt, ed., *Correspondance entre le Comte de Mirabeau et le Comte de La Marck*, 1851, 2 vols, II, 337.

8 Bertrand, I, 205.

9 A.N. C221 160 (148) pièce 19, quoted in P. and P. Girault de Coursac, eds, *Louis XVI à la parole*, 1989, 276.

10 Klinckowström, I, 269, Marie-Antoinette to Fersen, 7 December 1791.

11 J. Flammermont, *Negotiations secrètes de Louis XVI et du Baron de Breteuil avec la Cour de Berlin*, 1885, 17 and note.

12 Ibid., 9–10, the text of this letter.

13 A.A.E., Trèves, Sup. 4, fo. 22, cited in P. and P. Girault de Coursac, *Enquête sur le procès du Roi Louis XVI*, 1982, 338.

14 A.A.E., Autriche, 363 fos 53ff., cited in Girault de Coursac, *Enquête*, 373.

15 A.P. LIV, 488.

16 Bertrand, II, 51 and 58; Bacourt, II, 358.

17 A.P. LV, 539.

18 B.N. 40 Lb 39, 10536.

19 Letter of the King to the President of the Legislative Assembly, published in Feuillet de Conches, ed., *Louis XVI, Marie-Antoinette et Mme Elizabeth, lettres et documents inédits, 1864–9, 6 vols, VI, 245–6* — 'I yielded to the unanimous advice of my Council'; Bertrand, II, 145; Campan, *Mémoires sur la vie de Marie-Antoinette par Mme Campan*, 1849, 286–7; Mme de Staël, *Considérations sur la Révolution française*, op. post., 1843, I, 372.

20 Bertrand, II, 188.

21 A.N. C185 C II no. 32.

22 Ibid., nos 87–8; Campan, 279; Lescure, ed., *Correspondance secrète sur Louis XVI . . .* , 1866, 2 vols, II, 600.

23 F. Hue, *Dernières années de Louis XVI*, 3rd ed., 1860, 282; Mallet du Pan dates this note 3 August, Girault de Coursac, *Louis XVI à la parole*, 302.

24 Roederer, 50–3 and 76–8; Dumouriez, *Mémoires*, II, 153.

25 J. Arnaud-Bouteloup, *Le rôle politique de Marie-Antoinette*, 1924, 338.

26 Fersen to Taube, 29 July 1792, Klinckowström, II, 33.

27 La Fayette, *Mémoires*, 1837, 6 vols, III, 346.

28 Ibid., 357.

29 Bertrand, III, 10; La Fayette, III, 344.

30 Bertrand, III, 10; La Fayette, III, 346.

31 Mercy to Marie-Antoinette, 9 July 1792.

32 Note of 10 July, Klinckowström, II, 323.

33 Letter to Lally-Tollendal published by A. Thiers, *Histoire de la Révolution française*, Brussels, 1844, 2 vols, II, 374.

34 L. Pingaud, 'Un ministre de Louis XVI, Terrier de Monciel', in *Le*

Correspondant, August 1879, 590; A. Mathiez, 'Les Girondins à la veille du 10 août', in *Annales historiques de la Révolution française* (1931), 193–212, 194–5.

35 La Fayette, III, 348.
36 Bertrand, III, 10–45; Malouet, *Mémoires*, 1874, 2 vols, II, 220–6; Bacourt, II, 374, Montmorin to La Marck.
37 Mathiez, 'Les Girondins et la Cour . . .', *passim*.
38 Roederer, 299.
39 The following account of the rising is based mainly on Roederer, Mme de Tourzel and Reinhard.
40 Bertrand, III, 24.
41 Ibid., 38, conversation between Bertrand and Montmorin; Beaucourt, *Captivité de Louis XVI*, 1892, 2 vols, I, 289.
42 Mme de Tourzel, II, 228–9.

CHAPTER 16

1 Report of the Commune of 26 December, published in Marquis de Beaucourt, *Captivité de Louis XVI*, 1892, II, 23.
2 Beaucourt, I, 240; Cléry, *Journal de ce qui s'est passé à la tour du Temple pendant la captivité de Louis XVI, Roi de France*, London, 1798, 40 and 52.
3 Beaucourt, I, 214 and 240.
4 F. Hue, *Dernières années du règne de Louis XVI*, 3rd ed., 1860, 360; Cléry, 97.
5 Beaucourt, I, 235.
6 Cléry, 28–33.
7 Beaucourt, I, 241.
8 A. Soboul, *Le Procès de Louis XVI*, 1970, 86.
9 At least there are none in his papers either in the Archives Nationales or in the Public Record Office. A.P. LIV, 449 for the letter Louis annotated 'point répondu'.

10 Hue, 370 and 399–400; Campan, *Mémoires sur la vie de Marie-Antoinette par Mme Campan*, 1849, 285–6.
11 The record of Louis's appearance before the Convention is given in A.P. LV, 7–15.
12 Cléry, 152–3.
13 Beaucourt, II, 207.
14 Ibid., 181.
15 E. Seligman, *La Justice pendant la Révolution*, 1913, 2 vols, II, 420–2.
16 Miromesnil, *Correspondance politique*, ed. P. Le Verdier, 1899–, 4 vols, I, xvi, letter of 15 December to Barère.
17 A.N. C.243 dossier 305.7.
18 Beaucourt, I, 290 and II, 234.
19 Ibid., 231; Hue, 429 (from a manuscript given by Malesherbes to Hue in prison).
20 The speeches of Sèze and the King are given in A.P. LV, 617–34.
21 Beaucourt, II, 234 and I, 291.
22 Soboul, *Le Procès de Louis XVI*, 200–4.
23 Hue, 430–1.
24 Cléry, 207 and Hue, 439.
25 Cléry, 211–13.
26 Beaucourt, I, 291.
27 Ibid., 19–20.
28 Abbé Edgeworth de Firmont, *Dernières heures de Louis XVI*, 1816, 210–12 and 217.
29 Cléry, 226; Beaucourt, I, 215–16 and 240.
30 Beaucourt, I, 328 and 345; Edgeworth, 220.
31 Edgeworth, 225–7.
32 Beaucourt, II, 172, the account of the *Semaines Parisiennes*.
33 P. de Vaissière, *La mort du Roi*, 1910, 125 and 131–3; L.-B. Mercier, *Le nouveau Paris*, III, 4; Beaucourt, I, 398.
34 Beaucourt, I, 337 and 348; Comte d'Allonville, *Mémoires secrètes*, 1838–41, 10 vols, III, 159–60; *Le Républicain* for 22 January 1793.

Bibliography

MANUSCRIPT SOURCES

Louis XVI

Archives Nationales (A.N.) K161, 163 and 164, 'cartons des rois'; communications to the King vastly outnumber those from him; of special interest are K163 no. 8, a series of thirty-three letters from Miromesnil to the King, and K164, no. 3, correspondence with Vergennes.

A.N. C220–3 (Convention Nationale, Papiers des Tuileries); four boxes of letters from and to Louis XVI, mostly after 1789, captured after 10 August.

A.N. C183–5, papers found in the Armoire de fer; documents considered important by the Convention are printed in *Archives Parlementaires* (abbreviated A.P.), LIV, 428 ff.; there is a detailed inventory of the remainder in vol LV, 668 ff.

A.N. AE1–4, the King's diary, a microfilm copy of the original in the Musée des Archives.

A.N. KK375, *Registre de perte et gain des parties de billard faites par le Roi contre la Reine et Madame Elizabeth à commencer du trente juillet 1791.*

Bibliothèque Nationale (B.N.), B.N. Rés. Geo. C4349, *Reconnaissance des environs de Versailles faites par Monseigneur le Dauphin en 1769.*

Vergennes-Tugny Family Archives, *Letters de Louis XVI* (the complement to K164, no. 3).

Papers of Ministers and those in the Ministerial Milieu

D'AMÉCOURT, LEFEVRE, raporteur du Roi in the Parlement, B.N. nouv. ac. franc. 22103–12 (of special interest is his *Journal du règne de Louis XVI*, 22111, and the section *Ministres de Louis XVI* starting at folio 1).

BRIENNE A.N. 4 A.P.188.

CALONNE, A.N. 297 A.P. (especially 297 A.P.3 fos. 1–137 relating to the 1787 Assembly of Notables); PUBLIC RECORD OFFICE P.C.1/125.

CASTRIES, Arch. de la Marine, *Journal de Castries*, MS 182/7964. 1–2. A.N. A.P.306, the Castries Papers, especially 306.18–24.

JOLY DE FLEURY, B.N. fonds Joly de Fleury, 1432–44.

LENOIR, Bibliothèque municipale d'Orléans, MS 1421–3 (fragmentary memoirs left by the lieutenant de police).

MALESHERBES, A.N. 154 A.P.11.147.

MIROMESNIL, A.N. 158 A.P.3 *dossier* 16, seventeen letters from Miromesnil to the parlementaire Duval d'Epremesnil.

D'ORMESSON, A.N. 144 A.P.130–3; the minister's diary is in 130 and the minutes of the Comité des finances at 131 *dossier* 5.

VERGENNES, Archives des Affaires Étrangères, M.D. (France) 1375–1400.

VÉRI, Archives départementales de La Drôme (Valence), MSS Journal (unclassified); the archives also contain de Witte's copy of this diary of which *cahiers* 100–2 are missing in the original.

The Assembly of Notables of 1787

Bibliothèque de l'Arsenal

MS 3975–6; the minutes of the second bureau of the Assembly, presided over by the Comte d'Artois.

MS 3978; a fuller version of the preceding containing not only the formal opinions of the members but also the debates for the first two 'Divisions'.

MS 4546; a diary of the bureau kept by the Duc de Montmorency-Laval, one of its members.

PRINTED PRIMARY SOURCES

ADHÉMAR, COMTESSE D', *Souvenirs sur Marie-Antoinette* . . . , 1836, 4 vols.

ALLONVILLE, COMTE D', *Mémoires secrètes*, 1838–41, 10 vols.

D'ANGIVILLER, *Mémoires*, Copenhagen, 1933.

ARCHIVES PARLEMENTAIRES; the official record of parliamentary proceeding begins with the Assembly of Notables.

D'ARGENSON, *Mémoires*, ed. M.E.J.B Rathéry, 1859.

A. D'ARNETH, *Marie-Antoinette, Joseph II und Leopold II*, 1866.

A. D'ARNETH and J. FLAMMERMONT, eds, *Correspondance secrète du Comte de Mercy-Argenteau avec l'Empereur Joseph II et le Prince de Kaunitz*, 1891, 2 vols.

A. D'ARNETH and M.A. GEFFROY, eds, *Marie-Antoinette: Correspondance secrète entre Marie-Thérèse et le Comte de Mercy-Argenteau*, 2nd ed., 1875, 3 vols.

ASSEMBLÉE DES NOTABLES DE 1787, *Procès-verbal*, Paris, 1788.

J.M. AUGEARD, *Mémoires secrètes*, ed. E. Bavoux, 1866.

BACHAUMONT, *Mémoires secrètes pour servir à l'histoire de la République des Lettres*, London 1777–89.

A DE BACOURT, ed., *Correspondance entre le Comte de Mirabeau et le Comte de La Marck*, 1851, 2 vols.

BAILLY, *Mémoires*, ed. Berville et Barrière, 1821, 3 vols.

BARENTIN, *Lettres et bulletins à Louis XVI*, ed. A. Aulard, 1915.

BARENTIN, *Mémoire autographe sur les derniers Conseils du Roi Louis XVI*, ed. M. Champion, 1844.

BARNAVE, *Introduction à la Révolution française*, ed. G. Rudé, 1960.

A.F. BERTRAND DE MOLLEVILLE, *Mémoires secrètes pour servir à l'histoire de la dernière année du règne de Louis XVI, Roi de France*, London, 1797, 3 vols.

BESENVAL, BARON DE, *Mémoires*, ed. Berville et Barrière, 1821, 2 vols.

BOUILLÉ, MARQUIS DE, *Mémoires*, ed. Berville et Barrière, 1821.

BOUILLÉ (son of the General), *Souvenirs*, 1906.

BRIENNE, COMTE DE, and LOMÉNIE DE BRIENNE, *Journal de l'Assemblée des Notables de 1787*, ed. P. Chevalier, 1960.

CALONNE, C.A. DE [attrib.], *Les Comments*, 1781.
CALONNE, C.A. DE [attrib.], *Lettre du Marquis de Caraccioli à M. d'Alembert*, 1781.
CALONNE, C.A. DE, *Lettre au Roi*, London, 1789.
CAMPAN, *Mémoires sur la vie de Marie-Antoinette par Mme Campan*, 1849.
CHOISEUL, DUC DE, *Relation du départ de Louis XVI le 20 Juin 1791*, 1822.
CLÉRY, *Journal de ce qui s'est passé à la tour du Temple pendant la captivité de Louis XVI, Roi de France*, London, 1798.
CROŸ, DUC DE, *Journal, 1718–84*, ed. Grouchy et Cottin, 1906–7, 4 vols.
DUMOURIEZ, *Mémoires*, 1822–3, 4 vols.
DUQUESNOY, ADRIEN, *Journal*, 1894, 2 vols.
EDGEWORTH DE FIRMONT, ABBÉ, *Dernières heures de Louis XVI*, 1816.
ELIZABETH, MADAME, *Correspondance*, ed. Feuillet de Conches, 1868.
ÉTATS-GÉNÉRAUX. *Recueil des documents relatifs aux États-Généraux de 1789*, ed. G. Lefebvre, 1953–70, 4 vols.
FERSEN, COMTE DE, *Journal*, published by Klinckowström in *Le Comte de Fersen et la Cour de France*, 1878, 2 vols.
FRENCH REVOLUTION DOCUMENTS, vol. I, ed. J.M. Roberts, Blackwell, Oxford, 1966.
F. HUE, *Dernières années du règne de Louis XVI*, 3rd ed., 1860.
LA FAYETTE, MARQUIS DE, *Mémoires*, 1837, 6 vols.
LALLY-TOLLENDAL, article on Necker in the *Biographie-Michaud*.
LAMETH, THÉODORE DE, *Notes et souvenirs*, ed. E. Welvert, 1913.
LESCURE, ed., *Correspondance secrète sur Louis XVI . . .*, 1866, 2 vols.
LOUIS XV, *Lettres à son petit-fils . . .*, ed. Amiguet, 1938.
LOUIS XV, *Correspondance secrète inédite*, ed. M.E. Boutaric, 1866, 2 vols.
LOUIS XVI, *Réflexions sur mes entretiens avec M. le Duc de La Vauguyon*, ed. E. Falloux, 1851.
LOUIS XVI, *Louis XVI à la parole*, ed. P. and P. Girault de Coursac, 1989.
Louis XVI, Marie-Antoinette et Mme Elizabeth, lettres et documents inédits, ed. Feuillet de Conches, 1864–9, 6 vols.
LOUIS-PHILIPPE, *Memoirs*, ed. and trans. John Hardman, New York, 1977.
MALESHERBES, *Nouveaux documents inédits*, ed. P. Grosclaude, 1964.
MALLET DU PAN, *Mémoires et correspondances pour servir à l'histoire de la Révolution française*, ed. A. Sayous, 1851, 2 vols.
MALOUET, *Mémoires*, 1874, 2 vols.
MARIE-ANTOINETTE, *Lettres*, ed. La Rocheterie et Beaucourt, 1895–6, 2 vols.
MARIE-ANTOINETTE ET BARNAVE, correspondance secrète, ed. Alma Söderhjelm, 1934.
MARIE-ANTOINETTE, FERSEN ET BARNAVE, ed. O.-G. Heidenstam, 1913.
MARIE-ANTOINETTE, JOSEPH II UND LEOPOLD II, ed. A von Arneth, 2nd ed., Vienna, 1866.
MARMONTEL, *Mémoires*, ed. J. Renwick, 1972, 2 vols.
MIROMESNIL, *Correspondance politique*, ed. P. Le Verdier, 1899–, 4 vols.
MONTBAREY, Mémoires du Prince de, 1826–7, 3 vols.
MONTJOIE, *Éloge historique et funèbre de Louis XVI*, 1796.
MONTMORENCY-LUXEMBOURG, DUC DE, ed. Paul Filleul, 1939.
(MONTYON, AUGET DE) *Particularités . . . sur les Ministres des Finances les plus célèbres*, 1812.
J.N. MOREAU, *Mes souvenirs*, 1898–1901, 2 vols.
J. NECKER, *Sur l'administration de M. Necker par lui-même*, 1791.
J. NECKER, *De la Révolution française*, 1797.
RAIGECOURT-BOMBELLES, *Correspondance du Marquis et de la Marquise de*

Raigecourt avec le Marquis et la Marquise de Bombelles pendant l'émigration, 1790–1800,
ed. M. de la Rocheterie, 1892.

P.L. ROEDERER, *Chronique de cinquante jours*, 1832.

SAINT-PRIEST, COMTE DE, *Mémoires*, ed. Barante, 1929.

G.M. SALLIER, *Annales françaises . . . 1774–89*, 1813.

SÉGUR, Comte de, *Mémoires ou souvenirs et anecdotes*, 1827, 3 vols.

J.L. SOULAVIE, *Mémoires historiques et politiques du règne de Louis XVI*, 1801, 6 vols.

STAËL, MME DE, *Considérations sur . . . la Révolution française*, op. post., 1843.

TALLEYRAND, PRINCE DE, *Mémoires*, ed. Duc de Broglie, 1891–2, 5 vols.

TOURZEL, DUCHESSE DE, *Mémoires*, ed. Duc de Cars, 1904, 2 vols.

VAUDREUIL, *Correspondance intime du Comte de Vaudreuil et du Comte d'Artois*, ed.
L. Pingaud, 1889, 2 vols.

VÉRI, ABBÉ DE, *Journal, 1774–80*, ed. J. de Witte, 1928–30, 2 vols.

WEBER, *Mémoires concernant Marie-Antoinette*, ed. Berville et Barrière, 1822, 2 vols.

SECONDARY WORKS

M. ANTOINE, 'Les comités des ministres sous Louis XV', in *Rev. Hist. de Droit*,
1951.

J. ARNAUD-BOUTELOUP, *Le rôle politique de Marie-Antoinette*, 1924.

BEAUCOURT, MARQUIS DE, *Captivité de Louis XVI*, 1892.

BAKER, K.M., *Inventing the French Revolution*, Cambridge, 1990.

BAKER, K.M., ed., *The French Revolution and the Creation of Modern Political Culture*:
vol, I, *The Political Culture of the Ancien Régime*, Chicago, 1987; vol. II, *The Political
Culture of the French Revolution*, ed. C. Lucas, Oxford, 1988.

E. BIMBENET, *La fuite de Louis XVI à Varennes*, 1868.

J. BOSHER, *French Finances 1770–95*, Cambridge, 1970.

R. BROWNE, 'The Diamond Necklace Affair Revisited', in *Renaissance and Modern
Studies*, XXXIII, 1989.

P. BURLEY, 'Louis XVI and a new Monarchy', unpublished Ph.D. thesis, London
University, 1981.

P.R. CAMPBELL, 'Old Regime Politics', in *Renaissance and Modern Studies*, XXXIII,
1989.

P.R. CAMPBELL, 'Louis XVI King of the French', in C. Lucas (ed.), *The Political
Culture of the French Revolution*, Oxford, 1988.

P. CARON, 'La tentative de contre-révolution de Juin-Juillet 1789', in *Revue
d'Histoire moderne*, VIII (1906).

J.R. CENSER and J.D. POPKIN (eds), *Press and Politics in Pre-Revolutionary France*,
Berkeley, 1987.

A. CHÉREST, *La chute de l'Ancien Régime, 1787–9*, 1884–6, 3 vols.

COURSAC, P. GIRAULT DE, *L'éducation d'un roi, Louis XVI*, 1972.

COURSAC, P. and P. GIRAULT DE, *Enquête sur le procès du Roi Louis XVI*, 1982.

R. DARNTON, *The Literary Underground of the Old Régime*, Harvard, 1982.

H. DONIOL, *Histoire de la participation de la France à l'établissement des États-Unis
d'Amérique*, 1886–, 5 vols.

W. DOYLE, 'The Parlements of France and the Breakdown of the Old Regime,
1771–88', in *French Historical Studies*, VI (1970), 415–58.

W. DOYLE, 'The Parlements', in K.M. Baker, ed., *The Political Culture of the Ancien
Régime*, Chicago, 1987.

J.F.X. DROZ, *Histoire du règne de Louis XVI . . .*, Brussels, 1839.

D. ECHEVERRIA, *The Maupeou Revolution*, Baton Rouge, 1985.

Bibliography

J. ÉGRET, *La pré-Révolution française*, 1962.
J. ÉGRET, *Necker*, 1975.
B. FAŸ, *Louis XVI ou la fin d'un monde*, 1955.
J. FLAMMERMONT, *Négotiations secrètes de Louis XVI et du Baron de Breteuil avec la Cour de Berlin*, 1885.
R. GRIFFITHS, *Le Centre Perdu, Malouet et les 'monarchiens'*, Grenoble, 1988.
P. GROSCLAUDE, *Malesherbes*, 1961.
J. HARDMAN, 'Ministerial Politics from the Accession of Louis XVI to the Assembly of Notables, 1774–87', unpublished D.Phil thesis, Oxford, 1972.
J. HARDMAN, *The French Revolution . . . 1787–95*, Arnold, London, 1981.
R.D. HARRIS, *Necker*, University of California, 1979.
J.F. LABOURDETTE, *Vergennes*, 1990.
L. LAUGIER, *Un ministère réformateur sous Louis XV, Le Triumvirat*, 1975.
E. LEVER, *Louis XVI*, 1985.
LUÇAY, COMTE DE, *Les secrétaires d'État en France depuis les origines jusqu'à 1774*, 1881.
P. MANSELL, *The Court of France, 1789–1830*, Cambridge, 1988.
M. MARION, *Le garde des sceaux Lamoignon*, 1905.
G.T. MATHEWS, *The Royal General Farms*, New York, 1958.
A. MATHIEZ, 'Les Girondins et la Cour à la veille du 10 Août', in *Annales historiques de la Révolution française* (1931), 193–212.
J. DE MAUPEOU, *Le Chancelier Maupeou*, 1942.
G. MICHON, *Adrien Duport et le parti feuillant*, 1924.
L. MORTIMER-TERNAUX, *Histoire de la Terreur*, 1862–81, 8 vols.
A. MOUSSET, *Un témoin ignoré de la Révolution, Le Comte de Fernan Nunez*, 1924.
PIMODAN, COMTE DE, *Le Comte de Mercy-Argenteau*, 1911.
L. PINGAUD, 'Un ministre de Louis XVI, Terrier de Monciel', in *Le Correspondant*, August 1879.
M. PRICE, 'The Comte de Vergennes and the Baron de Breteuil', unpublished Ph.D thesis, Cambridge University, 1988.
M. PRICE, 'The "Ministry of the Hundred Hours": A Reappraisal', in *French History*, vol. 4 no. 3 (1990) 317–39.
O. RANUM, *Richelieu and the Councillors of Louis XIII*, Oxford, 1963.
M. REINHARD, *La chute de la royauté*, 1977.
J.M.J. ROGISTER, 'Conflict and Harmony in Eighteenth Century France: a reappraisal of the pattern of relations between Crown and Parlements under Louis XV', unpublished D.Phil. thesis, Oxford, 1972.
S.F. SCOTT, *The Response of the Royal Army to the French Revolution . . . 1787–93*, Oxford, 1973.
E. SELIGMAN, *La justice pendant la Révolution*, 1913, 2 vols.
A. SOBOUL, *Le Procès de Louis XVI*, 1970.
STONE. B, *The Parlement of Paris, 1774–89*, North Carolina, 1981.
STONE, B, *The French Parlements and the crisis of the Ancien Régime*, North Carolina, 1986.
A. THIERS, *Histoire de la Révolution française*, Brussels, 1844, 2 vols.
DE TOCQUEVILLE, A. DE, *The Ancien Régime and the French Revolution*, ed. H. Brogan, 1966.
P. DE VAISSIÈRE, *La mort du Roi*, 1910.
D. VAN KLEY, D., *The Jansenists and the Expulsion of the Jesuits from France, 1757–65*, New Haven, 1975.
D. WICK, 'The Court Nobility and the French Revolution: the Example of the Society of Thirty', in *Eighteenth Century Studies*, XIII (1980), 263–84.

Index